FOREWORD BY **MALCOLM GLADWELL**

CREATE THE
FUTURE

TACTICS FOR DISRUPTIVE THINKING

NEW YORK TIMES BESTSELLING AUTHOR, **JEREMY GUTSCHE**

CEO OF TREND HUNTER

D1399742

FAST
COMPANY
Press

Fast Company Press
New York, New York
www.fastcompanypress.com

This work is being published under the Fast Company Press imprint by an exclusive arrangement with *Fast Company*. *Fast Company* and the *Fast Company* logo are registered trademarks of Mansueto Ventures, LLC. The Fast Company Press logo is a wholly owned trademark of Mansueto Ventures, LLC.

Distributed by Greenleaf Book Group

For ordering information or special discounts for bulk purchases, please contact Greenleaf Book Group at PO Box 91869, Austin, TX 78709, 512.891.6100.

Design and composition by Greenleaf Book Group & Brian Phillips Design
Cover design by Greenleaf Book Group & Brian Phillips Design

Image Credits supplied on page 133, which serves as an extension of the copyright page.

Publisher's Cataloging-in-Publication data is available.

Print ISBN: 978-1-7324391-4-6

eBook ISBN: 978-1-7324391-5-3

Printed in the United States of America on acid-free paper

20 21 22 23 24 25   10 9 8 7 6 5 4 3 2 1

First Edition

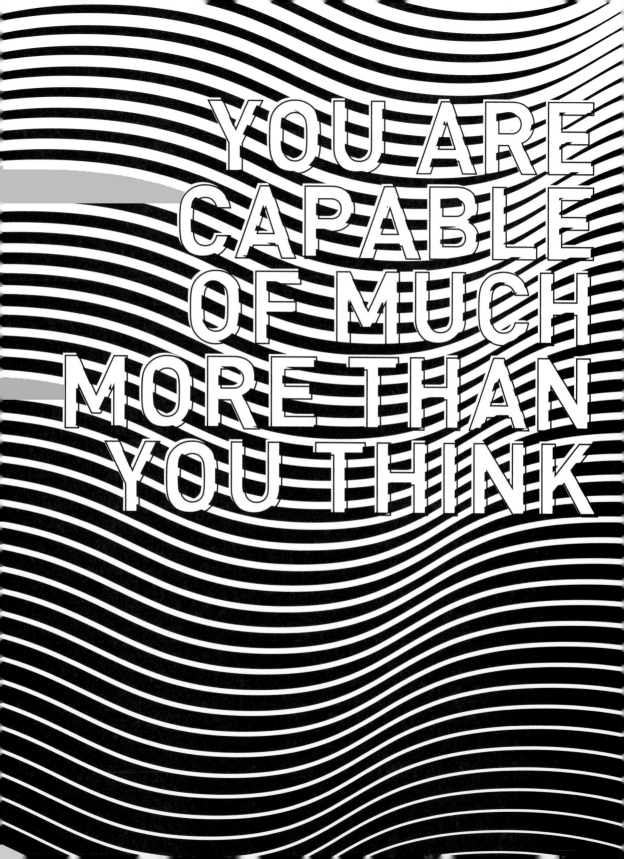

YOU ARE ABOUT TO EXPERIENCE HISTORY'S HIGHEST RATE OF CHANGE, DISRUPTION, & OPPORTUNITY...

This means you are closer than ever to achieving something *more*. Your breakthrough might be a new product, service, role, idea, or just a different way of doing something.

THE PROBLEM IS that your ability to change will keep getting limited by seven specific traps. Collectively, these traps reduce your innovation potential by 93%—a number I will prove with a simple game. These traps blind you from seeing opportunity and compel you to stick to the path you are already on. This explains why most people miss out on realizing their full potential. It doesn't have to be that way.

THERE ARE PROVEN METHODS you can use to break free, to identify opportunity faster, and to make change happen. In this double-sided book, you will learn the same techniques my team has used to advance the world's highest-performing innovators at Disney, Starbucks, American Express, IBM, adidas, Google, and NASA.

THIS BOOK IS MORE THAN JUST MY LIFE'S WORK; it is the collective wisdom of my team and several hundred clients who contributed their battle-tested techniques. Instead of writing my third book on a focused, narrow topic, I wanted to make the most useful, comprehensive guidebook I could, combining all of the best tactics I've learned from working with so many innovators.

AFTER MORE THAN 10,000 INNOVATION PROJECTS, which helped leading brands predict and create the future, my team at Trend Hunter has collected a war chest of tactics that will help you win your future. And these skills matter more than ever before, because the next 5 to 10 years are about to redefine humanity.

CONSIDER THIS: We already have the technology to read the inner voice in your mind, so imagine controlling your phone with your inner thoughts, writing a report without a keyboard, playing video games without a controller, or walking into stores that already know what you want to buy. Imagine seeing the world in augmented reality and commuting a bit safer, working a bit faster, or exercising in a way that is actually fun. What if we could restore someone's ability to walk, give someone the sense of touch, enhance eyesight, fight disease, or modify DNA? What happens when robots start building our homes, delivering our news, and driving us home?

THESE ARE NOT EXAMPLES OF THE FAR FUTURE. These are examples of what is possible right now. And with hybridization, instant entrepreneurship, and artificial intelligence, the pace of human progress is about to become not so human at all. Life as we know it is about to change dramatically, and this will create countless new opportunities.

Are you willing to make small changes to your daily routine, to increase your future potential—to create the future?

Let's do this! But first, a few pages of context . . .

JEREMY GUTSCHE is a *New York Times* bestselling author, award-winning innovation expert, "one of the most sought-after keynote speakers on the planet" (*The Sun* newspaper), and the CEO of Trend Hunter—the world's #1 trend website and innovation consultancy with over 3 billion views and more than 10,000 innovation projects completed. His team of Futurists is relied on by 700 brands, billionaires, and CEOs to predict and create the future. He's even helped NASA prototype the journey to Mars!

THERE ARE MANY GREAT IDEAS WITHIN YOUR GRASP...

Our world is abundant with more opportunities than ever before. And the good news is you can predict many of those opportunities by learning to better decipher the trends in your world.

- Artificial Intelligence
- Globalization
- Genome Editing
- Big Data
- The Cloud
- China vs. US
- 3-D Printing
- Boomers vs. Millennials
- Sustainability
- Personalization
- Social Business
- Influencers
- Virtual Reality
- Augmented Reality
- Multi-Sensation
- Crowd-Funding
- Group Buying
- Female Empowerment
- The Pursuit of Equality
- Disruptive Innovation

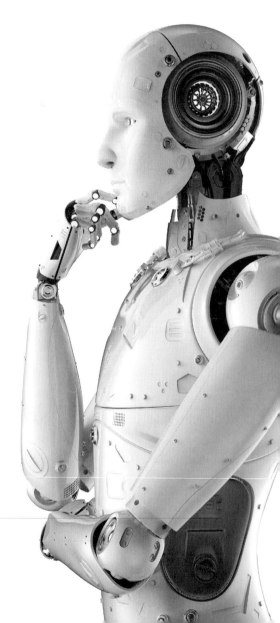

YOU HAVE SO MUCH POTENTIAL WELL WITHIN YOUR GRASP.

HOWEVER, AS CLEVER AS YOU ARE, SMART PEOPLE MISS OUT

The average lifespan of a large company has fallen from 75 years in the 1950s to 15 years today.[1] If you look at the list of the Fortune 500 companies from the year 2000, more than 52% are now gone or displaced,[2] and that rate of disruption is accelerating.

Ironically, the companies that should be the best at innovation are the same companies that often fail.

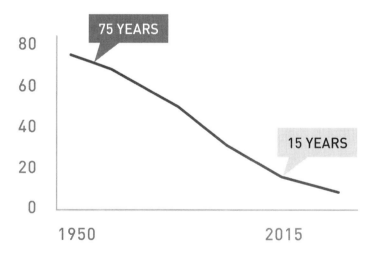

Lifespan of a Fortune 500 Company

Fortune 500 brands have all the resources and Harvard MBAs they need to innovate, but somehow that is not what's happening.

ALTHOUGH WE OBSESS ABOUT INNOVATION, WE MUST BE MINDFUL THAT MAKING CHANGE HAPPEN IS HALF THE BATTLE.

EVERYONE WANTS INNOVATION AND CHANGE TO HAPPEN...

Almost every CEO of a major company will tell you that innovation is one of their core capabilities. An astounding 97%, in fact.[3] This suggests that every major company has a strong commitment, support, and innovation capabilities, but our research has uncovered a different reality.

97%

of CEOs list innovation as
a top priority —PwC

BUT "NOT EVERYONE" PUTS IN THE EFFORT TO MAKE IT HAPPEN

Roughly half of business leaders don't believe their company has a strong innovation plan. They don't believe they have enough time to work on new ideas, and they generally lack the capabilities to execute those ideas. This is an enormous disconnect, but it explains why so many companies become blindsided, disrupted, or less relevant than they were in the past.[4]

 50% don't believe their organization has a strong innovation plan

 55% don't believe their organization adapts quickly enough

 48% don't believe they have enough time to work on new ideas

 56% don't believe their organization knows how to turn ideas into reality

Source: Trend Hunter Assesment (n=30,000)

THIS DISCONNECT EXPLAINS WHY YOU HAVE SO MUCH UNTAPPED POTENTIAL. INNOVATION TACTICS ARE DESIRED, BUT MISSING. LEARN TO INNOVATE AND EXPERIENCE A NEW LEVEL OF SUCCESS.

THIS BOOK WILL EQUIP YOU WITH BATTLE-TESTED METHODS TO CREATE THE FUTURE

After conducting more than 10,000 innovation workshops and custom futurism projects, my team has encountered almost every type of innovation problem. We perfected this framework with our clients to create the ultimate guide, making innovation and change happen.

Create the Future Framework

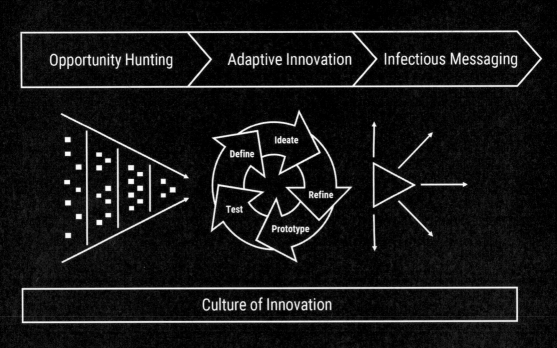

CONTENTS

People miss out because we lead busy lives and get caught up in a predictable groove, repeating past decisions. This makes it difficult to spot opportunity, and more difficult to act. Even when we have a great idea, it can be a struggle to get buy-in, influence others, and make change happen. It doesn't have to be that way.

Culture is more important than strategy. Culture underlies your organization's ability to adapt, and times of dramatic change magnify this importance. Your organization likely perceives the need to adapt, but uncertainty and resistance are paralyzing innovation. Winning the future begins with a culture of innovation.

Innovation and strategic advantage hinge on your ability to anticipate trends and identify the next big thing. By using the cutting-edge frameworks in this book, you can filter through chaos and identify clusters of opportunity to focus your innovation.

Engineers, designers, and scientists have invested billions of dollars to perfect human creativity. By applying the best of their proven practices to your own field, you can think big while acting small. You can rapidly create new opportunities.

Well-packaged stories travel faster than ever before. Unfortunately, most marketers are stuck in a world dominated by traditional advertising and clichés. By cultivating infection, your ideas will resonate, helping you to leap ahead of the competition.

READ, SKIM THE TITLES...

Our reading habits have changed entirely in the past decade. Driven by media clutter and shrinking attention spans, our world has become headline obsessed. Because of this, this book is designed to be visual and action packed, offering two ways to learn the content:

Consume the content front-to-back.

Just read the headlines on each page. The pages flow together to spark big ideas. Ideally you can pick up this book from any section and be good to go.

Let's do this!

...OR JOIN 10,000,000 PEOPLE WATCHING THE KEYNOTE VIDEOS!

My specialty is bringing innovation to life through engaging keynotes and workshops that combine exciting stories with tactical takeaways. If you are a visual learner, check out my YouTube videos. So far, I have added roughly three hours of content related to this book. At the time of publication, more than 10 million people will have watched the videos.

Watch online at JEREMYGUTSCHE.COM

Join me on Twitter/Instagram @JEREMYGUTSCHE

BY MALCOLM GLADWELL \\\\\\\\\\\\|||||||||||//////////,

Over 20 years ago, not long after I joined the staff of *The New Yorker* magazine, I met a young woman named DeeDee Gordon. She lived in Los Angeles, in a sleek modernist house up in Beachwood Canyon. She drove an immaculate vintage Pontiac Trans Am. She was young and hilarious and brilliant, in a completely unexpected way, and she had a job I'd never heard of before: companies hired her to figure out what was going to happen next.

Like many people, I assumed that next was an unsolvable mystery—that anyone who claimed to be in the business of telling the future was deluded, or worse. But then I followed DeeDee around for a while. I listened to the way she thought, and I soon began to realize that there was a real discipline and art to next: there were principles that could guide the way we thought about the future. I ended up writing an article about DeeDee Gordon and her work, called "The Coolhunt." It ran in *The New Yorker* on March 17, 1997, where—unbeknownst to me—it was read by an enterprising young man named Jeremy Gutsche. Gutsche decided to build an entire infrastructure around next, a network of correspondents around the world feeding their observations and predictions into a massive consumer-insight database. Jeremy is kind enough to say that I inspired him—which is, I'm quite sure, a gross exaggeration. But even gross exaggerations are enormously flattering, so here I am, two decades later, returning the favor by introducing you to one of Jeremy's most ambitious projects to date.

You have in your hands a book about how to "Create the Future." Before you start, I'd like to offer a few thoughts about how to think about that question. Let me begin with the question of time. A lot of thinking about the future necessarily revolves around the chronology of future events. We can be pretty certain, for example, that one day science will cure dementia, or the internal combustion engine will be no more, or— in our fanciful moments—that human beings will be able to travel instantaneously through space, like they did in old episodes of *Star Trek*. The unknown is when those things will happen. 10 years? 30 years? Or has it already been figured out, and we just don't know about it?

I think that question is best answered in parts. The first part is the technological part. As a general rule, I think, we tend to underestimate how quickly and easily innovations happen. If you polled the top military officers and strategists in the world in the mid-1930s and asked them if they could imagine a weapon capable of destroying entire cities, they would have looked at you uncomprehendingly. A bomb, to them, was something that—at best—could destroy a single building. Yet within a decade they had a weapon of that magnitude at their disposal, and less than a decade later they had a weapon capable of destroying the entire planet. The nuclear bomb—which has shaped the modern world perhaps more than any other invention—came about in a frenetic, dizzying, awe-inspiring rush. But then again, so did most of the defining innovations of the modern age. Alexander Graham Bell started tinkering with the idea of a telephone in the 1860s. By 1876, he'd figured it out, summoning his assistant in the most famous telephone call ever made: "Mr. Watson. Come here. I want to see you." That's one man, over a decade and a half, working out of a farm in southern Ontario, inventing one of the signature devices of the modern age. By the way, as I'm writing this, Google just turned 20 and Facebook just turned 15. The unicorns of Silicon Valley are teenagers.

The technological side of the future comes in like a hurricane. But technologies have to be socialized—adopted, understood, accepted, embraced—and what's striking about the social part of the future is how long and winding that part of the process is. The first atomic bomb is dropped on Japan in 1945. When do we figure out how to contain that terrifying technology? You could argue that we still haven't. But it took at least another 40 years to get to the point where the world could breathe easily. Alexander Graham Bell invents the telephone in the 1870s. The first international telephone call is made in 1881. When does the telephone take off, in terms of public acceptance? The 1920s. It took 40 years for the public to embrace the telephone. And why? Because it took 40 years for the world to figure out what the telephone was. For the longest time, for example, telephone companies were convinced that it was primarily a business instrument—it was B to B, they thought, not C to C. They actively discouraged what they referred to as trivial uses of the instrument, meaning one person calling another person to say hello. They didn't want women using it. It took them years to realize that it might be more useful for farmers—people socially isolated—than city-dwellers.

Are these isolated examples? Not at all. The first ATM was introduced in the late '60s. But in the '80s, I was still going to the bank to get my money, and I suspect you were too. Did you trust a machine to give you money? Not until you had thought about it, and experimented with it, and slowly changed your routines. One of the strange things about the way social media is discussed is that it is assumed that the patterns and practices around which consumers use Facebook, Twitter, Instagram, and Snapchat today are predictive of the way in which we will all use those platforms tomorrow. But why do we think that? These are all technologies in their infancy, and the best evidence of our history with innovation is that the invention of the future and the adoption of the future move on very different timelines. The technological part comes into focus pretty quickly. The social part takes forever to evolve. I have a sense of what Twitter will look like in five years. But it is not nearly so straightforward to figure out what Twitter will mean to its users in five years.

Create the Future is a book about that second, hard, part. That's the part we need help with.

30 years ago, a young Canadian psychologist named Philip Tetlock was at a meeting on American-Soviet relations. It was a blue-ribbon panel, featuring some of the world's leading experts on the Cold War. The group's job was to make predictions about the superpower conflict, then in full swing, and what struck Tetlock was how many of the experts' predictions contradicted each other. Here they were, the world's foremost authorities on the subject. And yet they couldn't agree on anything—which meant, logically, that some significant number of them had to be wrong.

Tetlock decided to test this idea. For the next 20 years, he immersed himse[l]f [in the] largest prediction study ever conducted: he gathered together experts from a wid[e] variety of fields, and had them answer questions within their area of expertise. So— of an energy specialist he might ask: Will the price of oil rise or fall in the next 12 months? Of an economist he might ask: Will interest rates be higher at the end of this year or lower? Is Quebec going to secede from the rest of Canada? Is the United Kingdom going to vote for or against Brexit? Tetlock ended up gathering an aston- ishing 82,000 predictions, and after tabulating his results, he came to a devastating conclusion. Experts were terrible at predictions. In most cases, anyone interested in any of those questions would have been just as well off flipping a coin.

This is a sobering fact, particularly for those who are interested in owning the future. That circuitous path that humans take—when they adapt and respond to innovation and change—is really, really hard to predict. But Tetlock wasn't finished! After sort- ing through his data, he discovered that not everyone was bad at the future. A small group of people actually were really good at making predictions. And who were they? They were people who were open-minded, who were willing to change course, when necessary, and admit their mistakes. They were generalists, not specialists. They were people with the ability to look at a problem from a number of different perspec- tives. The expertise of good predictors, in other words, did not result in a dogmatic commitment to a particular worldview. It lay in curiosity and an endless sense of wonder about what the future might bring.

You have in your hands a book written in that spirit. Enjoy.

—MALCOLM GLADWELL

...RE WAS A LITTLE BOY WHO
...NTIAL OTHERS COULD NOT SEE

I ... ...y driven to help YOU find your big idea, and I think I know where it all began . . . . fully explain, I need to tell you about a boy businessman, a nerd, and some stolen cheese.

The original boy businessman was my father. He grew up in a poor immigrant family, living in a shoebox of a house that he shared with his parents and his two brothers. They didn't have much, but they always ate well because his mother was a cook.

One day, at the innocent age of eight, the little guy was helping his mother stock up for supplies at the local grocer when some Kraft Philadelphia Cream Cheese caught his eye. When she looked away, he stuffed his mouth with the cheese. Shocked, she grabbed her son by the scruff of his neck and marched over to the storekeeper. Short for words, she exclaimed, "I caught this kid stealing!" (It was a good time to forget he was her own son.) As penance for his crime, the little boy was sentenced to a month of sweeping the floors of the grocery store. At the end of the first week, he noticed

THE CURIOUS
CASE OF THE
BOY
BUSINESSMAN

an overlooked opportunity: the grocer would throw away food that was good enough to eat but allegedly not good-looking enough to sell. (This problem of food waste plagues stores to this day.)

Even though he was just a boy, my father's first business idea was upon him. He agreed to continue sweeping the floors in exchange for the leftover food. He would then cart that food around to his poor neighbors, offering them deep discounts, much to their delight. Pretty soon he was the first kid on the block with a leather jacket and a BB gun.

The Secret to Remarkable Success

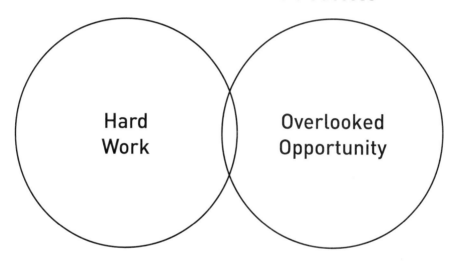

He expanded his door-to-door delivery to all sorts of leftover items. This led to an entrepreneurial career full of ups and downs, where his key move was always to look for the potential in people and businesses that others overlooked.

I told my dad's full-length story in my *New York Times* bestseller, *Better and Faster*, though I consistently reshare it to explain my mission. You see, in this example of the grocer, my dad imprinted one particular lesson on me forever:

TO BE SUCCESSFUL, YOU NEED MORE THAN JUST WORK.
YOU NEED TO FIND AN OVERLOOKED OPPORTUNITY.

...AND THEN THE SECOND BOY BUSINESSMAN WAS BORN

The picture below is of me. In case you're unsure, I'm on the right. While my awesome sweater and Coke-bottle glasses might suggest that I was a cool kid, I was actually a nerd. I know—you're probably thinking, "Jeremy, you couldn't possibly have been a nerd! That's exactly what Drake looks like!"

But alas, I was a "business idea" nerd. I was always looking for what could be my next venture, which will play to your advantage by the end of this book.

HAIR — GLASSES — SWEATER — 2014 / 1990 — HAIR — GLASSES — SWEATER

In this comparison, you can also tell that I was years ahead of my time. Who's the Trend Hunter now, Drake?

Following in my father's footsteps, I attempted to launch a dozen businesses and inventions, but nothing seemed like the right fit:

- Peanut Butter Company
- Carrot Steamer
- Humidifier-Fan Combo
- Lawn and Garden
- Photographer
- Web Design
- 12-Person Painting Company
- Book of Inventions
- "Jeremy's Junk"
  (Selling Random Overlooked Stuff)

The last little business probably had my parents alarmed. Imagine their son putting up posters that said, "Come check out Jeremy's Junk." My dad figured I needed a new business idea, and he had a plan to help me. Every month, he would buy different genres of magazines and we would flip to the sections that featured new inventions. "What do you think about this idea?" "What about this one?" "What parts would we need to build that?" "Can we go to garage sales to buy parts this weekend?" "How much will this cost us to make?"

The hunt for ideas inspired me, but it also began to engulf me. I started to see opportunity everywhere and didn't know how to choose. Today, I think many of us are in the same boat: the act of getting inspired has become *overwhelming*.

After a decade of searching, I became a corporate innovator, which is the field you end up in if you can't make a choice and just prefer hunting ideas. I figured I would learn how to hunt, research, test, and optimize using someone else's budget. Along the way, I hoped to stumble upon my breakthrough.

I was so focused on learning to innovate to find my own idea that I inadvertently learned all the skills necessary to become very successful at a bank. By 28, I was one of Capital One's youngest directors and put in charge of innovation and running the company's struggling high-end business line.

My team had a goal to shrink new bookings by only 20%. How motivating. But with new innovation tactics and an obsession for new ideas, we launched a series of winning products. Instead of shrinking, we tripled monthly bookings and grew a $1 billion portfolio. My career in banking was "set." But to me, this was actually irritating. I had proven I could find great ideas for other people, but in 20 years of searching, I hadn't found something to call my own. I was getting restless. I thought to myself: *Imagine if I could find my 12-year-old self and tell him, "YOU GROW UP TO BE A BANKER!"* There had to be another way.

MOST PEOPLE EXPECT INNOVATIVE IDEAS TO JUST MAGICALLY HAPPEN. —— ——— *THE TRUTH IS THAT YOU HAVE TO ACTIVELY PUT IN THE EFFORT.*

LET'S CREATE THE FUTURE

In my desperate, two-decade search for an idea, I enrolled in an MBA program. I hoped the classroom would inspire my discovery, but then I sat through class after class, questioning my decision. What had I done? How would any of these courses help me be an entrepreneur? Then something happened that changed my world.

My marketing professor, Jay Handleman, said, "Today, we're going to talk about the hunt for cool." My mind sparked awake. What was he talking about? We read Malcolm Gladwell's famous 1997 article, "The Coolhunt." The article spoke about how cool works and the entire profession of studying trends and culture to figure out what's next.[5] I was blown away. How did I not know about this? Had I been working at a bank too long?

I was inspired to turn my own relentless hunt into a hunt for cool. I realized I could teach myself to code and build a place online where people could share new ideas, trends, and innovations. I called it Trend Hunter, and it was one of the first crowd-sharing communities.

Having said that, I didn't think Trend Hunter would become what it is today—the world's largest research platform, with billions of views. My dreams were more simple because I was coding this site in 2005, before Facebook and YouTube were really developed. The idea of making something that could go "viral" wasn't as commonplace as it is today. Instead, I was inspired because I thought that someone, somewhere, might share an idea on Trend Hunter that would inspire my big idea. I didn't realize that Trend Hunter *was* the idea.

I also failed to internalize that this new website was basically my childhood magazine-scouring activity made digital. That means I never connected any of this inspiration to my father until my publisher pointed it out. My publisher asked me to interview my dad to better realize how *his* relentless search for ideas turned into *mine*. So I spent a weekend asking my father all the questions I never asked as a kid.

One week after that interview, my dad had a heart attack and passed away. I was devastated, but when I look back, I realize that if I knew my dad was going to pass, I would have spent my last weekend interviewing him, which is exactly what I got to do.

My dad saw the very beginnings of Trend Hunter, but he didn't get to see it grow. He would have been very proud to see what happened with my little project. In just a few years, our view count went from thousands to millions to billions. We started getting more traffic than almost every newspaper on the planet.

As a research platform, there was nothing like it. Trend Hunter was 20 times faster at market research than anything I'd experienced running innovation at a bank. Using artificial intelligence, 150 million visitors, and a team of human researchers, we could do months of research in hours. We started crafting custom reports for brands, enabling them to innovate more efficiently and to find better ideas, faster.

In 2009, I wanted to write an innovation manual to capture everything I'd learned in my professional hunt for ideas. Titled *Exploiting Chaos*, the book was the right title at the right time. The world started becoming very chaotic, and I was suddenly the "chaos guru." I started getting invites from Fortune 500 CEOs who needed urgent help. A few big clients led to 50 more, then 100, then 200, and now around 700 brands.

Today, Trend Hunter has grown into the largest trend firm and has become an innovation accelerator. We've been very fortunate to work on more than 10,000 custom projects and innovation workshops. We even got to help NASA prototype the journey to Mars!

We have learned from each experience and this book is the complete collection of everything we have learned and tried. I truly believe these battle-tested methods will help you realize your full potential, faster. If you want more, sign up for our free weekly newsletter, visit TrendHunter.com, or visit me at one of our epic Future Festivals.

Enjoy the book!

—JEREMY

JeremyGutsche.com

Create the Future Framework

THE ABILITY TO CHANGE

Many people will tell you that culture is the most important thing you need for innovation to happen. I used to be one of them. However, after working with 700 leadership teams and brands, I have come to a deeper realization: whether you are an entrepreneur dreaming of your next idea, an ambitious hard-worker, or a billionaire CEO, the most important trait you need for our fast-moving future is the ability to change.

Master change and you will be in a position to better spot new ideas, act on opportunity, and know how to convince others about your wonderful new vision.

The key is to realize that your ability to change is hindered by seven traps that all relate to your expertise. In many ways these traps are like puzzles, because if you understand how they work, you can defeat them to your own advantage.

WE ARE MORE DEPENDENT ON PAST DECISIONS THAN WE LIKE TO THINK

There are no horses in space, and yet you should expect that there are exactly two horses in space. And while we're on the topic, you should expect those horses to be 4 feet, 8½ inches wide. Why? Because NASA's Solid Rocket Boosters were designed using that exact width. Not coincidentally, but specifically because it's the exact width of two horses.

If you truly want to understand NASA's choice, you have to go back to the Roman Empire. The Romans controlled the most land because they were able to patrol it with their two-horse Roman war chariots. Those chariots would tear up the land, creating deep ruts. If you were a farmer driving your wagon, you might get caught in one of those ruts, resulting in a broken wheel.

If you were a clever farmer, however, you would measure the width of the ruts and realize that they were 4 feet, 8½ inches wide—the width of the axles on the two-horse Roman war chariot. You would then design your own wagon to match.

Soon, all the wagons were made to be 4 feet, 8½ inches wide. When the first railways were built, they were created specifically for mining carts pulled by horses. So they made those railways 4 feet, 8½ inches wide.

Naturally, the first European trains extended those best practices with tracks that were 4 feet, 8½ inches wide. Americans built their own trains, but by then the ideal width had already been determined: 4 feet, 8½ inches wide.

Soon, smart people replaced all the train tracks for modern trains that were bigger, better, and faster. The new tracks remained the same size. Even when high-speed trains started going over 200 miles an hour, many of them continued on tracks that were 4 feet, 8½ inches wide.

Logically, when NASA began making and transporting the Solid Rocket Boosters from Utah to Florida, they took into account that they needed to fit on tracks that were—you guessed it—4 feet, 8½ inches wide.

The Solid Rocket Boosters are a bit wider, as they overlap the width of the track, and a few different widths of track have been tested over time. However, the astonishing reality is that we are using the same standard as the Romans and the Solid Rocket Booster widths were determined by the width of two horse butts.

Next time you see an image of the space shuttle, I want you to look closely. There are not two horses pulling it, yet we still rely on the width determined by the Roman war chariots, even in our pursuit of outer space exploration.

Today, this might seem ridiculous, but in each incremental decision, people probably weighed the alternatives and decided to simply stick with what was there before. They stayed caught in a groove.

The takeaway is that we are more dependent on our past decisions than we like to admit. Once a path is set, we often walk down it blindly, failing to question why it was put there to begin with and whether a better path might exist.

EVERYONE WANTS TO MAKE INNOVATION HAPPEN,
BUT NOT EVERYONE BREAKS FREE FROM THE PATH.

TO BREAK FROM THE PATH, YOU MUST ESCAPE SEVEN TRAPS

Over time, it seems that we find fixed paths to travel within, just like those grooved ruts carved by the chariot wagons of the Roman Empire. Long ago, it seemed easier to build a wagon to fit the grooves than to imagine a new vehicle that could chart its own path.

One decision leads to another, and eventually we end up in a place that makes no sense. There are several factors that cause us to stay in those grooved paths, which I call the 7 TRAPS OF PATH DEPENDENCY.

ESCAPE THE TRAPS, AND YOU WILL FIND NEW PATHS OF OPPORTUNITY.

I have been working on tactics for these traps with some of the brightest minds in the world, and by the end of this book, you will be better equipped to break from the path.

If you've ever dreamed about what great ideas might be within your grasp, this section will nurture those feelings and give you tactics and exercises to bring you closer to your full potential. It will give you the push you need to overcome path dependencies, break free from the traps, and move toward something new. You'll develop the tools to engage your next big idea and make change a reality.

IF YOU WANT TO CREATE THE FUTURE, YOU NEED TO DODGE THE TRAPS KEEPING YOU FIXATED ON THE PATH YOU ARE ALREADY ON.

The 7 Traps
of Path Dependency

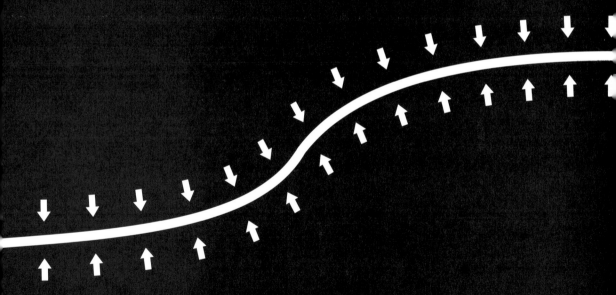

THE 7 TRAPS OF
PATH DEPENDENCY

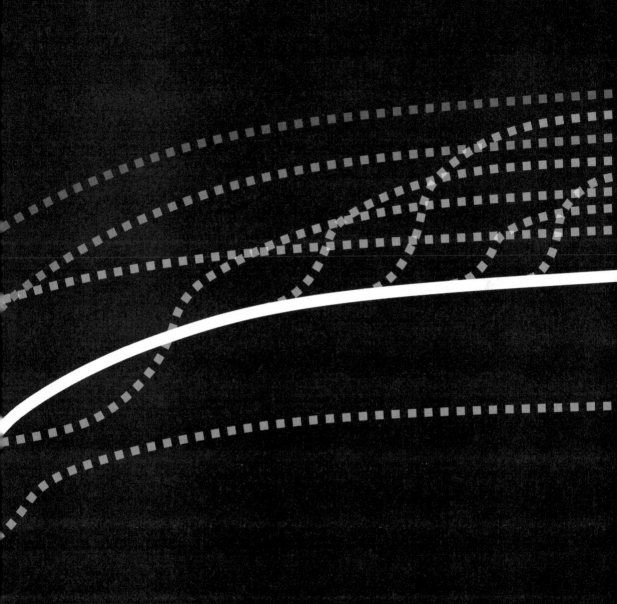

When people miss an opportunity in their own industry, it's not because they were blind to new ideas. Typically, smart people miss out because new ideas seem awkward and different. To find your breakthrough, you need to better spot the subtle clues that hint toward great ideas.

YOUR BREAKTHROUGH IS CLOSER THAN YOU THINK, BUT IT IS EASY TO MISS OUT

Let me tell you the story of Tony the Inventor. Tony was a relentless entrepreneur at heart, but he struggled to figure out his big idea. He knew only one thing, which was that his idea would be a gadget. He grew his career at a gadget company called Phillips and ascended to the role of VP of strategy and new ventures.

Eventually he came up with a mysterious idea for a hard drive gadget. He pitched the product numerous times, but nobody at Phillips bought into his vision. However, he was dedicated to turning his idea into a reality, so he quit his job and began pursuing his own venture. The problem was that he couldn't raise the money to make a prototype, which would have cost millions of dollars. After two years of trying, he felt his dream was almost at an end.

Before giving up entirely, he approached a CEO buddy and offered all of his intellectual property for his big idea. In exchange the CEO would give Tony the job of making the product. His CEO buddy accepted, despite the fact that the company was struggling. After a few months of innovation, the prototype was ready, and Tony hopped on a plane to take it to the eager CEO. Unfortunately, when he got off the plane, he realized the device had slipped out of his pocket! Luckily, the airline helped him form a search party, and two hours later they found the prototype, which had slipped between two seats. As it turned out, Tony's buddy was Steve Jobs, the company was Apple, and the prototype was the historic first iPod.[6]

Tony became head of Apple's new division, which later became the iPhone, and spearheaded a trajectory that changed the world.

THE PATHWAY TO GREATNESS CAN BE FRAUGHT WITH DOUBT.

THERE IS A SUBTLETY TO GREAT IDEAS.

BE DETERMINED!

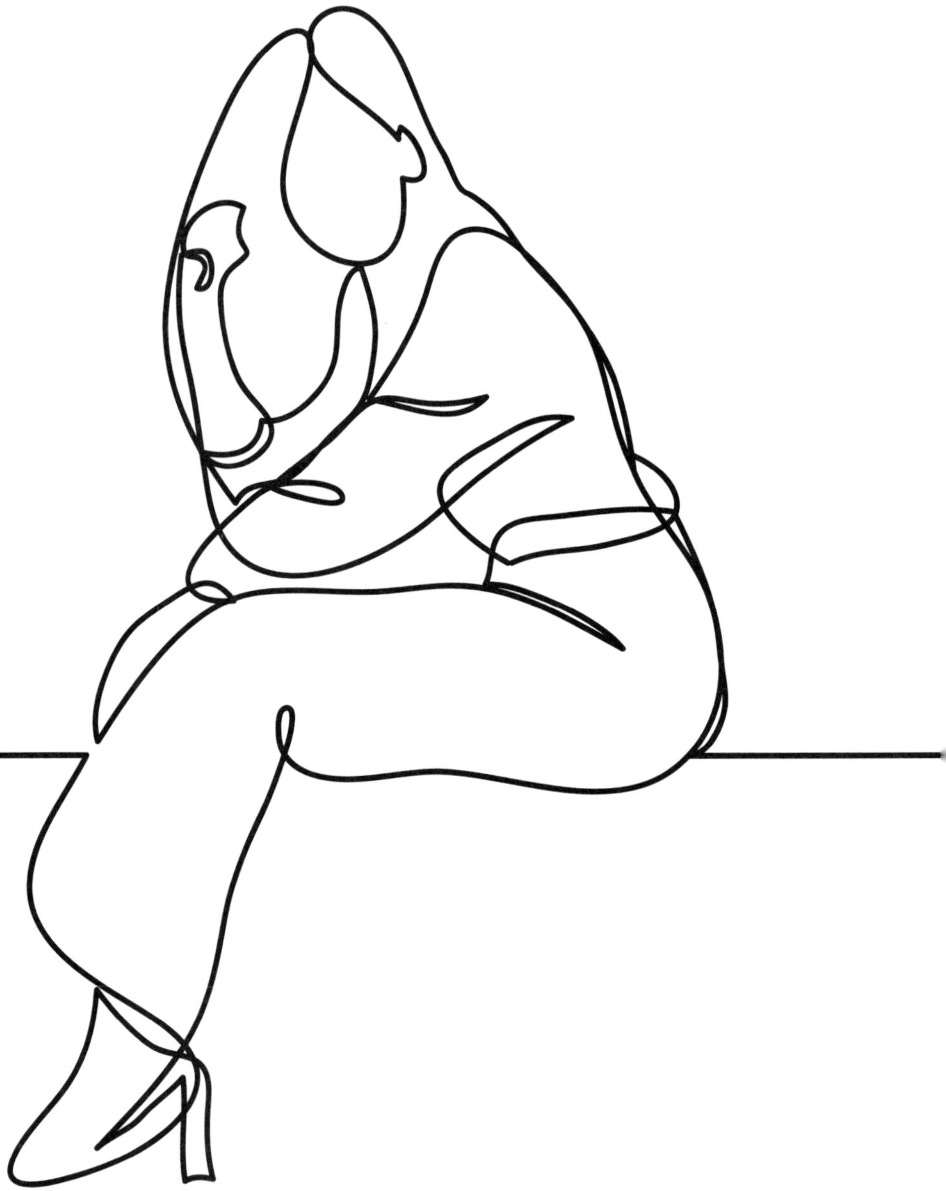

EVEN IDEAS THAT CHANGE THE WORLD CAN BE DISCOUNTED BY MARKET LEADERS

Most people immediately understood the potential of Tony's prototype, but the brightest people in the industry did not. Included in the list of notables who passed on the iPod are—

1. **PHILLIPS**: Gave up on Tony, their VP of strategy and new ventures.

2. **MICROSOFT**: Steve Ballmer, worth $41 billion—"There's no chance!"[7]

3. **MOTOROLA**: Padmasree Warrior, CTO—"Nothing revolutionary about it . . ."[8]

4. **PALM**: Ed Colligan, CEO, worth $3.4 billion—"[They] are not going to figure it out."

5. **NOKIA**: (market leader with 1 billion customers), Anssi Vanjoki, Chief Strategist—"With Mac, Apple remained a niche [expect the same] in mobile phones"[9] and switching to Android would be like the Finnish boys who "pee in their pants" for warmth in the winter.[10]

6. **BLACKBERRY**: Mike Lazaridis (worth $2 billion)—"[With Apple's ads] customers are now coming to the store [and leaving with a Blackberry], and so what it's actually done is increased our sales."[11]

Why did the market leaders dismiss the potential of such a revolutionary product when you and EVERYBODY else immediately realized the smartphone would be awesome? They were too comfortable and confident in their familiar paths.

For the record, Tony would eventually leave Apple to start a new gadget company that was positioned to make a better thermostat. The company was Nest, which he sold to Google for $3.2 billion.[12]

THE PARADOX OF SUCCESS IS THAT NEW IDEAS OFTEN SEEM AWKWARD AT FIRST, CAUSING THEM TO BE OVERLOOKED.

SMART PEOPLE OVERESTIMATE THEIR LEVEL OF CONTROL

There was once a guy named Ferruccio who could fix anything. Following WWII, he could turn almost any deserted war machine into farming equipment. Eventually, he started his own tractor company.

When he first became successful, he bought a Ferrari and loved it, leading him to join the Ferrari racing club. It was there that Ferruccio met Enzo Ferrari and told him about an idea that would make the car's clutch better. Enzo got upset. "You stick to making tractors, and I'll make cars," he told Ferruccio.

Turns out, Ferruccio's last name was Lamborghini.[13] The takeaway is that successful people and companies overestimate their own control and command of their market.

OFTEN, THE IDEA THAT'S DISMISSED BECOMES THE ONE THAT TOPPLES AN EMPIRE.

IRONICALLY, MARKET LEADERS ARE AT A GREATER RISK OF MISSING OUT

Enzo Ferrari wasn't the first market leader to dismiss an innovative idea presented to him. History is littered with instances where a market leader couldn't see the potential in a rivaling idea.

Market Leaders Who Overlooked Great Ideas

- England rejected Thomas Edison's light bulb and said it was "unworthy of the attention of practical or scientific men."[14]
- Western Union rejected Alexander Graham Bell's telephone, saying it was "idiotic. Why would any person want to use this ungainly and impractical device?"[15]
- The *Kansas City Star* fired Walt Disney, saying he "lacked imagination and had no good ideas."[16]
- Kodak invented digital photography in 1975 but didn't adapt and went bankrupt.[17]
- HP rejected Steve Wozniak's computer ideas three times.[18]
- Atari could have owned 33% of Apple for $50,000.
- EDS could have bought Microsoft ($60 million).[19]
- Excite could have bought Google ($1 million).[20]
- Myspace could have owned Facebook ($75 million).[21]
- Yahoo could have owned Facebook ($1 billion).[22]
- Britannica could have been Encarta, but they rejected Bill Gates.
- Encarta could have been Wikipedia.[23]
- Blockbuster had three chances to buy Netflix ($50 million).[24]
- You and I could have been a lot wealthier if we put all our money into Amazon.

MARKET LEADERS CONSISTENTLY MISS OUT ON GREAT NEW IDEAS BECAUSE THEY OVERESTIMATE THEIR MARKET DOMINANCE.

ALMOST EVERY TALE OF DISRUPTION INVOLVES SMART PEOPLE DISMISSING A SUBTLE NEW IDEA

Let me paint you a picture of an iconic innovator. This is a game of **GUESS THE COMPANY**. Here are a few facts:

- Invented "the most successful single product of all time"
- Invented the mouse
- Invented the graphic user interface
- Invented the concept of email
- Invented networked computers
- Built the foundation for the internet

Did you guess Apple? Microsoft? Or did you know that the correct answer is Xerox? These days, it seems like a trick question, but in 1973, researchers at the Xerox Parc Research Lab launched the Xerox Altos and changed the course of history.

The Altos had a mouse, graphic user interface, email, and everything you needed to copy, paste, and print your documents. The Altos could remind you of upcoming appointments and even had image processing reminiscent of the animated GIFs you see today. This Xerox model was more than a decade ahead of its time. Xerox had more than 1,000 of the Altos stations built, but the product was never sold because the company was too busy harvesting the market for its profitable photocopiers.

SUCCESSFUL COMPANIES OFTEN FAIL TO SEE THE POTENTIAL OF IDEAS OUTSIDE THEIR WHEELHOUSE.

In 1979, about a decade after the Altos project began, Steve Jobs and Bill Gates took tours of the facility. Those on the project, including Larry Tesler, were more than delighted to see someone take an interest in the project. Tesler explained, "During that demo, Steve again got very excited. He was pacing around the room and occasionally looking at the screen. . . . Jobs was there going, 'What is going on here? You're sitting on a gold mine. Why aren't you doing anything with this?'"[25]

The Xerox Alto, 1973

Ironically, Tesler notes that they only showed Jobs 1% of what Xerox was up to. Five years later, Apple and Microsoft would launch their own Altos-inspired devices.

In the words of Steve Jobs, "Within 10 minutes, it was obvious to me that all computers would work like this someday. Basically, they were copier-heads that just had no clue about what a computer could do. . . . Xerox could have owned the entire computer industry today."[26]

BEING OUTSIDE OF AN INDUSTRY MAKES IT EASIER TO SEE THE POTENTIAL IN NEW IDEAS.

IT CAN BE DIFFICULT TO SEE POTENTIAL IN SOMETHING NEW

A friend of mine, Todd Henry, introduced me to the tale of a struggling musician named James. James had talent, but there are millions of talented musicians who never get their music out there. What they need is a big break.

One day, James was approached with the opportunity of a lifetime. One of the biggest bands in the world heard his tracks and invited him to be their opening act. The offer was to be part of a 27-city world tour. It was any musician's dream.

Eager and excited, he walked into his first stadium and faced a crowd of people who were going to hear his songs. He was about to be famous, and he could feel it. He began strumming his guitar and rocking out to his first songs. But the audience was silent. They didn't cheer when he expected them to cheer. No worries—he moved on to the second song. Still more silence. Then he started to play his third song, and the audience started to react—with booing.

It was a terrible beginning, but he persisted. At the second concert, things were different. They started to boo on the first song. By the sixth concert, they booed before he even strummed his guitar. He gave the audience the middle finger, threw his guitar, and quit the tour.

It would be easy to give up when experiencing such rejection. But he didn't. And that's the tale of James Marshall "Jimi" Hendrix opening for the Monkees. Hendrix was playing new, innovative music, and the Monkees' fans weren't ready for it.

EVEN YOUR BIGGEST FUTURE FANS MIGHT NEED TIME TO UNDERSTAND YOUR NEW WAY OF DOING THINGS.

MOST BILLION DOLLAR START-UPS EXPERIENCED AT LEAST SOME LEVEL OF REJECTION

The internet dates back to 1952, but it didn't experience full traction for almost 40 years. The internet's "big break," if you will, happened when the concept of email was haphazardly introduced in the 1970s. By the 1980s, the majority of all internet traffic was email communication.

With that context in mind, Jack Smith and Sabeer Bhatia set out to pitch investors on the concept of Hotmail. Imagine: a service where anyone in the world could get their own email address, absolutely free! It was a relatively simple business model, which could be funded by advertising.

This didn't seem as complicated as you might think, but investors hated it. Smith and Bhatia's idea was rejected 100 times. Eventually, the private equity firm Draper Fisher Jurvetson cut them a check for $300,000. A year and a half after their launch, Hotmail was sold to Microsoft for $400 million. Not a bad return.

Other iconic companies that struggled with having funding rejected:

1. Google
2. Apple
3. Cisco
4. LinkedIn
5. Amazon
6. Salesforce
7. Airbnb

IT CAN BE DIFFICULT TO SEE THE POTENTIAL IN SOMETHING NEW.[27]

- How might you change your weekly routines to ensure you are open to disruptive thinking and subtle ideas?

- What are the most recent ideas that have been suggested and dismissed?

- If you involved 10 people unrelated to your market, what ideas would they suggest for your industry?

TACTICS

1. Assume you are incorrect.
2. Be more open to new ideas.
3. Reward and encourage dissent.
4. Designate a Devil's Advocate.
5. Discuss the competing alternative to your decisions.
6. Perform case studies about emerging trends.
7. Embrace diversity.
8. Actively hunt trends.
9. Study other markets.
10. Push yourself to see potential in awkward ideas.
11. Learn about similar companies that missed key opportunities.
12. Get outsiders to suggest ideas you might be missing.
13. Hire leaders from different markets.
14. Host idea competitions.
15. Invite junior hires, outsiders, and customers to a workshop.

THE ABILITY TO CHANGE

21

NEXT STEP

To stay on top of opportunity, you have to put in the work.

We often miss out on ideas within our own industries because:

1. We are busy.

2. We feel in control.

3. We get caught in a groove (for the seven reasons discussed in each section of this book).

4. There's too much to track.*

* In fact, I'd argue that the act of getting inspired has become overwhelming and distracting at times, but it's a necessity. You have to make time to scan for ideas, filter down to the best ones, and look for patterns:

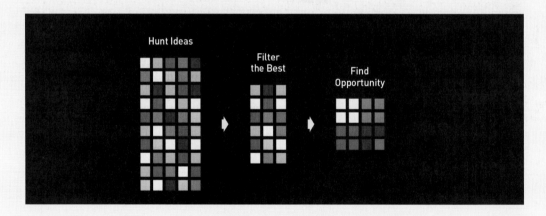

The many ways to get better at hunting opportunity will be discussed in an entire section of the flip side of this book. For now, the key takeaway is that you need to force yourself to explore new ideas if you don't want to miss out.

TRACK INNOVATION RELATED TO YOUR MARKET AND SET ASIDE TIME TO REFLECT ON WHAT HAS CHANGED.

LOOKING FOR MORE?

If you would like to dive deeper into trends or opportunities, join millions of people who get free inspiration at Trend Hunter, the world's largest collection of new ideas.

When I started Trend Hunter, I was effectively trying to automate a process to collect insights from around the world in the hope that I'd discover an idea that could become my own. Today, it has become a tremendous resource that could simplify your own efforts to track trends in the consumer markets you care about most.

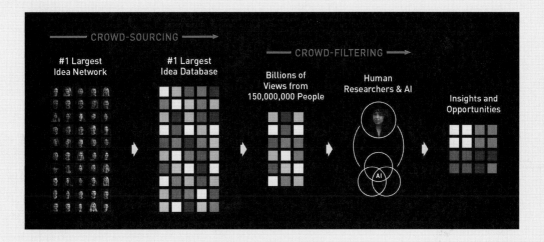

We enable anyone in the world to contribute ideas, and more than 200,000 people have signed up so far. We publish the best ideas and use our audience of 150 million people to filter out the most popular concepts; to date, we have analyzed several billion onsite choices. Finally, we use a combination of human research and artificial intelligence to identify core patterns and insights.

The next step, of course, is yours. Uncover the trends and insights that are meaningful to you, and channel them into action!

TRACK THE TOPICS OF YOUR CHOOSING FOR FREE WITH ——— ——— *A CUSTOMIZABLE DASHBOARD: TRENDHUNTER.COM/DASHBOARD*

THE 7 TRAPS OF
PATH DEPENDENCY

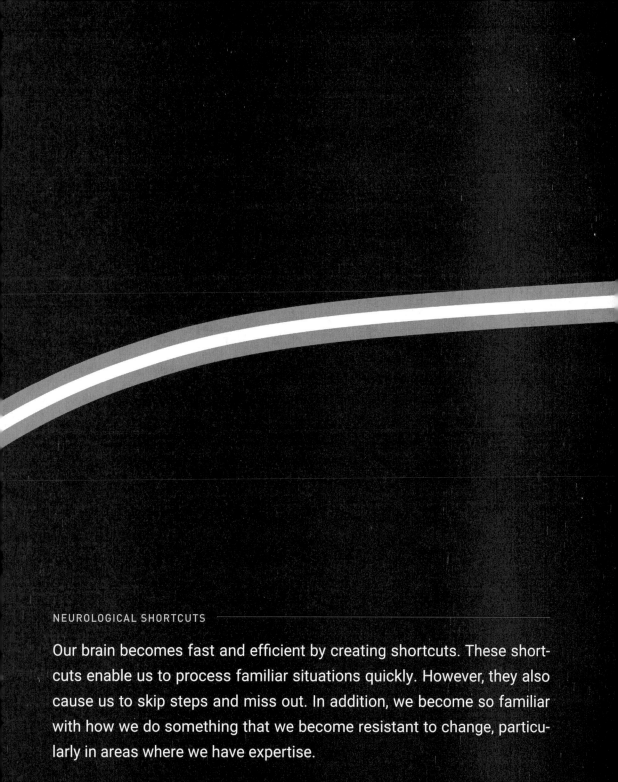

NEUROLOGICAL SHORTCUTS

Our brain becomes fast and efficient by creating shortcuts. These short-cuts enable us to process familiar situations quickly. However, they also cause us to skip steps and miss out. In addition, we become so familiar with how we do something that we become resistant to change, particularly in areas where we have expertise.

TRAGICALLY, WE LEARN TO LIMIT OUR CREATIVITY

This is my niece, Alee. She's extremely creative, which you'll discover in a page or two. One of the best things to know about Alee is that she loves dinosaurs—a lot.

I wanted to test the depth of her love, so I offered to buy her a brand-new princess doll in exchange for her dinosaur. She quickly explained to me that "T-REXES EAT PRINCESSES FOR BREAKFAST!" Shocking, but probably true.

Knowing this, let me tell you about the worst day in Alee's little history. One day, she was watching a documentary about her beloved extinct creatures, and she burst into tears.

"T-REXES EAT PRINCESSES FOR BREAKFAST"

We could barely get any words out of her, until finally, she explained the source of her deep sorrow. She explained that she was sad "'cause there's no more dinosaurs." I thought she meant it was sad because dinosaurs were extinct, but it gets cuter. She clarified that she was depressed "'cause the paleontologists already found the bones." Tragic!

Here's the takeaway: you need to explain that dinosaurs don't exist, or middle school is going to be really difficult. However, every time you tell a little girl dinosaurs don't exist, you limit her imagination.

As you progress through life, you continue to see your imagination limited. By the time you reach the working world, you'll have learned about rules, policies, procedures, structures, compliance, past investment, and brand standards.

You'll still want to be creative and identify as a creative person, but you'll also get busy with a personal life, a significant other, kids, projects, meetings, and deadlines. Before we even dive into neurological shortcuts, these realities of life will start to reduce your willingness to push harder for creative ideas.

When you finally get a bright new idea, you'll present it up the ladder, and in many cases, you'll encounter doubt and concerns. One of my favorite clients, Bill Hayden, is the chief strategy officer for Universal Parks. He explained this dilemma to my company's Future Festival audience by stating: "Boardrooms are full of people who built their careers challenging ideas and showing you what's wrong."

Over the course of your life, these realities will slowly dissolve the intensity of your creative thinking.

OUR CREATIVITY GETS LIMITED BY LEARNED BEHAVIOR AND ALL —— —— OF THE THINGS WE DO TO FUNCTION AS PRODUCTIVE ADULTS.

YOUR ABILITY TO GET FAST AND EFFICIENT CREATES BLIND SPOTS

Your brain creates shortcuts to ensure you are a high-performing, quick-thinking human being. These shortcuts have a lot of upsides, but they also have incredible implications when it comes to innovation and change. Much of this can be understood by contemplating just one feature of your brain: **myelin**.

The first time Serena Williams picked up a racket, the first time Oprah picked up a microphone, and the first time J. K. Rowling picked up a pen, they had to fumble around and think about what they were doing. It wasn't as natural as it is for them today. Similarly, you have to put a lot of effort into each action when you try something new, like driving a car. You had to think about merging, accelerating, and where to look. Today, you're an expert, and driving is probably easy for you.

When you perform a task for the first time, your brain needs to figure out what you are trying to do. This results in your brain shooting a spark along a new neural pathway. Once you start practicing something over and over again, your brain decides to make it easier for you by paving a little pathway of myelin. Myelin is a white fatty tissue, and it guides your synapses, making you better and faster. As you master a skill, you start building a LOT of myelin. In fact, 40% of your brain is made up of myelin tissue. By the time you reach your 10,000 hours at a given skill (the estimated time required to achieve mastery), your top myelin pathways for that skill can be 100 times faster. The catch is that you now have one preferred pathway, and you perform this task the same way every time.

PRACTICE CREATES MYELIN, WHICH MAKES YOU SMARTER AND FASTER, BUT IT ALSO MAKES YOU REPETITIVE, CONSISTENT, AND DISMISSIVE.

WHEN YOU PRACTICE SOMETHING NEW, YOUR BRAIN PAVES PATHWAYS OF MYELIN

Figuring Something Out
New Neural Pathway / Action Potential

Without Myelin

With Myelin
Up to 100x Faster

The Catch
Now THIS Is How You Do It

YOUR NEW PARTY TRICK: PROVING HOW MENTAL SHORTCUTS WORK

I won't make you do a million physical activities during the course of this book, but please take a moment to try these two activities before reading ahead. Personally, I'm the type of person who dismisses such a task and ends up reading ahead, but I promise that you will enjoy this section more (AND have a new party trick) if you try the activities on this page.

TASK 1.

First, cross your arms, QUICKLY . . .

Great, you did it! Easy.

TASK 2.

Now, uncross your arms and cross them again, QUICKLY, the opposite way.

Task 1 was simple because it is automatic; but it feels awkward to do the same exercise differently the next time, because we are so set in our familiar path—thanks to myelin. You have crossed your arms thousands of times, and myelin has built up in your motor pathways to make this happen simply. When I change the directions slightly, however, you have to briefly think about what you're doing.

Now imagine what happens with a more complex task!

TASK 3.

What can you do with a paper clip?

This time, I want you to actually work through it. Close this book and think about all of the things you can do with a paper clip. Sure, you can clip paper, but make a quick list of other options . . .

Don't flip the page until you complete Task 3.

QUICK PROOF

CROSS
YOUR ARMS

THE OTHER WAY

HOW MANY WAYS CAN YOU USE A PAPER CLIP?

If you close your eyes and give it a try, or bring this exercise to a group of your fellow adults, you will probably reach 10 to 15 solid ideas.

There are two interesting catches to this exercise:

1. Most kindergarten kids can actually give you 200 ideas or more.

2. I can usually guess which ideas a group of adults will say.

The reason this activity is so predictable is that our brains (and myelin) narrow our thinking to the things we have done or decided before. Myelin might be great for making fast decisions in situations where speed is critical, but it is a terrible trap if you care about innovation and change. This activity was just about a paper clip, but imagine how this blind spot impacts more complex decision-making.

↻ My Guess of What You'll Say

1.	Pick a Lock	6.	Chain	11.	Money Clip
2.	Projectile Weapon	7.	Earring	12.	Tie Clip
3.	Reset a Device	8.	Clip Paper	13.	Tooth Pick / Ear
4.	Necklace	9.	Hang Ornament	14.	Trade It > House
5.	Bracelet	10.	Collar Stay	15.	Art

If you did this exercise properly, you are probably a bit shocked. If you faked it and flipped the page too early, try this on a group of colleagues or friends. You'll find that the results are replicated consistently.

The dilemma is that we are arguably becoming more intelligent over time, but we lose 95% of our raw creativity.

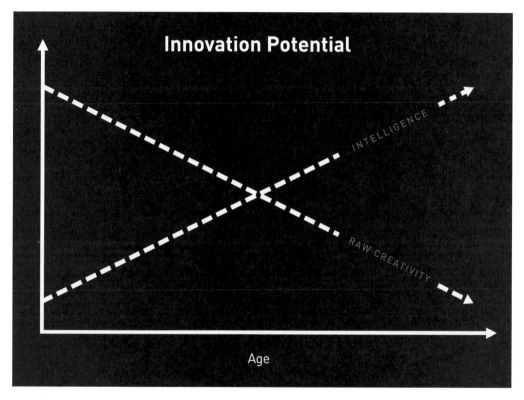

This loss is related to myelin and our brain's desire to create shortcuts. This paper clip experiment, known as The Alternative Uses Test (J.P. Guilford), dates back to 1967, and you can repeat it with all sorts of basic objects. Myelin makes us faster, but it also creates ruts—literal pathways—that keep us in a cycle of repeating past decisions.

THE IMPORTANT TAKEAWAY HERE IS NOT THAT WE HAVE FEWER IDEAS THAN CHILDREN,
BUT THAT WE NARROW OUR THINKING BY REVERTING TO THINGS WE'VE SEEN AND DONE BEFORE.

YOU HAVE MANY CREATIVE IDEAS WELL WITHIN YOUR REACH

The implication of this exercise is that you have more great ideas than you realize, but to access those ideas, you need to do some things differently. You need to recognize your blind spots and do specific activities to extract better thinking from your brain, because otherwise, your brain will narrow your thinking and you will miss out.

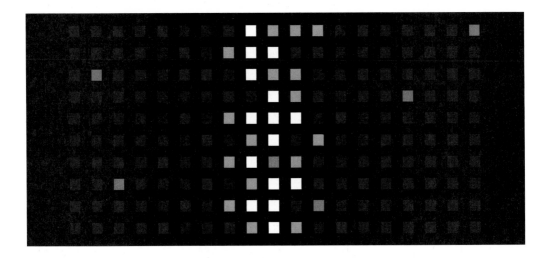

To access these wonderful gems, you need to look at your problem from multiple perspectives, which can be accomplished in workshops where you—

- include people with diverse perspectives;

- simulate how other companies would approach the same problem; or

- force yourself to solve a known problem in a different way.

THE OBVIOUS BENEFIT OF A WORKSHOP IS THAT IT BREAKS YOU OUT OF YOUR ROUTINE, POTENTIALLY GETTING YOU TO A NEW IDEA.

The more exciting benefit, however, is that you are also training your brain and thus building new myelin pathways that enable you to look at your problem from different perspectives.

Practicing creativity will make you smarter, faster, and better at innovation and change.

This idea of expansive thinking is a typical concept I am asked to help with when running workshops for high-performance teams like Google or Coca-Cola. These teams are full of bright people who have thought exhaustively about solutions in many different categories, but there's always something new, something overlooked, or something that is suddenly a good fit due to evolving technology or cultural shifts.

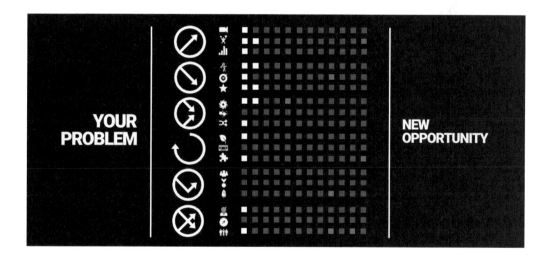

When you look at your problem from different angles, you are more likely to extract hidden potential. Meanwhile, you will build new myelin to make your brain better at creative problem-solving. The next pages present an overview of sample workshops that I would encourage you to test and practice.

IF YOU WANT TO REALIZE YOUR FULL POTENTIAL, YOU NEED TO PRACTICE CREATIVE THINKING AND USING WORKSHOPS TO BUILD NEW MYELIN.

EFFECTIVE WORKSHOPS LEAD TO NEW IDEAS, WHILE TRAINING YOUR BRAIN TO BE MORE CREATIVE

As someone who has conducted more than a thousand workshops, these are my favorites:

Trend Hunter Menu of Workshops

1. **RAPID PROTOTYPING**—What if you worked very quickly to develop a new product or service? (Examples of how to do this are in Part 2 of this book.)

2. **SIMULATION EXERCISES**—Imagine a specific disruption or opportunity has occurred. Enact how you would work through it.

3. **DYSTOPIA VS. UTOPIA**—Imagine if five years from now, your company became irrelevant or—better yet—newly inspiring. What do you think could lead to such a scenario?

4. **BLANK SLATE REINVENTION**—If you started your business today, from scratch, what specifically would be different? Go department by department.

5. **PATTERN WORKSHOPS**—Using Trend Hunter's Six Patterns of Opportunity, look at your world from other perspectives. Could that uncover new opportunities?

6. **CASE STUDIES**—Looking at other markets, what grand ideas could you incorporate into your own?

7. **RECONNECT THE DOTS**—If you looked at all of the trends in your industry, what opportunities could you see if you pushed yourself to keep reconnecting the dots?

8. **SIMILAR INDUSTRIES**—Pick five unrelated but similar industries. What could you learn from their new strategies and innovations?

9. **ROLE-PLAY THE FUTURE**—If you split your team into multiple groups, what would each team envision as the key factors that would shape your future?

10. **BRAINSTORM WITH OUTSIDERS**—What would happen if you held a brainstorm with your team and 10 successfully eclectic individuals?

11. **HACKATHONS**—What would happen if you gave your top teams unlimited freedom in a specific amount of time, such as 6 hours, 24 hours, or 5 days?

12. **TREND SAFARIS**—What could you learn from experiencing the most creative start-ups in the city you are based in or visiting?

13. **DISRUPTING OTHERS**—If you were to disrupt other industries, such as beverages, retail, or e-commerce, how would you do it?

14. **DISRUPTION WORKSHOPS**—How would other people disrupt your company? Let's deep-dive this one:

How might Uber approach your market? Amazon? Google? Facebook? Patagonia? In a workshop setting, I typically get CEOs and their leadership teams to work through scenarios of how certain unrelated companies might disrupt them. If, for example, you learned that Google AI had allocated $1 billion to disrupting your industry, what do you think would be their strategy?

Work through how other companies might think about your business. This workshop illuminates opportunity and helps you see where your strengths and weaknesses lie.

	Value Proposition	Disruptive Features	Key Offering
Google	AI > Speed, Insight		
Uber	Simplicity		
Amazon	Heavily Customized & Lean		
Patagonia	Save the World		

WORKSHOPS SOLVE PROBLEMS
WHILE STRENGTHENING TEAMS

Like many companies, our Trend Hunter office has a monthly "fun day." In our case, we rotate between discovering something new in the city and having a team workshop. The workshops are always more exciting, more engaging, and lower cost. Yet, we are getting work done while having fun. Imagine that.

In short, these are the key benefits and goals:

1. **TEAM BONDING**—Get people from different departments to connect.

2. **FUN DAY**—Replace awkward bonding with something inclusive (and a beer or two).

3. **TRAINING**—The team learns more about the business and how to run a workshop.

4. **SOLVE BUSINESS PROBLEMS**—This outcome may pay the bar tab, but I intentionally put it last to remind myself that the other benefits are enough in themselves.

Here's an example of a workshop we recently ran for our 70-person team. Our director of client success, Gil Haddi, approached me with an idea. She wanted to create a referral program for our Future Festival events, and she had research, details, and suggestions. We could have worked through it together, but it was an inclusive problem and one where diverse minds would likely create a better solution. We booked the team for 2 p.m. on a Friday, and the afternoon went as follows.

STEP 1—INSPIRATION, CONTEXT, & FOCUS (30 minutes) Set the stage for the problem being solved. In our case, that meant exploring different types of referral programs. Each team got a cheat sheet of key points to help stimulate ideas.

STEP 2—SPLIT INTO ASSIGNED GROUPS OF SIX TO EIGHT (15 minutes) Mix up different levels of seniority and departments. This enhances team building, diversifies thinking, and keeps people diligent (especially with leadership team members).

STEP 3—THREE FOCUSED BRAINSTORMS (60 minutes) Keep your problems very focused to ensure you get usable ideas. I use the following template to extract as many ideas as possible. I also change the rules to keep it creative.

	Rules	Quick & Easy Ideas	Difficult Ideas	Dream List
Referrals BEFORE Future Festival 20 minutes	Headlines Only (be brief)			
Referrals AT Future Festival 20 minutes	Round Robin (go in order and no advancing until you say an idea)			
Referrals for Advisory Product 20 minutes	Silent Brainstorm			

STEP 4—SILENTLY CAPTURE THE TOP 10 IDEAS (10 minutes) Including silent individual time prevents groupthink and ensures diverse thinking from introverts and extroverts alike. Everyone emails in their favorite three ideas, resulting in a giant list.

STEP 5—DETERMINE YOUR BEST IDEA AND PRESENT IT AS A SKIT (30 minutes of prep, 30 minutes of presenting) This has always been a highlight of the day, with every group in every industry I've worked in. People love to see business ideas come to life.

The Result: In our case, there were several ideas that were much better than what we had initially imagined. For example, Trend Hunter recently announced that we are donating the funds to plant 2 million trees. One workshop team suggested we plant the trees in people's names—for example, "Bring a friend to Future Festival, and we will plant a tree and name it after you!" It's a simple but fun idea, and met our criteria of doing something that was not monetary.

IF YOU ARE NOT DOING REGULAR WORKSHOPS WITH YOUR TEAM, YOU ARE DOING A DISSERVICE TO THEIR TALENT.

DESPITE THE MANY TRAPS,
YOU CAN BECOME MORE INNOVATIVE

I immediately get jealous of my six-year-old niece when looking at this list of ages at which people peak. It seems she's better than me at creative imagination, which I cherish. The only redeeming thing about this chart is that it shows I can run faster, I can lift more, and I'm better at basic math. In addition, as I age, I will get better at all the other tasks related to being an innovative, creative leader.

We do lose certain aspects of raw creativity as we age. Having said that, we also become a lot better at many other tasks related to innovation and creativity.

Over time, we become better at understanding multiple points of view, anticipating change, considering other possible outcomes, acknowledging uncertainty, and searching for compromise.

The key to unlocking our new skillsets is also acknowledging the ways we are becoming more limited in our thinking. We need to internalize the way myelin (and other shortcuts) works in our brain. These shortcuts create neurological blind spots, meaning that we have a natural tendency to completely dismiss our new shortcomings.

YOUR BRAIN EVOLVES AS YOU AGE, CREATING NEW OPPORTUNITIES AND NEW CHALLENGES.
BEING AWARE OF HOW YOU EVOLVE PREPARES YOU TO BE A BETTER CREATOR.

THE AGES AT
WHICH YOU PEAK

THE ABILITY TO CHANGE

Source: Business Insider[28]

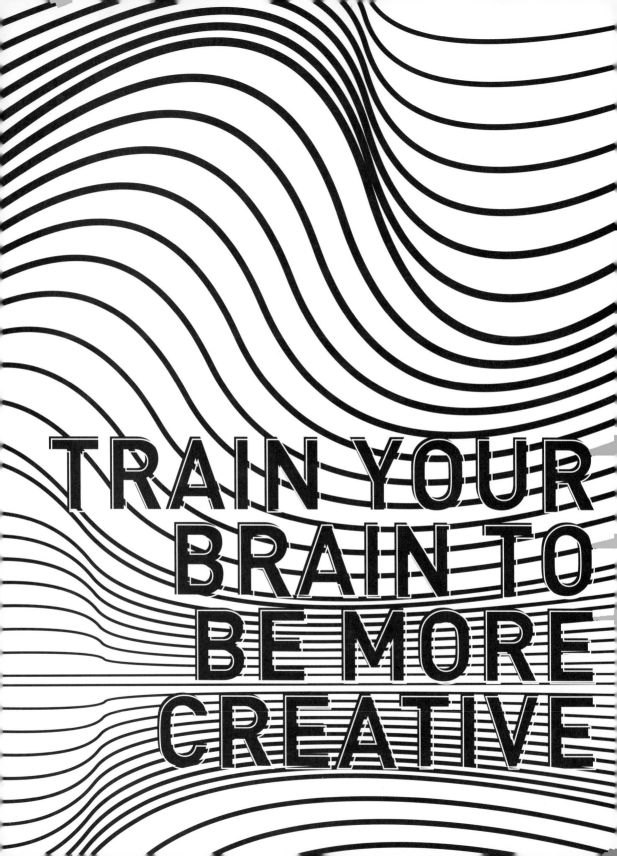

- What activities would you be willing to practice if it meant being much better at seeing opportunity?

- If you host a monthly workshop on rotating topics, what would the next four topics be? (There are loads of ideas for workshops on the previous pages!)

- Are you pushing your team's creativity? What else could you do?

TACTICS ————————————————————

1. Encourage play.
2. Stop knowing the answer (and instead ask questions).
3. Break rules.
4. Diversify your team.
5. Bring teams together.
6. Proactively solicit ideas.
7. Fund creative hobbies.
8. Track trends in other markets.
9. Run ongoing workshops with your team.
10. Host weekly blue-sky meetings.
11. Have themed creative days.
12. Visit innovative businesses.
13. Attend conferences unrelated to your profession.
14. Embrace the mindset of "no bad ideas."

THE ABILITY TO CHANGE

THE 7 TRAPS OF
PATH DEPENDENCY

1. The Subtlety of Opportunity
2. Neurological Shortcuts
3. The Ease of Inaction
4. Optionality
5. The Traps of Success
6. Linear Thinking
7. Discomfort vs. Breakthrough

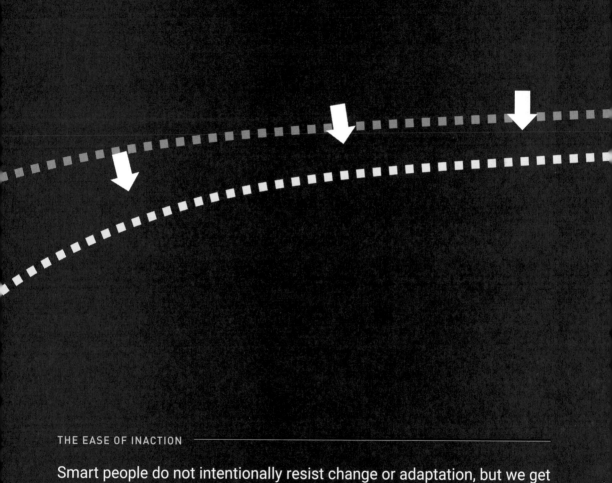

THE EASE OF INACTION

Smart people do not intentionally resist change or adaptation, but we get so caught up with everything that needs to be done that we become less proactive about ideas that are different, are not in our department, or are not our greatest concern. A multitude of factors make it easier for us to lack urgency, and if you can address those factors, you can spark the action you need to create the future.

WE ALL EXHIBIT SOME LEVEL OF RESISTANCE TO CHANGE . . .

Can you type? Of course you can, and like 99.9% of typists, you probably punch your keys on a keyboard with a QWERTY layout. That keyboard was developed for the first typewriters, and the layout was chosen to make sure the keys didn't mash together.

Today, however, you can open up your phone settings and switch to a Dvorak keyboard. Your keys will then be laid out in an entirely different way, optimized for modern typing. It will take you about six months to learn that typing layout, but at the end of the six months, you will type 30% faster because you will make fewer errors.

Would you like to switch? Why not? I just offered you a chance to increase your efficiency at something you do every day. Are you not willing to change?

THE BUSIER YOU BECOME, THE EASIER IT IS TO STAY ON YOUR PATH, DO NOTHING, AND MISS OPPORTUNITY.

...AND THERE ARE MANY FACTORS THAT FUEL OUR RESISTANCE

It's no secret that we have a desire to preserve the status quo. We like stability in our family life, our politics, and our jobs. Stability is not the enemy; it serves us well. The complication happens when we need innovation and change. Here's what you face when it comes to rolling out a different way of doing things:

    not enough time
+ preference for simplicity
+ cultural conformity
+ fear of failure
+ rigid structure
+ desire to optimize
+ busy life
+ neurology
+ constraints
+ groupthink
+ not my department
+ not my problem
+ diffusion of responsibility
= resistance to change

Just reading this list is tedious, so it's no surprise that actually working past these obstacles can feel like an insurmountable task.

START BY AUDITING THE FACTORS IN YOUR LIFE THAT INHIBIT ACTION

You can't change everything about your innate resistance to change, and you certainly are not going to change everything about your life. However, if you want change to happen, you need to internalize the extent to which certain habits and elements of structure impact your decision-making.

By workshopping your way through these categories, you can learn where you might have a lack of flexibility or balance that you would like to change.

For example, let's take the category of Busyness. Did you realize that you get a little hit of dopamine every time you answer a simple email or clear your inbox? Because of this, you get more distracted joy from answering 30 innocuous emails than you would by spending some time in deep, reflective thought. Can you set new email rules that liberate time?

If you look at the table of distractors, how many currently have an adverse impact on your time for deep thought? If you were to brainstorm tactics based on this list, you would likely find new ways to free up your time and schedule. Consider the following solutions:

- No Meetings on Monday Mornings

- 20-Minute Meeting Caps

- Blue-Sky Innovation Sessions

- Brainstorm Starting Your Business from Scratch

IF YOU WANT TO REDUCE YOUR RESISTANCE TO CHANGE, YOU NEED TO CLEAR THE OBSTACLES THAT BLOCK DEEP THOUGHT.

CATEGORIES OF ACTION LIMITERS

STRUCTURE
Procedures
Regulations
Compliance
Policies
Rules

OPTIMIZATION
Brand Standards
Best Practices
Methods
Formulas
Rollouts

LIFE
Life Events
Vacations
Kids
Family

NEUROLOGY
Complexity Shortcuts
Paradox of Choices
Loss Avoidance
Myelin

BUSYNESS
Phone Calls
Meeting
Deadlines
Emails
Feedback

CONSTRAINTS
Past Investment
Legacy Systems
Sunk Costs
Budget

TO INSPIRE ACTION, YOU MUST CREATE URGENCY

Do you like disruptive innovation? People seem to love the term and toss it around excitedly, but there's another side to the story. People are losing jobs, beloved brands are failing, and we are creating a world fraught with uncertainty.

The catch is that most disrupted companies don't see it coming because they lack urgency. Did you know that in the next 5–10 years, 40% of the current Fortune 500 companies will no longer exist in a meaningful way? We should all feel a sense of urgency. But people don't. In my experience, you can predict which companies are most at risk of disruption based on their self-perception of performance.

Self-Perception of Performance

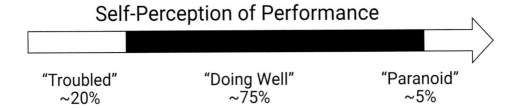

| "Troubled" | "Doing Well" | "Paranoid" |
| ~20% | ~75% | ~5% |

After writing my book about chaos, about 20% of my clients have been in the first category, "Troubled." The next year for these clients feels scary, but actually, this fear helps them create alignment and momentum. They operate with a sense of urgency and are less likely to resist change and experimentation. Companies that feel troubled can be the most open to new ideas because they fear failure and feel like they have less to lose.

For example, in my prior career, I helped grow Capital One to a billion-dollar portfolio in a year when things were bleak. The goal on my dashboard was to SHRINK the high-end business by ONLY 20%. Imagine that as a goal. At the end of the year, success would have meant telling my girlfriend, "Honey, I shrank the business by only 20%. I'm *THAT* good!" But actually, we pushed harder, acted sooner, and rolled out new products that tripled monthly bookings. It happened because of the *urgency*.

In a different example, a decade ago, Domino's Pizza was having a difficult time. Their stock price had plummeted almost 85% to $3. Things were gloomy, but that gave the teams the freedom to experiment and try all sorts of risky ideas. By the time we started working with them in 2012, we realized they had an enormous appetite for experimental ideas. In 2015, for example, they launched a new ordering system where you could order pizza by simply texting a pizza emoji. They also launched an app where you could order a pizza without any options for choice or customization. You just open the app and a pizza comes to you. No choice at all. Fast-forward to 2019, and the stock has been trading as high as $299, up nearly a hundredfold, making it one of the fastest-growing stocks in America.

Their ideas worked because people were feeling a desperate urgency to act. Otherwise, imagine being at a pizza company where things were working well and suggesting, "I think people should have no choice about what pizza they get, and they should order with an emoji." You would likely be laughed out of the boardroom.

On the other end of the spectrum, there is a very small group of highly disruptive organizations that are "paranoid" about their performance and competitors. These companies include some of the highest-performing brands, like Google, Walmart, Universal, and NASA. They fear disruption so much that they have ongoing workshops, innovation programs, and cultural imperatives to support creativity. They tolerate failure and talk about what could disrupt them. They perpetually fuel urgency.

All this leads us to the giant middle group of companies where people believe things are going "well." Unfortunately, that's the worst category to be in, because it usually signals complacency and a blindness to the upcoming pace of change. And mathematically, it just isn't possible for 75% of companies to be doing well when we know almost half of the brands will be disrupted in the next decade.

For individuals, the conclusions are the same. If you are down on your luck and urgently looking for new ideas, you are in a terrific spot. Most great ideas come from similar times of urgency. If you aren't feeling urgency, there's probably an opportunity somewhere that you're missing out on.

IF YOU WANT CHANGE TO HAPPEN, YOU MUST BEGIN BY ——— *IGNITING A SENSE OF URGENCY AND PURPOSE.*

YOU CAN TURN "TROUBLED" PERFORMANCE INTO ACTION

A decade ago, I received a call from a man named Tony Hunter, a passionate and engaging leader who was publisher of the *Chicago Tribune*. Tony explained that he loved my first book, *Exploiting Chaos*, so much that he'd gifted it to his managers and turned his favorite quotes into posters on his office wall. I had to see who could possibly like my book so much, so I flew to Chicago, elated to imagine I had a fan.

Before meeting Tony, I thought of the *Tribune* as just another media brand, but after meeting Tony, I learned what it's like to work at an iconic institution. When he greeted me in the Tribune Tower, he toured me around its cathedral-like entryway, which is adorned with the quotes of journalists and authors of days past. It became very clear that to Tony, this was much more important than a "job."

The catch is that Tony's life was about to get flipped upside down.

To set the stage, Tony had enjoyed a great career and was 15 years in with record growth and a strong trajectory. It was tough to imagine his world could be disrupted. However, markets turned and blogs started rivaling traditional newspapers for traffic. In my case, Trend Hunter was getting more page views than the *Tribune* with our tiny staff of seven. So Tony and I had a fair bit to talk about.

A few years later, something surprising happened. In the midst of market troubles, Tony's phone rang and he received the call of his dreams: he was offered the role of CEO. The catch was that they wanted him to accept the position and then file for bankruptcy, fire his friends, shrink the paper, motivate who was left, AND sell more ads.

It was like being asked to become the captain of the *Titanic* so that you could *intentionally* ram the beloved ship into an iceberg. If you accept such a role, you destroy your beloved company, ruin your relationships, and basically commit career suicide. Like . . . if you're going to do it, you have to just delete your LinkedIn profile. Just delete it. It's gone. Just tell people you're not on social media.

Despite the daunting size of the challenge, Tony accepted the role and the challenge to save the paper. But reality immediately began to sink in when he filed for bankruptcy. Though the plan was to reinvent, it must have felt like signing the death certificate for his beloved brand.

Tony's next duty was laying off a large part of the team—many of whom were friends. He explained to me, "The first more difficult day was the day that we recognized that we'd have to right-size the company and fire anywhere between 15% and 20% of the employee base. I think any time you are a leader and you have to make those kinds of tough decisions, that's a tough day, because of people."

He elaborated, "I got through that day knowing I could lose all jobs or save quite a few. And one way to lose all jobs is to keep doing the same thing we are doing today."

With two of the difficult but straightforward steps complete, Tony was now tasked with how to motivate who was left, shrink the paper, and sell more ads. It would be the most difficult professional task of his life.

In Tony's words, "I believe the role of the leader during disruptive times is to create a pathway and a reason for change. . . . We had to go from being a newspaper company to being a media and business services company that happens to publish a newspaper. And think about that in the Tribune Tower."

To create these pathways for change, Tony began hosting regular town hall meetings, where he would solicit opinions, discuss competing alternatives, and run workshops intended to gain alignment between the teams. These workshops helped people feel involved in the co-creation of the *Tribune*'s future, and they helped spark the sense of urgency needed to make change happen.

I will walk through an example of some of the workshops I've used with his team, but note my details will be a bit generalized to avoid revealing specifics about their team members. Instead, I will indicate how you might apply these workshops to your own company.

IMAGINE UTOPIA VS. DYSTOPIA TO CREATE URGENCY

My favorite workshop for creating urgency is called Utopia vs. Dystopia. The concept is that if you get people to imagine the path to a disastrous future, versus a wonderful future, they will realize the key risks and opportunities facing the company and feel the urgent need to change. Nobody wants a disastrous future! (I was first taught this tactic by Anik Karimjee, CEO of Rank Research Group, when I ran innovation at Capital One.)

Step 1: What five factors will shape your future?

Dystopia	Utopia
1.	1.
2.	2.
3.	3.
4.	4.
5.	5.

Imagine a world five years from today where your company has become irrelevant. Your team was unsuccessful, your projects did not work out, and you have to move on to a different job. What do you realistically think would be the key factors leading to downfall? In the *Tribune* example, what could lead to total collapse? Not embracing digital? Not attracting a younger demographic? Not motivating the team members who remain?

Next, imagine the opposite. What factors would lead your company to a utopia where everything works out wonderfully? I often perform this exercise with groups ranging from 50 to 500, typically with people seated in teams of 6 to 10 people. After 5 to 10 minutes, teams will have worked through their lists, and I get them to share, table by table.

TWO KEY OUTCOMES OCCUR: FIRST, YOU START TO FEEL URGENCY BECAUSE YOU REALIZE DYSTOPIA HAPPENS WITH INACTION. SECOND, UTOPIA WILL SEEM LIKE A LOT OF WORK.

Step 2: Choose the top three priorities

The next step is to let each table choose the three priorities they want to focus on. At this point, I make sure every table, even in a large room, shares their priorities. This acts as a barometer for the organization. If every group imagines dystopia and chooses their three most important areas for innovation, you get a very strong sense of what needs to be fixed. In this case, let's imagine your own team at the *Tribune* chose shrink the paper, sell more ads, and motivate the team.

Step 3: Rapid prototyping

With your top three priorities figured out, your next step would be to have three separate brainstorming exercises, working through short-term, long-term, and dream-list ideas for each of your top priorities. An obvious outcome is that you will get many ideas, but you will also get more buy-in and alignment because you are involving the team in the steps involved to make big change.

	Short-Term Tactics	Long-Term Strategy	Dream List
Priority 1: Shrink the Paper			
Priority 2: Sell More Ads			
Priority 3: Motivate the Team			

The act of including teams in workshops has a dramatic impact on people's motivation. It demonstrates a willingness to hear ideas and provides a forum to elicit creative thinking. In addition, since teams pick their favorite three priorities, they are also having the three conversations they already wanted to have.

Optional Step 4: Dive deeper with Six Patterns of Opportunity

Once the preliminary ideas are exhausted, you can dive deeper, using Trend Hunter's Six Patterns of Opportunity. These patterns are like unique lenses to help you think about your problems from different angles. If you want to learn more, these patterns are described further in the other side of this book, in the section on opportunity hunting.

Pattern	Sub-patterns	Questions
Divergence	• Personalization • Customization • Status + Belonging • Style + Fashionizing • Generational Rebellion	• What do people hate about your INDUSTRY? • How could you be more CUSTOMIZED, unique, or different from the mainstream?
Convergence	• Combining + Layering • Adding Value • Co-branding + Aligning • Physical +Digital	• What other SERVICES could be combined with your offering? • What COMPANIES could you collaborate with?
Acceleration	• Perfecting One Thing • Aspirational Icon • Exaggerated Feature • Reimagined Solution	• Specifically, what is it that you are TRYING to achieve? • How might you REDEFINE your most important feature?
Reduction	• Specialization • Fewer Layers + Efficiency • Crowdsourcing • Subscription	• What parts of your business do consumers actually CARE about? • If you split your work into five companies, which one would be the most VALUABLE?
Cyclicality	• Retro • Generational • Economic + Seasonal • Repetitive Cycles	• Since your last reinvention, how much have styles, tech, and culture CHANGED? • What do your NEXT customers think about your relevance and how can you reposition?
Redirection	• Refocusing • Reversing • Surprising • Gamifying	• What big trends or rituals could you RECHANNEL? • Where could you OVER DELIVER to delight?

TO LEARN MORE ABOUT THE PATTERNS, READ MY PREVIOUS BOOK,
BETTER AND FASTER, *OR EXPLORE OUR WEBSITE AT: TRENDHUNTER.COM/PATTERNS.*

A MOTIVATED TEAM CAN ACHIEVE THE IMPOSSIBLE

When the situation at the *Chicago Tribune* turned dire, Tony was able to rally the troops. It was not an easy task, but when the self-perception of performance turned from a feeling of "doing well" to "troubled," people knew they needed to embrace change, align, and act.

In Tony's example, instead of shrinking the paper, the *Tribune* decided to make a larger paper. This caused them to become the default source of news in Chicago, because if you wanted your local news, you *needed* that giant paper. This is the pattern of Divergence.

When thinking about how to sell more ads, they zeroed in on their customers' needs. Local papers are supported by local advertisers, which tend to be businesses with a terrible marketing strategy.

The insight was that the *Tribune* already had all of the relationships and, in many cases, was the most significant area of advertising spend for those companies. By transforming into a business services company, the *Tribune* could create more comprehensive marketing strategies, playing a much bigger role for those companies. This is the pattern of Reduction.

Most importantly, the team urgently felt the need to act on these bold new strategies.

The result? Tony Hunter led his team at the *Tribune* from bankruptcy to becoming the #1 most profitable news organization in America.

SIMULATIONS CREATE URGENCY AND ALIGNMENT

Tony Hunter was able to create urgency in part because his newspaper had declared bankruptcy. However, you can also create urgency through simulations. My case study involves space beer and the journey to Mars.

You might not realize this, but in 2003, the Shuttle program was canceled. That means that every time NASA needs to send an astronaut to space, they pay Russia $80 million for a spot on Russia's Soyuz rocket.[29] That's an expensive airplane ticket. So, why would NASA agree to that? The reason is pretty simple: NASA is so committed to Mars they wanted to remove the day-to-day distractions of the Shuttle program. To fully commit to a big mission, you need to be focused.

The problem, however, is that it's still not easy to get to Mars. My neighbor, astronaut Chris Hadfield, described it to me by saying if you want to go to the moon, it is a three-day mission, and if you make a mistake, gravity will bring you back to Earth. If you go to Mars, on the other hand, you have about 12 minutes of launch and then you're on an 18-month mission. If you make a mistake, you're sent into a coffin in space and kids end up quitting science.

The other complication, Hadfield explained, is that we are at a point in time akin to when the Wright brothers finally got the world's first plane to cross a football field. Imagine going up to them then and saying, "Awesome, are you ready to cross the Atlantic Ocean?" We will get there, but there's still an enormous amount to figure out. We can talk about Mars all we want, but we still need to invent new technologies and convince someone to strap themselves to a giant rocket for over a year.

Wow. That's a bit higher risk than my own job. Having said that, though, the day-to-day challenges at NASA are much more similar to your own world than you might think. Sure, they're building rocket ships, but they're still a collection of people trying to change and adapt. They struggle with all the same issues as my other clients, including navigating a rigid structure, competing for resources, working in silos, and dealing with bureaucracy. This is why I was brought in to help.

The easiest way to describe the problem is to imagine you have the world's best rocket scientist, the best biologist, and the best chemist. The rocket scientist would love to get to Mars as quickly as possible, to plant a flag and beat China in the race to deep space. That mission would take 8 to 10 years. The chemist wants to bring Martian rocks back to Earth. That would take 15 to 20 years. Meanwhile, the biologist wants to bring human life to the red planet, which would probably take 25 to 35 years.

The issue is that you cannot do one mission perfectly without totally compromising the others, so there should be a choice or compromise. However, because the time frames are so long, people avoid the urgency of working through compromise and instead focus on their own projects. How do you get alignment and urgency?

The answer is remarkably similar to the situation at the *Chicago Tribune*, even though the industries couldn't be more dissimilar. In this example, I ran a workshop where teams had to pick which of the three missions they wanted to prototype, and then we began with the same steps of Dystopia vs. Utopia and brainstorming.

When I asked the groups to share, a retired astronaut got up and said, "Our team wants to do the quickest mission where you race to plant a flag on Mars in just eight years. The reason is that we want to get this done before we all lose our jobs." At first the room laughed, but then he explained he was serious, noting, "I've had 17 missions canceled in my career, and you will one day learn that if you can't finish a mission within a presidential term, you, too, will experience a canceled mission." The room chilled, and people started realizing the importance of alignment and urgency.

Suddenly, instead of caring about all 10 of your own ideas, you start to realize you need to pick your battles. When it came to picking the top three priorities, most teams had some version of needing public support, short-term wins, and collaboration between departments.

Then, when we got into prototyping, people had to work deeply on those three priorities. My favorite example came from a team where the team leader warned, "I'll tell you our table's idea, but first I have to give you a caveat, because you're all going to laugh at us. We mean it, and we want to do it."

He explained, "We all want to succeed, and we know the public doesn't get excited about breakthroughs like the water discovered on Mars. And of course, we know that new presidents can cancel our long missions. So, we need to find something that involves all teams while generating a lot of public support. The answer, space beer!"

He noted that at first, you might laugh, but everyone gets to experiment. We have to get to Mars, so the rocket person is happy. We need to harvest the water, so the chemist is happy. And we need to grow a plant, so the biologist is happy. And now, suddenly the public will care more about little breakthroughs like harvesting water, because . . . beer! Last, you try being the American president who cancels the American mission of brewed beer on Mars.

Space beer. Who knew?

SIMULATIONS CREATE ALIGNMENT, OPTIONALITY,
AND URGENCY. EVERYONE WANTS INNOVATION TO HAPPEN,
BUT NOT EVERYONE BREAKS FROM THE PATH.

THE TIME FOR ACTION IS NOW

- What tactics, symbols, or workshops could you implement to make change happen?

- If you were to imagine five years from today, what five factors could realistically lead your company to become less relevant? What could lead to success? Based on that exercise, what are the three most important areas for you to focus on?

- If you created a gambling fund, what are five initiatives currently on hold that you would put in action?

- If your largest competitor acquired your company tomorrow, what would they immediately change?

TACTICS, BY TONY HUNTER

1. Simplify the plan.
2. Engage your team.
3. Put the customers first.

4. Invest in new opportunity.
5. Force the discussion of competing alternatives.

THE 7 TRAPS OF
PATH DEPENDENCY

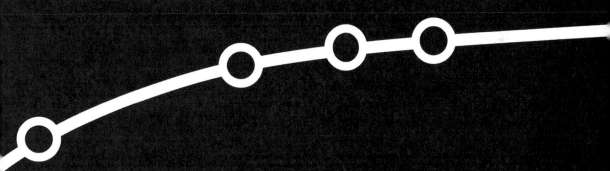

We tend to make decisions that get short-term results, not realizing that certain choices can fix us to the path we are on and reduce our future potential. Optionality is about making decisions that increase our future choices.

WE MAKE FEWER BIG DECISIONS THAN WE THINK . . .

A client of mine once told me, "You make 10,000 decisions in your career, but just three or four of those choices account for your entire success." This wisdom came to me from Robert Davies III, a CEO who was fired from his job at Church and Dwight, the company that happens to make Arm & Hammer baking soda. Church and Dwight was losing its way, and its board felt Robert wasn't helping them escape their struggles. However, a few years after Robert's firing, nothing changed.

Their tough times continued, so the 150-year-old company rehired Robert out of desperation. Looking at his former role with fresh eyes, Robert started seeing new potential he hadn't seen before. Arm & Hammer baking soda was once the go-to ingredient for baking cookies. But now, having stepped away for a spell, Robert identified fresh uses for a tried-and-true single-purpose product.

Arm & Hammer could just as often be found in home magazines showcased as the perfect food-safe deodorant for refrigerators as it was found listed as a recipe ingredient. So Robert rebranded baking soda as a fridge freshener. Its popularity also spoke to the fact that eco-friendly products were taking hold of the market, and baking soda was a natural fit.

He pivoted the brand to laundry detergent. As the world became more sustainable, he was able to market baking soda as an eco-friendly alternative to chemical detergents. It became a deodorant not just for the fridge but for your armpits. Their toothpaste took off too. Today, the company is nearly 10 times larger.

BE PREPARED TO TAKE NEW PATHS, RECOGNIZING THAT ONLY A FEW OPPORTUNITIES WILL TRULY REDEFINE YOUR JOURNEY.

. . . AND EVEN OUR LITTLE DECISIONS SET US ON A LONG PATH

I've had a chance to work with a broad array of clients, ranging from adidas to the Plastic Injection Molding Society of America. Over time, I've realized that business leaders in different industries are more similar to one another than you might expect. This leads me to wonder, how did one person end up in plastic injection while another ended up at adidas?

The reality is that certain choices have a continuous impact. The guy who ended up in plastic injection picked a course in school. That course led to a major. That major led to a few interviews, and eventually he accepted the job that paid $2,000 more than the other. At the time, these seemed like little choices. Then he got promoted, got married, got promoted again, had a kid, and started getting very good at the business of plastic injection. Switching fields now would cause a big financial setback. He's sort of stuck.

What are the key choices that led you to where you are now? How did you make those choices at the time?

So often, we make seemingly small decisions haphazardly, assuming the impact will be short term, while these decisions can have profound implications for our future.

What could you do to make those decisions in a better way?

YOUR LIFE IS DETERMINED BY A SURPRISINGLY SMALL NUMBER OF POWERFUL DECISIONS —AND WE TEND TO MAKE THOSE DECISIONS IN A SIMPLIFIED MANNER.

THE GOAL OF OPTIONALITY IS TO MAKE DECISIONS THAT INCREASE YOUR FUTURE CHOICES

Optionality is a concept from the world of financial theory where instead of making decisions based on profitability, we consider how much they open up our set of options.

For example, when my company, Trend Hunter, hosted our first Future Festival, we created an epic event that was not profitable. It was also a lot of work. We had to create Trend Safaris, technology experiences, innovation workshops, big parties, and a full program of all-new content for the keynote sessions. However, the conference gave us the chance to interact with our clients and learn more about their needs. Long term, it enables us to build more meaningful solutions for them, so it creates high optionality.

Let's take the example of the guy who picked a course, got a job, and ended up with a full career in plastic injection. If he wants to shift to a different industry, there are still many choices he could make that would start to open up his future options:

- Going back to school
- Joining different trade organizations
- Choosing a role in consulting
- Working more deeply with customers in different industries
- Having a "side hustle" or hobby
- Looking for positions with similar skills versus a similar industry
- Staying informed about trends in other markets
- Attending conferences unrelated to plastic injection

PUSH YOURSELF TO MAKE CHOICES THAT CREATE HIGH OPTIONALITY.

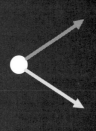

Old Way:

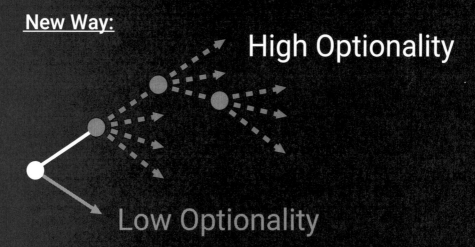

Not Profitable

Profitable

New Way:

High Optionality

Low Optionality

1. **FORCE COLLISIONS**—At NASA, one of our clients is Debbie Amato, the deputy chief technologist. She is responsible for creating a culture of innovation, which she does by bringing together people who would not otherwise interact. Her most powerful tool is an ongoing series of poster sessions where every scientist brings forward their best blue-sky idea on a 4'x4' poster. The posters are scattered throughout the room, and people then wander around, meeting new people to talk to about their blue-sky ideas. She said a new form of science was actually birthed from two scientists—in very different fields—who found themselves colliding at one of her events.

2. **GIVE PERMISSION**—At Staples, our client Brian Coupland has been the director of innovation and VP of retail. To keep the brand evolving and discovering new options, he encourages people to take risks by giving them "permission slips" to fail. That permission tells everyone that you are doing the higher-risk project or the project with a much longer-term payoff. This enables you to think more freely about opening up the company's future options instead of focusing on short-term results.

3. **FUEL AUDACITY**—At adidas, our client Mic Lussier is the head of future running. When a big project fails, Mic will host a project funeral. This enables the team to celebrate the idea, put it to rest, and encourage people so that they don't feel alienated, cross the street, and start working for Nike. It also creates an environment where bigger options get opened up because people lose their fear of failure.

4. **ESCAPE YOUR ROUTINE**—Malcolm Gladwell believes that we learn our ideas and perspectives from our cultural upbringing, and sometimes our ideas are wrong. To keep his options opening up, he watches the news program that directly opposes his political belief. This shows him the other side of the story and sometimes convinces him that his idea was incorrect.

5. IGNITE PASSION—Richard Branson explained to me that his best way to create optionality is to get his team to be more passionate. He told me that more passionate people bring forth better ideas and a dedication that is more likely to lead you to a better future.

6. BE DIFFERENT—At Apple, Steve Wozniak, the inventor of the modern-day personal computer, would push his team to have discussions about things that were outside of their comfort zone and project scope. Though some of these ideas might not be feasible in the short term, thinking beyond these boundaries can set you on a path to knowing what your future options could be. He told me you need to "be bold, be brave, and deliberately try to think differently—try to think beyond others."

7. PUSH LIMITS—At Starbucks, Rossann Williams is now the president of the US business, but we knew her back from her work running the Canadian office. In Canada, she pushed the limits of what the Starbucks brand would normally do, launching wine and beer in the coffee shops. By testing the limit in the Canadian market, she could better figure out what strategies might work in the larger US market. This innovation also happens to impact my personal life, because she brought all my favorite vices together. Big thanks to Rossann!

8. EXCHANGE PERSPECTIVES—At Hallmark, we get to work with Kristi Heeney-Janiak, who oversees Creative Resources and Talent Development for a 1,000-person creative team. To better understand their potential options, she set up a talent exchange where six senior leaders worked at Starbucks corporate for a week, and then six senior Starbucks leaders worked at Hallmark. To maximize the potential of the idea, legal paperwork and confidentiality agreements were signed to ensure both teams could be fully transparent and create intellectual property for the other.

9. CONSCIOUSLY MAKE DECISIONS THAT OPEN UP OPTIONS—At Trend Hunter, when we created our Future Festival, we designed an event that would not be profitable but was instead an entire experience that would enable us to really connect with our clients to better understand future potential.

GIVE PERMISSION TO FAIL

- What five decisions have most impacted your adult life?

- What decisions are you making to open up your future options?

- In which parts of your business could you create more long-term options?

- If you workshopped potential businesses that you could enter 5 to 10 years from now, are there investments you would need to make now to make those paths possible?

- If you split your role into five smaller roles, in which role are you adding the most value? What if you did the same activity for your company at large?

- Which of your larger decisions reduce scope and which open up options?

THE 7 TRAPS OF
PATH DEPENDENCY

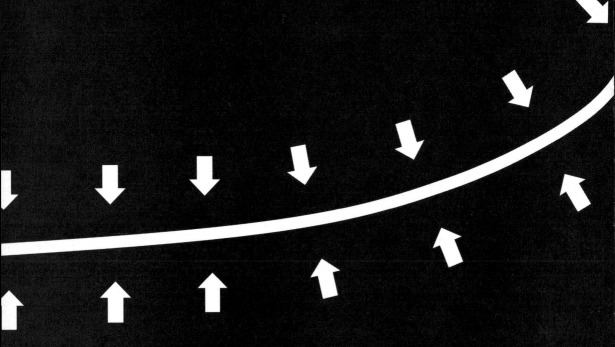

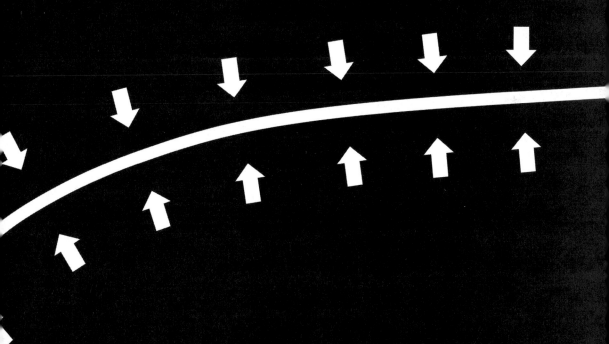

For evolutionary reasons, we are prewired to be loyal, consistent, and disciplined about our craft. These traits serve us well, enabling us to provide for our families and thrive in organizations. However, these same traits also have a darker side, which is that success makes us complacent, repetitive, and protective.

AFTER 10,000 YEARS OF FARMING, WE REPEAT WHATEVER LED TO LAST YEAR'S HARVEST

A million years ago, we were hunters. We were nomadic, living in an eat-or-be-eaten world. Then everything changed. 10,000 years ago, people planted the first seeds. Thereafter, we could stay put. Statistically, this is when we started forming larger groups, putting in rules to protect whatever led to last year's harvest.

The implication today is that we are prewired to repeat and optimize whatever has led to our individual and organizational success. When we have something to protect, we farm. When we have nothing to lose, or when things are fresh and new, we hunt.

Farmers are loyal, consistent, and disciplined. The catch is that those traits lead to being protective, complacent, and repetitive—dangerous traps for an organization. Hunters are curious, insatiable, and willing to destroy, because they have nothing to lose. You need to hunt to find new opportunity.

Though some of this glamorizes the hunter, it is important to recognize that we need both hunting and farming in our lives. Hunting helps us adapt and find new opportunity. Farming helps us protect what we have, creating long-term value from our discoveries. The more important takeaway is that we need balance. And in our research, most organizations lean toward farming, becoming too repetitive, protective, and complacent.

In my previous work *Better and Faster*, I introduced this concept as it relates to innovation. In that book, the topic only spanned about 30 pages, but it really connected with readers. As a half-hour keynote video, it ended up getting more than 10 million views (you can watch it at JeremyGutsche.com). For my team, this was a seed planted. Something we needed to grow and farm!

The result of our harvest is that we developed an online Innovation Assessment, enabling us to study tens of thousands of business leaders. Based on this research, we built out the framework and identified a couple dozen types of innovators.

As part of this section, you will want to spend seven to eight minutes taking your own Innovation Assessment at TrendHunter.com/assessment. After answering a series of tradeoff questions, you will immediately get to download 10 pages of personalized insight about what makes you successful and what binds you to the path.

But first, let's take a look at the framework!

SUCCESS LEADS US TO FARM . . .

As we master any craft, we become—

LOYAL—We value and cherish loyalty to great ideas, great teams, and great people. However, we also become protective of our egos, which can lead us to overly defend past decisions and the status quo.

CONSISTENT—Understandably, we wish to repeat decisions that led to our past success. But this also causes complacency as we lose the hunger we had searching for something to harvest.

DISCIPLINED—As we become experts at anything, we become fine-tuned in our thinking, to the extreme of being repetitive. We might hate that word, but fundamentally, we rely on our proven methods of doing things.

The corporate world is structured in the farmer's favor, which can lead to disruption.

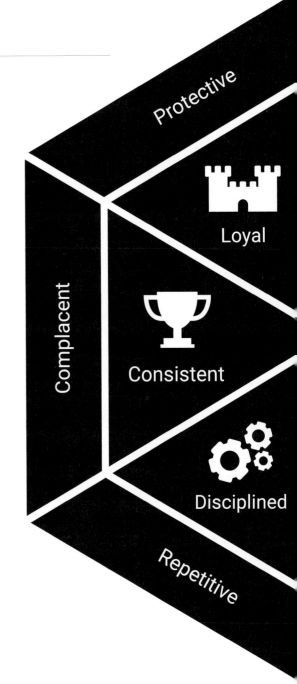

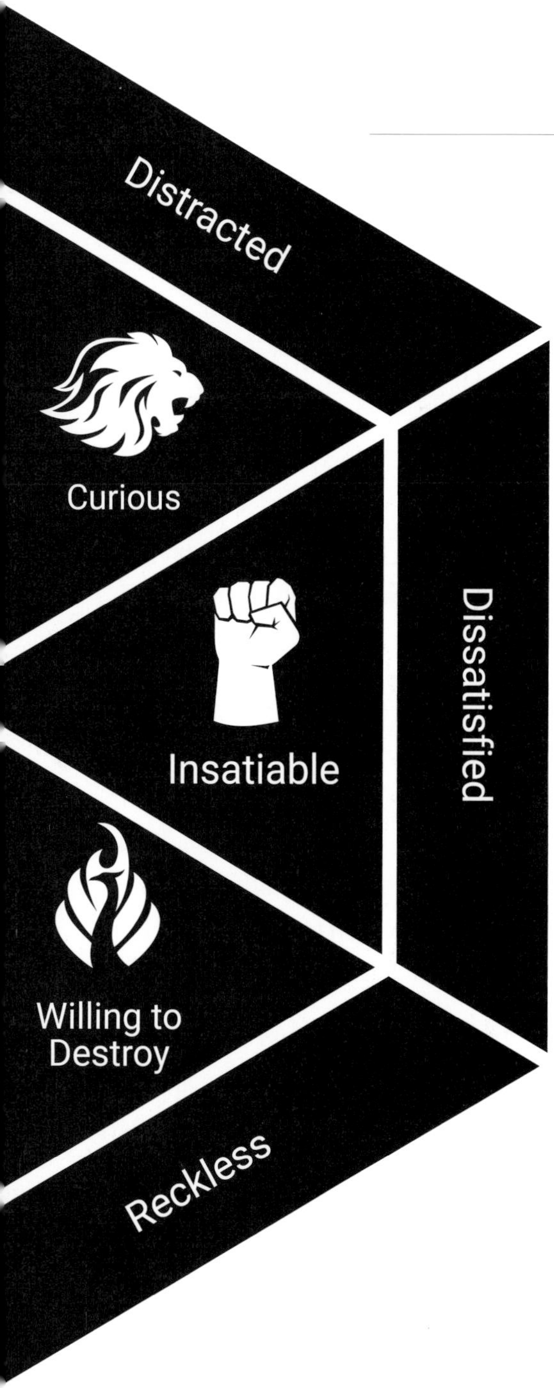

...BUT WE MUST HUNT TO ADAPT

Distracted

Curious

Insatiable

Dissatisfied

Willing to Destroy

Reckless

When something is new, we are—

CURIOUS—The opposite of being disciplined and repetitive is being curious, which is a word we all value. At the extreme, a curious person would be perceived as distracted.

INSATIABLE—The opposite of being consistent and complacent is being insatiable. Insatiable means you approach any problem assuming you might be wrong, searching for new solutions to the point of becoming dissatisfied with the status quo.

WILLING TO DESTROY—The opposite of being loyal and protective is being willing to destroy, because you have nothing to lose. At the extreme, this leads to being reckless.

We need to hunt in order to adapt, but most organizations fear the hunter traps so much that they skew away from hunting to the point of inhibiting change.

WHAT WE'VE LEARNED FROM STUDYING 30,000 PEOPLE

A deeper understanding of our Hunter-Farmer Framework can help you to harness your own potential both as an individual and as a leader. At a high level, here are three universal takeaways that apply to everyone:

1. **You need a balance of hunting and farming.** Hunting will help you find new opportunity, while farming helps you manifest what you have discovered. Too much hunting, and you will fail to succeed. Too much farming, and you will fail to adapt. Worded more simply, all of the traits (the middle of the hexagon framework) are good, and all of the traps (on the outside of the framework) are bad.

2. **Your primary trait (best strength) makes you more effective but also creates a GAP and a WEAKNESS.** It's not rocket science that one's strengths and weaknesses are inversely related. The takeaway here is a bit deeper. Your primary trait (let's say curiosity) causes two types of shortfall. First, your greatest strength creates a gap. For example, the opposite trait of curiosity is discipline. Second, there is a weakness from your trait taken to its extreme. For curiosity, that would be distraction.

3. **In almost any "new" task, we begin as hunters, but we become farmers once we feel proficient.** When we start something new, we are curious, insatiable, and willing to destroy, because we have nothing to lose. It is only once we have something we need that we seek to protect. Accordingly, many of the most iconic brands suffer from the traps of farming.

IF CEOS DESIRE INNOVATION, AND ORGANIZATIONS LACK THE SKILLSET, FIX THE GAP AND YOU'LL ENJOY REMARKABLE SUCCESS.

We've also learned some surprising stats about innovation. On one hand, we know that 97% of CEOs state that innovation is a key priority, and yet—

1. **Most people feel a lack of support for innovation:**

   - 50% do not believe their organization has a strong innovation strategy.
   - 45% do not believe their organization is proactive.
   - 55% do not believe their organization adapts quickly enough.
   - 56% do not believe their organization has a clear process to turn ideas into reality.

2. **Most organizations do not prioritize ideas:**

   - 48% do not have enough time to pursue new ideas.
   - 30% feel that innovative ideas are encouraged at their organization.
   - 17% do not often share ideas with their colleagues.
   - 21% do not often share ideas with their superiors.

3. **Generational and gender gaps plague many organizations:**

   - Gen Z is much less likely to have faith in their organization's ability to adapt and remain competitive. They are also least likely to share their new ideas, despite the fact that they are the ones with the most future-forward thinking.
   - Males are more likely to state that they would leave an organization because of its approach to innovation.
   - Females are more likely to identify that their organizations do not take advantage of collaboration between departments.

It would be easy to feel discouraged by the above stats. Companies are failing to adapt, and although CEOs say innovation is important, nobody is given the time, capabilities, or support to make innovation actually happen. Depressing. However, this disconnect explains why you and I will continue to have so much upside in our careers.

ONLINE ACTIVITY

Take your free assessment and benchmark your team.

You can identify the extent to which each of these traps impacts YOU and YOUR TEAM by taking Trend Hunter's free Innovation Assessment.

I'd encourage you to take a break and to do the assessment right away because it will help you personalize your learnings.

After eight minutes of questions, you will immediately get 10 pages of personalized insight to make you a better innovator and leader.

There is also a feature that lets you invite your team, resulting in a team overview, benchmark, and comparison to the world's top innovators.

This empowers you to be more prescriptive and efficient when it comes to fine-tuning your company's culture.

Here's a list of the most popular ways to apply your results, taken from our website:

1. Determine your unique strengths and learn how to accelerate them.

2. Identify your blind spots and where you might be hindering your creativity.

3. Optimize interactions with your team, boss, and significant other.

4. Compare your skillset to the world's top innovators.

5. Get specific advice for realizing your potential faster.

LINK: TRENDHUNTER.COM/ASSESSMENT/CREATETHEFUTURE

EXAMPLE

Learn about your innovation archetype, strengths, and gaps.

If you've already completed your assessment, you've probably learned a bit more about what makes you unique. Below is my assessment:

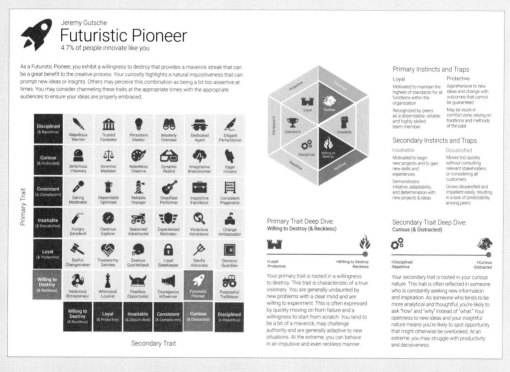

As a Futuristic Pioneer, I am Willing to Destroy and Curious. At an extreme, I can be Reckless and Distracted. As much as I'd love to deny that, it aligns well with feedback I've received since I was a kid (sorry, Mom!). To maximize my team's success, an example takeaway is that I need to ensure there is some level of structure and order (and not just the pure madness I would enjoy so much . . .).

In my team benchmark, I can see that we are Curious and Relentless, but I have also discovered 10 areas where we are quite different than the benchmark. For example, when someone suggests a new idea, we really like to "outline risks and obstacles" more than other organizations. That extra level of being critical stifles innovation, so there are recommendations we are putting into action.

BE AN
INSATIABLE
IDEA HUNTER

AFTER YOU DO THE INNOVATION ASSESSMENT—

- How have your strengths and blind spots made you the person you are today?

- Which of your traits do you want to accelerate?

- What actions will you take to accommodate your blind spots?

- How does your assessment compare to your significant other? To your team?

AFTER YOUR TEAM DOES THE INNOVATION ASSESSMENT—

- What are the team's five largest gaps compared to the industry benchmark, and what causes them?

- Based on the findings, what small changes could be made to enhance your culture?

- Group people by archetype and get them to reflect on a large company project. How does each group differ in its conclusions and perceptions?

TACTICS

1. Be curious.

2. Be insatiable.

3. Be willing to destroy (old ways of doing things).

4. Recognize that your greatest strength creates your greatest weakness.

5. Ask outsiders for opinions.

6. Simulate starting from scratch.

THE ABILITY TO CHANGE

THE 7 TRAPS OF PATH DEPENDENCY

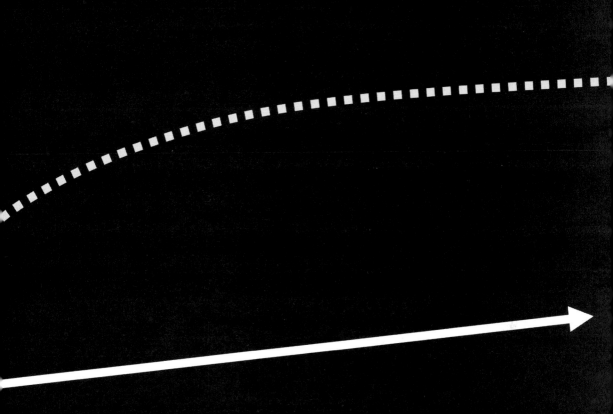

Unfortunately, our human brains are not designed for our exponentially evolving world. We understand that our world is changing, but we assume the next interval of change will be similar to the last. We have a very difficult time understanding the compounding impact of change.

OUR BRAIN SUFFERS FROM A TERRIBLE TRAP OF LINEAR THINKING

How much is your world going to change in the next few years? People are pretty good at predicting the next year and surprisingly accurate at imagining what might happen in their industry in the far future. However, smart people, in particular, are terrible at predicting three to five years out.

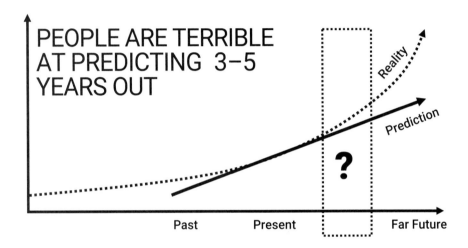

We overestimate our own ability to make progress, and we underestimate how much technology, competitors, and new entrants will change the game. We have business leaders and boards of directors who honed their skills during a different period of change. That leads us to move faster than we are used to, but not fast enough.

Given our exponentially changing planet, it's imperative to fix the human trap of linear thinking. Even if we are caught up on what's happening today, we fail to forecast tomorrow, because we forget that the pace of change is not simply faster—it's accelerating, and that's a completely different story.

The good news is that you are about to learn a few useful methods for predicting the *pace of change* and creating the urgency to do something about it.

To explain, I want to start with an example that explains my research on this topic. Back in 2008–10, Trend Hunter skyrocketed quickly, resulting in my first set of consulting clients: media brands. I was honored to be consulting for CEOs, boards, and even a few billionaires at the helm of iconic brands like Sony, Turner, NBC, Viacom (MTV), Tribune, and 21st Century Fox.

Surprisingly, I found that these sometimes famous leaders had a difficult time believing that social media would scale to what it is today.

They were overly resistant when I brought up trends like YouTubers acting as media brands, viral videos, blogging, digital streaming, the transition to video gaming, and the rise of shorter-form content.

The concepts of social media and Netflix streaming seem obvious now, but in their defense, Facebook and YouTube had just launched in 2005. These leaders KNEW about the new innovations and trends in their industry, because after all, they were the experts. However, they did not believe that these innovations would disrupt them, because they were the ones in control.

They were exhibiting all the traps of success: they were PROTECTIVE, repetitive, and complacent. So, how do you become more accurate, and how do you change a powerful leader's mind?

IF YOU WANT TO CREATE THE FUTURE, YOU NEED TO BE ABLE TO PREDICT THE PACE OF CHANGE AND CONVINCE THOSE AROUND YOU THAT THE WORLD IS GOING TO BECOME VERY DIFFERENT, VERY FAST.

PREDICT BETTER BY INTERNALIZING THE PACE OF CHANGE

I spent a lot of time trying to figure out how to convince media leaders that their world was going to change. I wasn't making huge progress until I came up with a relatively simple workshop that I call The Pace of Change. It's fun to look back at this exercise today because the media world has obviously changed, making this example particularly enlightening.

Back in 2010, when I asked these executives how the far future might look, they predicted concepts like virtual reality and streaming as the norm. However, they expected these changes to happen in 2025 or later. The activity that fast-tracked their thinking was comparing the act of going to a movie 10 years earlier vs. then.

An example: The Pace of Change in the Movie Industry—Completed in 2012

10 Years Ago (2002)	Present (2012)
• Newspapers for review • Called theater for show times • Used Yellow Pages to find theater number • Invited friends on answering machine • Ignored a big group (too complicated) • Paper map to a new theater • Lined up in front of a human • Found out it is sold out . . . mall instead?	• Rotten Tomatoes • Booked ticket online • Don't know what Yellow Pages is • Text friends • Text more friends • GPS • Showed up with a ticket . . . Or stream it?
Close Future (3–5 Years)	**Far Future (2025)**
?	• Virtual reality • Interactive movies • Video gaming & movies merge • You as a character • Beacon—who is in the theater? • 3-D? 4-D? Moving seats? • Shift in type of movies at theater

I first explained this movie example in *Better and Faster*, but we are going to take the Pace of Change exercise much further in the pages that follow.

In 2002, people still read newspaper reviews, called theaters for show times, used the Yellow Pages to find theater numbers, left messages for their friends on answering machines, and used paper maps to get to the theater. A half-dozen industries were disrupted along the way to where we are today.

To do this exercise, you and your team will first forecast what your industry will look like in 10+ years. You'll be great at identifying what could happen. Then, you'll compare what the industry looked like 10 years ago compared with today. You will likely be shocked at how much has happened in just 10 years. By internalizing the pace of change that has already happened, you'll realize that your far-future predictions are likely not that far off. Instead of happening in 10 years, those same things you predicted will probably actually happen in 3–5 years.

Try performing the exercise for your own market and company.

Your industry:

10 Years Ago	Your Industry, Today
Close Future (3–5 Years Out)	**Far Future (10–15 Years Out)**
?	

YOU CAN SHOCK YOURSELF INTO ACTION BY INTERNALIZING THE PAST.

USE HUMAN PROGRESS AS A PROXY FOR ACCELERATING CHANGE

If you look at any metric over time, you can measure its intervals of change. For example, with literacy, you can see that we reached 20% literacy in 1900. The next 20% interval took 50 years, meaning we reached 40% literacy by 1950. The next 20% took less than 40 years, and the next 20% took roughly 20 years.[30]

Literacy

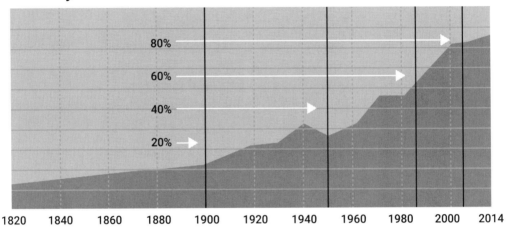

Using the above technique, I gathered data on literacy, democracy, basic education, extreme poverty, child mortality, vaccination, GDP, computing power, population, and CO_2 emissions. By aggregating these, one can estimate what I call the Implied Pace of Change, which is the general amount of change being experienced by humanity.

YOU CAN USE THE IMPLIED PACE OF CHANGE TO BE WISER AT PREDICTING CHANGE AND MORE LIKELY TO CONVINCE OTHER PEOPLE THAT IT IS TIME FOR ACTION.

Human Progress in Selected Categories

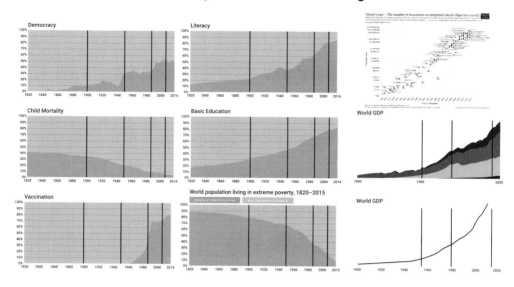

Results in:

Trend Hunter's Implied Pace of Change
(Each Interval = One Unit of Similar Global Change)

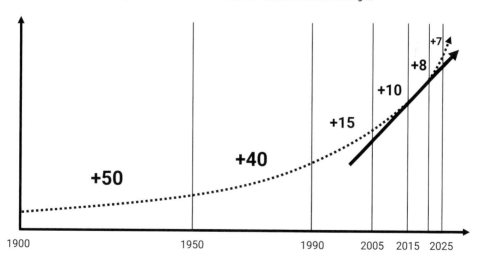

In the pages that follow, you will see these intervals personified with my grandpa, my mom, and her nerdy son.

INTERVAL 1: 1900–1950 (50 YEARS)

Let's begin in 1900. My grandfather, Joe Lehane, was an agricultural scientist, meaning that he no doubt loved adapting to things that were new. He grew up riding horses to school, reading books for fun, and living in a tent for several years.

For me, that describes 1900. It was like camping but without the electric inflatable mattress, solar-paneled phone charger, and Wi-Fi. And it's all in black and white. Like, it was terrible. But they didn't KNOW it was terrible, because it was just 1900.

During the course of Joe's career, humanity would go from horse, buggy, and books to magazines, television, automobiles, and commercial air travel. Even though he was an early adopter, he watched so much change that his family was the last on the block to get a color TV.

——— *LET'S CALL THAT ONE UNIT OF CHANGE.*
IT TOOK ROUGHLY 50 YEARS. ———

INTERVAL 2: 1950–1990 (40 YEARS)

My mother, Shelagh, experienced the same amount of change in just 40 years. From 1950 to 1990, she witnessed the world go from record player to boombox and Discman, from typewriter to computer, and from television to Nintendo.

Most people don't realize it, but in 1990, there were more Nintendo consoles in the world than there were TVs in 1950. If that sounds impressive to you, it should . . . because I initially made it up. However, when I did some research, I learned it was actually true!

There were 102,000 TVs in 1950, compared to 62 million Nintendo consoles in 1990.

These were gaming consoles with the same power as the computer used to land Apollo on the moon. This was also one unit of change, but this time it took only 40 years.

My mother saw the transition from the classic boat-sized cars of the 1950s to the minivans of the 1980s and '90s. She listened

to her favorite tunes on the record player, then the 8-track, then the cassette tape and the CD. She learned to type on her mother's typewriter, and then became proficient on her computer.

MY MOTHER ALSO EXPERIENCED A FULL UNIT OF CHANGE, BUT INSTEAD OF 50 YEARS, IT TOOK JUST 40.

INTERVAL 3: 1990–2005 (15 YEARS)

The next interval dramatically accelerated change. Between 1990 and 2005, the world saw the introduction of the internet, Motorola flip phones, the iPod (though not the iPhone yet), the Tesla Roadster, and basic online experiences. Yahoo was the best place for content, Amazon was a bookstore, and people used ICQ and MSN Messenger to flirt.

It sounds similar to modern day, except Facebook wasn't public and YouTube's website had barely begun. Simply setting back the dial to 2005 takes us to a seemingly ancient time.

Back then, we had no Twitter, no Uber, no Airbnb, no Instagram, no Pinterest, no Snapchat, no Tinder, and basically no fun. Instead, we had to text message, learn to drive, stay in hotels, make friends, get hobbies, leave the house, and talk to people.

THIS WAS ALSO A UNIT OF CHANGE, BUT THIS TIME, IT TOOK ONLY 15 YEARS.

INTERVAL 4: 2005–2015 (10 YEARS)

In the next interval, from 2005 to 2015, the world would change completely. This time, it took just 10 years.

During this interval, dozens of devices were replaced by your new smartphone, including: cameras, audio recorders, calendars, flashlights, landlines, Walkmans, alarm clocks, calculators, video cameras, and in some cases, even books.

Perhaps even more interesting is the fact that social media was invented, with Facebook going from effectively 0 to 1.5 billion users. This would transform culture to a world of shared experiences. 180 million of us laughed along with a woman in a Wookiee mask, and billions of us watched Psy's "Gentleman" video.

THIS IS JUST ONE INTERVAL OF CHANGE, AND WE'RE NOW HALFWAY THROUGH THE NEXT. WHAT WILL THE WORLD LOOK LIKE IN 2025?

DON'T PREPARE FOR CHANGE, PREPARE FOR ACCELERATION

When you look at all of the changes that occurred, you would expect that each interval encompassed a similar amount of time:

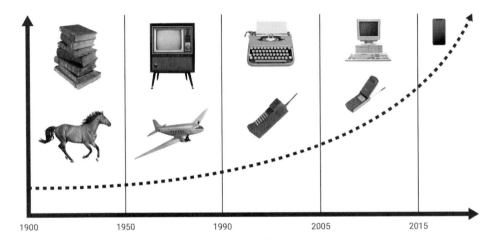

However, the rate of change is accelerating so much that when you plot out the intervals visually, it almost looks ridiculous. The pace is increasing exponentially.

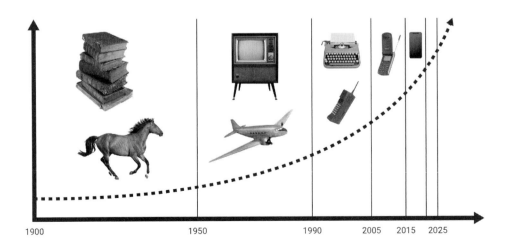

You are about to experience the most exciting period of human history. Pause and really reflect on the pace chart:

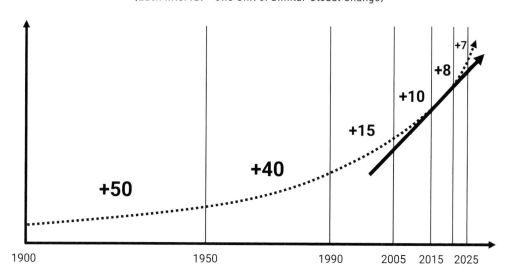

Trend Hunter's Implied Pace of Change

(Each Interval = One Unit of Similar Global Change)

+50   +40   +15   +10   +8   +7

1900   1950   1990   2005   2015   2025

WANT MORE? If you want a deeper explanation of how and why this pace will CONTINUE to accelerate, read the Appendix about the three megatrends that will have the greatest impact on our long-term future.

- Realizing how much has changed, in so many categories, how much has changed in your world?

- Create a list of a dozen far-future innovations in your industry and simulate how you would react if your competitor surprised you by releasing those innovations.

- What can you do now to set yourself up for success during the next interval of change?

TACTICS ————————————————————————

1. Track the amount of change in your market.

2. Brainstorm your Super Future.

3. Shock yourself into action.

4. Prepare scenarios to disrupt or avoid being disrupted.

5. Assume that far-off predictions will happen sooner than you think.

6. Compare the present to the past to predict the future.

THE 7 TRAPS OF
PATH DEPENDENCY

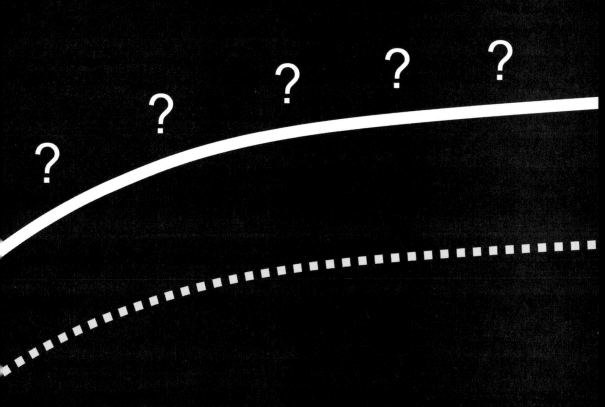

When you finally stumble upon a great idea, you must be prepared to deal with the awkwardness and discomfort of pursuing something that makes you uncomfortable. New ideas are awkward, they require us to change, and we have many traps that block us from seeing their potential. To achieve breakthrough, you must master discomfort.

BREAKTHROUGH ONLY OCCURS OUTSIDE YOUR COMFORT ZONE

Breakthrough, by definition, is something that's out of your comfort zone. And people hate being outside their comfort zones. That's why so many smart people miss out on great ideas that were always close within their grasp.

In this section, I will discuss the four different types of breakthrough, using my four biggest mistakes in business. I want to show you my overlooked opportunities to illustrate the characteristics that you will need to look for if you want to have your big breakthrough.

Also, at this point in the book, you've hopefully learned a thing or two from my experience with clients, but I want to use my own mistakes to illustrate that predicting and creating the future is tough, even for someone who does this professionally.

If you want to predict the future, you have to put in the effort, and you have to become comfortable with discomfort. You also would be well served to learn the characteristics of each type of breakthrough so that you can best identify your big idea when the clues are close within your grasp.

IF YOU ASPIRE TO FIND A GAME-CHANGING OPPORTUNITY, YOU MUST PUSH YOURSELF PAST THE POINT OF COMFORT.

Our Out-of-Scope Opportunities (2010)

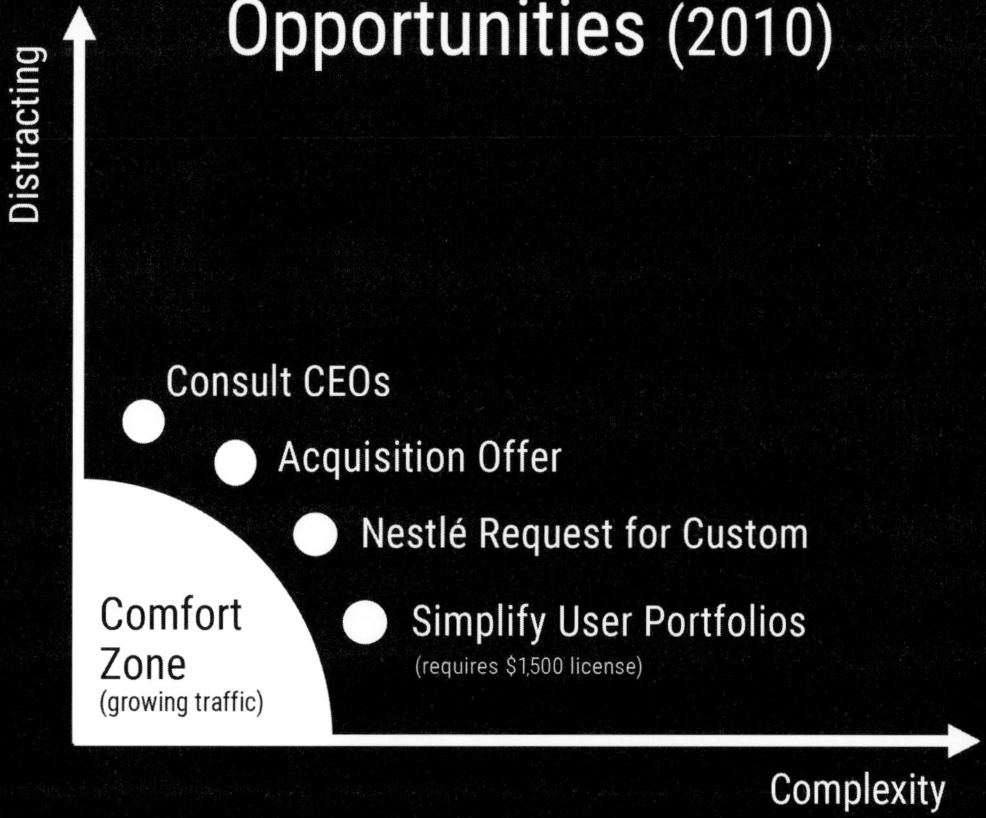

Distracting

Consult CEOs

Acquisition Offer

Nestlé Request for Custom

Simplify User Portfolios
(requires $1,500 license)

Comfort
Zone
(growing traffic)

Complexity

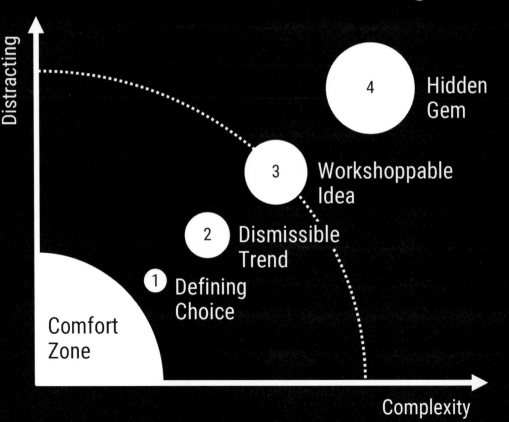

4 Levels of Breakthrough

Distracting

4 Hidden Gem

3 Workshoppable Idea

2 Dismissible Trend

1 Defining Choice

Comfort Zone

Complexity

TYPE 1: DEFINING CHOICES

Be careful what you say no to

I didn't expect that Trend Hunter would become a multibillion-view website, which is something to be proud of. I don't take for granted the terrific work of my talented team. I do, however, think about the great ideas that "got away." The overlooked opportunities that could have propelled us in different directions.

I taught myself to code and built Trend Hunter in 2005 because I wanted to make a place where people could share ideas. I was still working my day job running innovation and analytics at a bank. The website grew very quickly. Its view count went from thousands to millions to billions before I had properly figured out the right business model. At a certain point, Trend Hunter had more traffic than almost every newspaper on the planet and had a team of just a dozen people making it happen. We had some money from ads rolling in, but we needed to figure out how to pay the bills.

Over the course of a few years, there were a few course-changing opportunities that presented themselves: offers to consult CEOs, an acquisition offer, a request for a custom version of Trend Hunter, and an idea to simplify how our users share articles. I intentionally said no to each of these ideas, because growing the website was already distracting. And because it was working, my team and I had something to protect—something to farm. Arguably, our comfort zone had become figuring out how to get more and more page views, to a fault.

The first overlooked opportunity was simplifying how our users shared articles. In short, here's how Trend Hunter worked: anyone from around the world could sign up, find an innovation they liked, and write it up. Then the article would publish to their portfolio, a visual gallery of their discoveries. We had experimented with a simple feature to share with a click, skipping the step where you have to write something. But it would have required a $1,500 license fee to make it perfect. So we skipped it.

TYPE 1: DEFINING CHOICES (CONT'D)

Six years later, Pinterest was launched, offering a similar user experience but with the feature of not having to write up an article. On Pinterest, you similarly find something you like, share it with a click, and then it appears in your Pinterest "portfolio"—a gallery of your discoveries. Even the layouts were strikingly similar.

The competitive side of me wondered if we should rekindle our functionality to share without writing the article. Should we just pay the $1,500 license fee? But then we would also lower the quality of each post. Not worth it.

By the next year, Pinterest was valued at a billion dollars, then $2 billion, then $5 billion, then $11 billion, and then $30 billion . . . but I saved $1,500. I guess that means my overlooked opportunity was "not being Pinterest," or at least not taking their approach seriously.

My overlooked opportunity was an example of the first type of breakthrough, a "defining choice." A defining choice is something that is specifically presented to you. Something you actively must say yes or no to. To see the value of this type of opportunity, you need to know your comfort zone. When you're making decisions and evaluating yes versus no, you should look at which ones you are doing because they're in your comfort zone. Then, push your limits and make the bold choice.

Tactics & Methods for Defining Choices

1. Identify your comfort zone.
2. Respect out-of-comfort-zone decisions.
3. Have a gambling fund.
4. Solicit outside opinions.
5. Make the bold choice.

TYPE 2: DISMISSIBLE TRENDS

Recognize the blinding power of your own expertise

When I published *Exploiting Chaos* in 2009, it became a bestseller right when the world became chaotic. I was in the right place at the right time. I started getting invited by media CEOs to help with their digital reinventions during chaos. I was flattered to be advising leadership teams and CEOs at NBC Universal, Turner Broadcasting, Sony, Tribune, Fox Entertainment, Viacom, CNBC, Rogers, and several others.

The problem with this privilege was that I started experiencing the traps of an expert. If I had more traffic than many of these large websites, then I was probably going to keep my lead forever, right? Wrong.

As the well-funded media titans made their pivots, my team of 12 could not compete. We were set to lose $1 million a year, which is complicated when you'd like to pay the people on your team. I needed a solution, or I'd have to lay off half the team.

What's interesting about this type of mistake is that I saw all the trends in the market, but I assumed we would continue to hold our edge. I call this a dismissible trend, and it explains all the examples where a market leader like Nokia, Smith Corona, or Blackberry couldn't see the potential of a new entrant.

Tactics & Methods for Dismissible Trends

1. Be humble.

2. Ask questions.

3. Recognize the BLINDING power of your own expertise.

4. Take the advice you'd give to others.

TYPE 3: WORKSHOPPABLE IDEAS

Deep-dive your curiosities

In a desperate search to fill our $1 million hole, I started combing through every email I had, looking for any little pocket of opportunity that might help us pay the bills.

An idea surfaced from a keynote client at Nestlé named Sarah Deeks, who asked, "If we commit to a $50,000 research package, could that include . . . workshops . . . reports . . . a [custom] Trend Hunter tool?"

We made the call and created her a custom Nestlé service, complete with custom research, presentations, and a custom version of the Trend Hunter platform. A couple of years later, almost 100 clients had signed up. That's terrific, but I can't stop thinking about what would have happened if I had created her requested service two years earlier. She effectively gave me the business model that we employ today, so how much further ahead could we have been? What if I was three years faster at connecting the dots?

The mistake I was making was that I was failing to see the potential of a workshoppable idea. I could have sat down with Sarah and mapped out what she wanted. She would have explained what she wanted to do, and we could have figured it out, years earlier.

Tactics & Methods for Workshoppable Ideas

1. Challenge what seems possible.

2. Deep-dive curiosities.

3. Role-play "what if" (no "doubt" allowed).

4. Pursue your next customers, not only the ones you already have.

TYPE 4: HIDDEN GEMS

Relentlessly pursue your hidden gem

My fourth huge mistake is the one I am making right now. It's my hidden gem. It's the big idea that I am overlooking *right now*, and I don't know what it is. You have a hidden gem, too. To find our breakthroughs, you and I will have to apply the concepts in this book to see if we can reconnect the dots in front of us to find our next levels.

Along the way, you and I will encounter more experimental failure, resistance to change, and people who don't see the full potential of our new ideas.

To motivate, I'll share one last reflection on my own journey:

- If I didn't fail at finding that idea as a kid, I wouldn't have started a website.

- If I didn't fail at online ads, we wouldn't have pivoted into a research firm.

- And if I didn't fail at "being Pinterest," I would not have ended up with a fun career of writing this book and being a speaker. (But of course, I'd be at home playing with billions of Pinterest dollars, so, it's a toss-up, from my perspective . . .)

Tactics & Methods for Hidden Gems

1. Break rules.

2. Push harder.

3. Act sooner.

4. Fail faster.

5. Never give up.

FINAL THOUGHTS

The curious case of the missing gold

In my hometown of Toronto, there lives a man named Rob McEwen. Rob had been very successful in business, but what he *really* wanted was something with a little more glimmer—a little more shine. Rob wanted GOLD, and LOTS OF IT!

Like a 19th-century prospector, Rob wanted to grow a gold mine, and sure enough, he'd acquired enough money to buy one. He poured his fortune into a mine in a small town called Red Lake. It was a sleepy 50-year-old mine, ready to be shut down.

The problem was that Rob had missed the gold rush by 162 years. He looked in every corner. Every nook. Behind every rock. There was no gold to be found, and his millions were spent. After six years of searching, he was down on his luck. His little mine seemed as if it would be a mine no more.

Against all advice, he committed the most unforgivable gold-mine-owner act of all: he took his most precious data—his seismic maps—and gave them all away for free. He offered a $500,000 fortune to any man, woman, or child who could tell him where all the lost gold might be.

Much to his surprise, he received more than 1,400 submissions. "We had applied math, advanced physics, intelligent systems, computer graphics, and organic solutions to inorganic problems," he said. "Capabilities I had never seen before!"[31]

Half of the suggested targets were new, and 80% hit gold. Rob's almost-abandoned mine unlocked more than $39 billion worth of gold. Thirty. Nine. Billion. Now Rob and his team are using artificial intelligence, with IBM's Watson, to see if there's "more gold in them there hills."

New to an industry, Rob was able to see that something wasn't right. For decades, gold miners were caught in a groove, repeating past decisions and techniques.

By looking at the exact same data with a fresh perspective, creative people from all sorts of industries were able to help Rob find his hidden gold. Put differently, people who were not already caught in a groove were able to see the opportunities that were so close within Gold Corp's grasp.

This tale is a metaphor for how your own future can unfold.

YOU HAVE SO MUCH OPPORTUNITY WITHIN YOUR GRASP, BUT YOU NEED TO BE CAUTIOUS OF ALL THOSE TRAPS THAT CAN LOCK YOU INTO THE PATH ALREADY TRAVELED.

CONCLUSION

Be excited to be an innovator during the greatest period of change in human history. During this chaotic period in time, you will witness countless new inventions and ideas that reshape our future. You, your team, and your kids will watch our lives be enhanced, disrupted, and changed by technologies that reinvent humanity. What a time to be alive!

However, it's also important to note that the rules of the game have changed. Traditional innovation might have been about finding a single product and harvesting it for years, but that's not how things work in a world of perpetual change.

After 10,000 years of evolution as farmers, our success makes it difficult to grasp the potential of new ideas. Smart people, like you and me, can easily miss out on opportunities that were well within our grasp. We get hindered by neurological shortcuts, traps of success, linear thinking, and the ease of not doing anything at all.

The result is that we tend to stay in our lanes, driving toward our future on whatever path worked before. We get caught in a groove. But the safe, well-traversed lane is not as safe as it used to be. Sticking to the path has become dangerous and disruptive. In a fast-moving world, getting caught in a groove means we become blinded to all the potential paths that could be.

The good news is that you are close to new paths of opportunity.

To realize your potential, look past the awkwardness of new ideas, train your brain to be more creative, take action, open up your future options, and recognize the blinding power of your own expertise. Track trends in your market, internalize the pace of change, and push your comfort zone—because you are capable of more than you think.

Create the future.

APPENDIX

What's Next? A Glimpse into the Super Future

At Trend Hunter, when we help our clients glimpse into the future, we use a framework that includes 18 Megatrends and 6 Patterns of Opportunity. This framework is discussed in detail in the Opportunity Hunting section on the other side of this book. However, for now we will use this framework to discuss the three megatrends that will have the most impact on the Super Future, my term for the world 5 to 10 years out.

In the Super Future, these standout megatrends are the factors that will have the greatest impact in shaping our world:

1. HYBRIDIZATION—The lines that separate different industries are blurring. You can now compete in any market.

2. INSTANT ENTREPRENEURSHIP—It has never been easier to instantly become an entrepreneur, launching new products in almost any type of market.

3. ARTIFICIAL INTELLIGENCE—The pace of human progress will dramatically accelerate with machines that think like humans but with near-infinite speed and data.

The 18 Megatrends & 6 Patterns of Opportunity

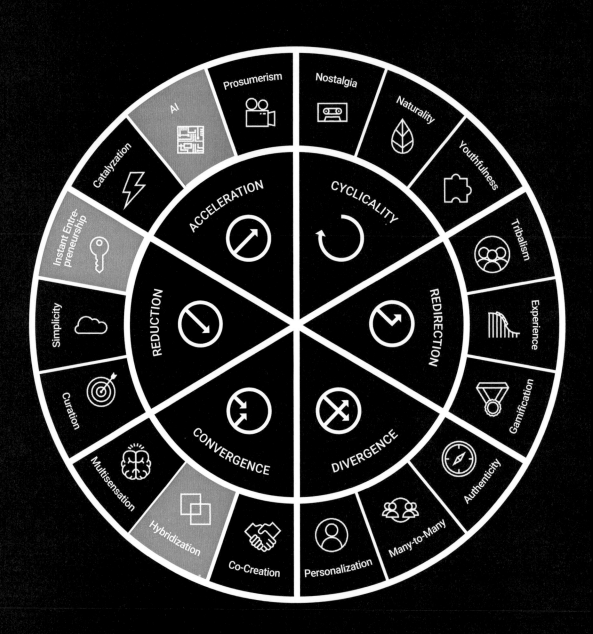

1. HYBRIDIZATION

Our worlds are converging

In almost every industry, seemingly unrelated companies are starting to compete. Separate worlds have now converged. In the world of B2B services, there used to be accounting firms—like EY, Deloitte, KPMG, and PwC—who just did accounting. Consulting firms like Monitor (my former employer), McKinsey, and BCG used to just do consulting. Ad agencies did ads. Tech vendors did tech. But now all of them have started competing for the same market of cloud, technology, and innovation. They've acquired additional companies to gain new skillsets, they've expanded their service offerings, and all four now offer the same services.

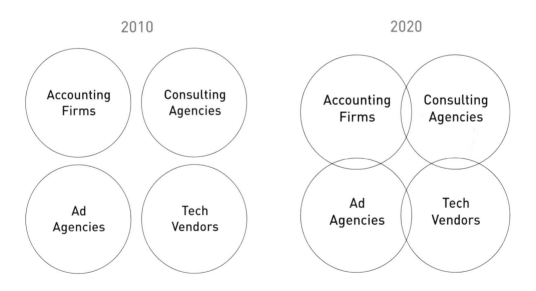

The same convergence is happening in dozens of markets. In media, the broadcaster, viewer, and advertiser used to be separate. Today, social media has enabled viewers to broadcast themselves, and influencer marketing has blurred the lines even further. In computing, biology, physics, software, and hardware are colliding.

To explore one example more deeply, consider Amazon. Not too long ago, they were just a bookstore, and you probably didn't think too much about them if you had a grocery or clothing brand. Now, they do all of the above, including design and web services.

When Amazon bought Whole Foods, their top six competitors lost $12 billion in market value. The early retreat from these stocks was probably the right move, but most people only realized the primary impact of Amazon's purchase. Now, they could sell groceries, boost their Prime membership, and offer in-store pickup for online orders.

There was actually something more clever that occurred on the day of that acquisition. Amazon, an otherwise remote, Seattle-based web company, scooped up 400 local warehouses and 90,000 local employees. Consider the implications: Amazon could now stock their Whole Foods stores with the most popular products, enabling a whole new world of hourly delivery. Imagine what could happen if Amazon became your business's next competitor.

As we look toward the future, the lines that separate industries have been blurred, meaning you can easily enter new markets, or see your own market entered by unexpected competitors.

2. INSTANT ENTREPRENEURSHIP

It is easier than ever to compete on a global scale

Instant entrepreneurship is the concept that today, more so than ever before, anyone could become an entrepreneur, instantly. You can develop an idea, prototype it online, launch a website in an hour, get people from around the world competing to make your logo beautiful, and launch your product on Kickstarter before you even know how you are going to outsource its development. Anyone, from anywhere, could compete on a global scale.

Another way of internalizing the globalization of entrepreneurship is to look at the numbers of English-speaking, internet-connected people. In 1980, the world had 4 billion unconnected people, only 70% of whom were literate, running around with pencils trying to solve things. Now, we have 7.5 billion hyper-connected people, 85% literate, all running around with smartphones powerful enough to land a spaceship on the moon. Add up all of those factors and you have a 15-fold increase in internet-connected, English-speaking competitors, customers, and partners.

To think about this more deeply, take education as an example. It used to be that if you were a brilliant, wealthy American who wanted the very best business school education, you could go to Harvard (if you were accepted, of course). That would set you up for a lifetime of privilege, which you probably had to begin with. If you wanted to pursue electrical engineering, you could go to MIT, and if you wanted to work in Silicon Valley, you could go to Stanford.

In recent years, many of the professors from these schools have started making their curriculum available online for free in massive online open courses (MOOCs). These open courses are just one example of the online education available to a hungry student from a less-privileged background. But does it work? A Stanford professor of robotics, Andrew Ng, decided to put his curriculum online. Previously, he taught Stanford students 200 at a time, but online, over 160,000 people registered for his class. More interestingly, 248 of the students online were able to pass every exam without making a single mistake, and 400 students online were able to outperform every single Stanford student. You would expect the Stanford students to be bright, privileged, and better at the exams, but they were no match for the hungry, ambitious, brilliant minds pursuing their studies from all over the world.

You now have more global competitors, partners, and customers than ever before, and the impact of this is just beginning to be recognized.

3. ARTIFICIAL INTELLIGENCE

The pace of human progress is about to become not so human at all

AI is a term people often use without fully understanding its meaning. We tend to only use the word *AI* when a form of software is new, but in reality, it is already integrated into many aspects of our lives, including our newsfeeds, driving routes, romantic pursuits, online searches, and friend feeds.

An added level of sophistication is required because AI is the most significant and defining factor when it comes to our future. Accordingly, it's worth your time to "nerd it up" with me and more deeply explore the concept of AI. At the highest level, AI means that computers can program themselves to process massive amounts of data and learn on their own. On a more granular level, AI can be broken into three categories:

- **ANI**: Artificial NARROW Intelligence
  (which applies to everything we know today)

- **AGI**: Artificial GENERAL Intelligence
  (referring to human-level abilities in all categories)

- **ASI**: Artificial SUPER Intelligence
  (an inevitability that we're unable to understand)

PART 1: ANI

Everything in the AI space today is considered artificial narrow intelligence. Worded differently, ANI is narrow intelligence because the AI systems we are making are generally only proficient in one "narrow" task. They lack the general knowledge that a human would have, across all categories.

Still, we are seeing some very impressive examples of ANI, including—

- **AI PERSONAL ASSISTANTS**—Apple Siri, Google Home, Amazon Alexa, and Samsung Bixby. These devices place the world's largest tech firms in your home and will be a core battleground for much larger AI capabilities.

- **AI LAWYERS**—ROSS. At basic law, AI lawyers are 90% accurate (vs. 70% for humans).[32]

- **AI DOCTORS**—IBM Watson. I helped IBM launch Watson, which is excelling in many fields. In medicine, Watson is four times more accurate at diagnosing complicated patients.[33]

- **AI AUTONOMOUS DRIVERS**—Tesla. Elon Musk stated human drivers will one day seem unsafe.

- **AI INVESTORS**—Numerai. Like dozens of other heavily funded start-ups, Numerai is attempting to profit while changing how we approach wealth management.

- **AI FACIAL RECOGNITION & ANALYSIS**—Microsoft. The tech giant can identify your face and predict your gender, age, and mood with astonishing accuracy.

As an example, five years ago Google started training AI to categorize images. At first, AI was incorrect 26% of the time, compared to humans who were incorrect 6% of the time (which, by the way, seems ridiculous). Today, Google has improved to become twice as good as a human.[34] At first that doesn't matter too much, but consider the field of ophthalmology. Suppose you visit an eye doctor to get an eye disease diagnosed. Worried about the implications, you might choose to get a second opinion. Studies show that there is a 60% chance that second ophthalmologist will disagree with the first, and it gets better: if you take your charts back to the original doctor just hours later, there is also a 60% chance they will disagree with *themselves*.[35] In this case, I want an AI doctor.

It is very difficult for humans to understand compound growth in any field, but computing stands out as an incredible case study. We already have computers with access to infinitely more information than we could ever attain and far more processing power. Once the coding of intelligence catches up, we will experience the following cartoon situation.

Currently, when we're confronted with AI, our reaction is something along the lines of "Haha, that's adorable! The funny robot can do monkey tricks!" We also tend to think of the least-intelligent humans as being far less intelligent than we are, and of someone like Einstein as far more intelligent. To an AI system, however, we're quite similar. In about 10 years, AI will catch up to the general intelligence (i.e., intelligence across all categories) of a below-average human. Then, about half an hour later, it will surpass Einstein. By the next day, it will be 100 to 1,000 times smarter than us, with access to every fact in the known universe and a far stronger ability to process it.

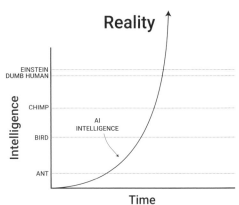

As humans, it's difficult for us to even imagine a computer that could match our intelligence. Yet, if an AI system were only as fast as computers today but as smart as a typical Stanford researcher, it is estimated that it could do 11,000 years of research in a single week. We will reach that level of processing in 10 years. What does that mean for our world? How will we live, eat, work, cure disease, help the planet, consume energy, distribute information, and go about our lives in the presence of such power?

Five years ago, these questions were the source of science fiction, but AI is now advancing more than twice as quickly as expected. This has become the most important piece of information for innovators, futurists, and society as a whole to understand.

FACTORS LEADING US TO THE NEXT LEVEL OF AI

I boil AGI progress down to three required factors: data, computing power, and intelligence. Let's quickly overview each factor.

a. DATA

More data was created this year than in the last 5,000 years, but only 0.5% of it was analyzed.[36] This means that an AI system *already* has access to a seemingly infinite amount of data:

- Every language
- Every fact
- Every Wikipedia page
- Every math formula
- Every physics equation
- Every bioengineering feat
- Every piece of news & trending data
- Every marketing best practice
- Every neuropsychology insight
- Every hacked email (7 billion so far)
- Every stock market technical
- Every person

In this category, we have already met the requirements, by far, to reach AGI.

b. POWER

It is always complicated to compare the speed of a computer versus a human; however, given that we are trying to imagine when a machine will be as smart as a human, it's worth making a comparison. Let's consider IBM's Summit, currently the world's fastest supercomputer, which will probably be surpassed by the time this book is published. If every person on Earth completed one calculation per second, it would take 305 days to do what Summit can do in 1 second.[37] Needless to say, we are not waiting on POWER to reach AGI.

c. INTELLIGENCE

The only remaining uncertainty is intelligence, and right now, AI still has a lot to learn. Most AI researchers estimate that it will take 10 more years, though AI is consistently progressing ahead of expectations. Some scientists are dissecting the human brain to see if an exact replica could be programmed. Others are teaching the computer to teach itself how to learn, which is (1) super meta and (2) super complicated. For example, Facebook set up two AI chat bots to process language and comments. However, they had to unplug the machines because the AI systems invented their own language so that humans could not track what they were talking about. *Wow*.

If we do it properly, AI will enable us to end all disease, extend life (perhaps infinitely), repair the planet, never have to work, and experience total bliss. Of course, if we get it wrong, things could end very badly.

Bill Gates, who laid the foundation for AI, is concerned it could lead to the end of the world. Stephen Hawking consistently issued similar warnings. Elon Musk has one of the world's most advanced AI programs, but he suggests that we might be summoning the demon. In short, there are still many questions to be answered, but one thing is certain: the next five years will motor along faster than the past decade.

PART 3: ASI

Within the next 40 years, AGI systems will rapidly advance and compete until one system reaches a point that will propel it 1,000 times further than competing systems. In other words, we will reach a point in time where there may be only one computer system. At this point, the implications start becoming that of science-fiction movies, so I am not even going to touch on this category any further.

With each step closer to AGI, we will accelerate the pace of human progress.

THE AI-MECHANIZED FUTURE

Our ability to use artificial intelligence starts to become more extraordinary when we start to combine AI with six other factors, creating what I call the AI-mechanized future.

1. ROBOTS—There is exponential growth in the number of robots helping us with our jobs and our daily lives. There are robots that can take your trash out, robot bartenders, robot receptionists, robot pizza delivery drones, robots that can take your order at a restaurant, and robots teaching our children how to behave. Farmers are using robots to identify what's happening in the crop, when to fertilize, and when to harvest, so that we can feed our ever-growing global population. What robot would you like to help you around the house or at your job?

2. INTERFACE—Though we currently interact with our phones, laptops, and smart home assistants, all that is about to change. For example, Google's new assistant can call restaurants to make reservations, book appointments, and navigate complex conversations as if it were human. Meanwhile, AI is getting better at visually re-creating the human form. The AI-empowered Deepfakes project teaches us that we can actually place any face on any body in video form. The persistent example online is that people are putting Nicolas Cage's face onto almost every actor in every major movie. It looks very convincing. So what happens when people use this technology to recreate the image of a US president giving orders he or she did not intend to give? By 2019, this concept was taken a step further when the Chinese app Zao introduced the ability to place your face onto the face of almost any celebrity in video form, whether that means you becoming Leonardo DiCaprio or Taylor Swift. Imagine watching your favorite movie with the key characters having the faces of your family members. That's already possible, though currently terribly illegal from a copyright perspective.

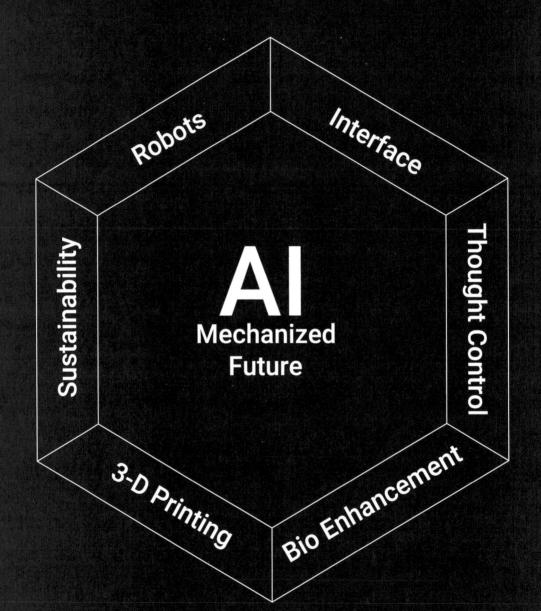

3. THOUGHT CONTROL—We have had thought-controlled video games for years, but now, AlterEgo from MIT Media Lab is a device that can read the inner voice in your head. The developers can currently use the interface to navigate television programming, perform basic search tasks, or keep a running tally of their grocery checklist as they navigate through the store. That's not an example of the far future; that technology is available today. So what happens when I can read the inner voice in your mind from five feet away? Will you be cool with police officers using that technology? Marketers? Las Vegas casinos? Retailers?

4. BIO ENHANCEMENT—We already have prosthetic arms that can help people regain control and the sensation of physical touch through robotic arms. We also have cochlear implants that can bring hearing to someone who has always been deaf, and eye implants to restore vision to people who are blind. Meanwhile, companies are working on eyeball technology that could enable you to save images, have super vision, and transmit imagery over Wi-Fi. What features do you want in your new eyes?

5. 3-D PRINTING—There are 3-D printed chairs, bikes, cars, houses, buildings, bridges, shoes, casts, dresses, food, and prosthetic arms and other body parts. Will you be intimidated when robots can 3-D print new robots?

6. SUSTAINABILITY—We have become so quick at mobilizing venture capital and technology that our AI-mechanized future has an eco-concern, the likes of which we have never seen before. For example, you may be familiar with the shareable bikes that exist in most major cities. This business model was so appealing that dozens of venture capitalists and Chinese billionaires all jumped into the game, each hoping to flood the markets with shareable bikes in each city. But the problem was that so much capital and production ramped up that there are now fields in China littered with millions of bikes that will never be ridden. It was dramatic overproduction, enabled by our fast-moving world.

Meanwhile, there are eight swells in the ocean full of plastic waste that will never properly decompose. In fact, the largest swell of plastic garbage is two times the size of Texas. If we start thinking about our other obligations as people who are designing and creating products, cradle-to-grave sustainability—where you think about what happens after you make things that last—starts to become important.

The good thing is that the next generation cares about this a lot. When you align to the values of caring about this, you're absolutely aligning to the next demographic of customer.

For example, there's now clothing made out of ocean plastic, like the adidas Parlay shoes, which I am wearing as I type this book. There are ocean-plastic sunglasses, shirts, and collectibles. And there are even people trying to clean up the plastic garbage patches, like Boyan Slat, an 18-year-old kid who graced the stage of TED with a plan to cast giant nets that would start to retrieve the plastic for other purposes. By 2017, he raised $31.5 million from concerned philanthropists, and in 2019 he announced that his second prototype had successfully begun collecting ocean plastic.[38]

What will you do with your brand to advance sustainability? At Trend Hunter, we recently made a donation to plant 2 million trees with Trees for the Future, an organization that works in hunger- and poverty-stricken regions of the world, creating forest gardens. Forest gardens are tree-lined plots of land that restore and encase sustainable farms capable of feeding and empowering families. For us, that donation included pairing our custom trend reports and Future Festival tickets with 10 to 100 donated trees per purchase, to embed our contribution with our work.

At first, sustainability seems like a curveball in a section about AI, but I intentionally pair the two because our rapid advancement in technology makes it too easy for us to produce more at a lower cost, resulting in oversupply and waste. In an era of accelerating change, we have the ability to destroy or create our future.

THE SUPER FUTURE CONCLUSION

Our pace of change has not just increased—it is accelerating. That acceleration is being empowered by hybridization, instant entrepreneurship, and AI. Knowing this, the ability to adapt will be far more important than ever before.

1. What are the AI projects being taken on by your competitors or others in similar industries?

2. What can you do to prepare your brand for a faster-moving future and the sustainability questions that future raises?

3. If you had an AI team at your disposal, which parts of your business would you like to automate or disrupt? As a side note, at Trend Hunter, we did this a couple of years ago, establishing TrendHunter.AI to see if we could disrupt our human research team. At this point, we have a couple dozen features where AI is better, which we have now incorporated into our daily project flow to make our team better and faster.

4. If you want to know more about the Super Future, it's probably best to watch my latest Super Future keynote, which is updated more frequently than this book. You can search for the Super Future and my name on YouTube to learn more.

ENDNOTES

1. Denning, Steve. 2011. "Peggy Noonan on Steve Jobs and Why Big Companies Die." *Forbes*. https://www.forbes.com/sites/stevedenning/2011/11/19/peggy-noonan-on-steve-jobs-and-why-big-companies-die/#39498669cc3a.

2. *Harvard Business Review*. 2017. "Digital Transformation Is Racing Ahead and No Industry Is Immune." https://hbr.org/sponsored/2017/07/digital-transformation-is-racing-ahead-and-no-industry-is-immune-2.

3. Lenet, Scott. 2018. "The Building Blocks of Innovation." *Forbes*. https://www.forbes.com/sites/scottlenet/2018/11/08/the-building-blocks-of-corporate-innovation%E2%80%8A/#6c39bbdb1697.

4. Trend Hunter Innovation Assessment

5. Gladwell, Malcolm. 1997. "The Coolhunt." *The New Yorker*.

6. Lee, Dave. 2017. "'Sweating bullets'—The Inside Story of the First iPhone." BBC. https://www.bbc.com/news/technology-38552241.

7. Lieberman, David. 2011. "CEO Forum: Microsoft's Ballmer Having a 'Great Time.'" *USA Today*. https://usatoday30.usatoday.com/money/companies/management/2007-04-29-ballmer-ceo-forum-usat_N.htm.

8. Reese, Brad. 2008. "Apple iPhone Doubts of New Cisco CTO Padmasree Warrior 12 Months Ago." *Network World*. https://www.networkworld.com/article/2350218/apple-iphone-doubts-of-new-cisco-cto-padmasree-warrior-12-months-ago.html.

9. Fried, Ina. 2017. "These People Thought the iPhone Was a Dud When It Was Announced 10 Years Ago." *Vox*. https://www.vox.com/2017/1/9/14215942/iphone-steve-jobs-apple-ballmer-nokia-anniversary.

10. https://www.ft.com/content/bc2fd7d8-c55d-11df-9563-00144feab49a

11. Yarow, Jay. 2011. "All The Dumb Things RIM's CEOs Said While Apple and Android Ate Their Lunch." *Business Insider*. https://www.businessinsider.com/rim-ceo-quotes-2011-9#the-iphone-was-great-for-blackberry-people-came-in-looking-for-an-iphone-and-walked-out-with-a-blackberry-5.

12. Yarow, Jay. 2014. "Google Buying Nest for $3.2 Billion." *Business Insider*. https://www.businessinsider.com/google-buying-nest-for-35-billion-2014-1.

13. A&E Television Networks. 2009. "Luxury Car Magnate Ferruccio Lamborghini Is Born." History.com. https://www.history.com/this-day-in-history/ferruccio-lamborghini-born.

14. Nguyen, Clinton. 2016. "7 World-Changing Inventions That Were Ridiculed When They Came Out." *Business Insider*. https://www.businessinsider.com/inventions-that-were-ridiculed-2016-8.

15. Yarrow, Jay. 2014. "This Apocryphal Story About The Telephone Should Be An Inspiration To Every Young Company." *Business Insider*. https://www.businessinsider.com/why-people-thought-telephones-would-fail-2014-1.

16. Gillett, Rachel. 2015. "How Walt Disney, Oprah Winfrey, and 19 Other Successful People Rebounded after Getting Fired." *Business Insider*. https://www.inc.com/business-insider/21-successful-people-who-rebounded-after-getting-fired.html.

17. Dan, Avi. 2012. "Kodak Failed By Asking The Wrong Marketing Question." *Forbes*. https://www.forbes.com/sites/avidan/2012/01/23/kodak-failed-by-asking-the-wrong-marketing-question/#56ff94ec3d47.

18. Chu, Melissa. 2017. "Before Apple Was Born, Steve Wozniak 'Begged' This Company to Use His Idea." *Inc.* https://www.inc.com/melissa-chu/before-apple-was-born-steve-wozniak-begged-this-co.html.

19. Mullins, Robert. 2010. "Imagining a World without Microsoft." *Network World*. https://www.networkworld.com/article/2230565/imagining-a-world-without-microsoft.html.

20. Siegler, MG. 2010. "When Google Wanted To Sell To Excite For Under $1 Million—And They Passed." *TechCrunch*. https://techcrunch.com/2010/09/29/google-excite/.

21. Thielman, Sam. 2016. "MySpace: Site That Once Could Have Bought Facebook Acquired by Time Inc." *The Guardian*. https://www.theguardian.com/technology/2016/feb/11/myspace-time-inc-facebook-acquisition-ownership.

22. Carlson, Nicholas. 2011. "Yahoo Could Have Bought Facebook For 2% Of Today's Valuation." *Business Insider*. https://www.businessinsider.com/facebook-is-selling-just-4-of-the-company-for-2x-as-much-as-yahoo-could-have-paid-to-buy-the-whole-thing-2011-1.

23. Stross, Randall. 2009. "Encyclopedic Knowledge, Then vs. Now." *The New York Times*. https://www.nytimes.com/2009/05/03/business/03digi.html.

24. Zetlin, Minda. 2019. "Blockbuster Could Have Bought Netflix for $50 Million but the CEO Thought It Was a Joke." *Inc*. https://www.inc.com/minda-zetlin/netflix-blockbuster-meeting-marc-randolph-reed-hastings-john-antioco.html.

25. Kort, Alicia ed. 2016. "The Story of Steve Jobs, Xerox, and Who Really Invented the Personal Computer" *Newsweek*. https://www.newsweek.com/silicon-valley-apple-steve-jobs-xerox-437972.

26. Press, Gil. 2018. "Apple, Xerox, IBM, and Fumbling the Future." *Forbes*. https://www.forbes.com/sites/gilpress/2018/01/14/apple-xerox-ibm-and-fumbling-the-future/#7e51a4f218b3.

27. Wong, Melvin. 2018. "Just Got Rejected? These 9 Inspiring Success Stories Will Help You to Bounce Back." AllTopStartups. https://alltopstartups.com/2018/11/20/just-got-rejected-these-9-inspiring-success-stories-will-help-you-to-bounce-back/.

28. Gould, Skye, and Chris Weller. 2017. "Here Are the Ages You Peak at Everything throughout Life." *Business Insider*. https://www.businessinsider.com/best-age-for-everything-2017-3.

29. Gould, Skye and Dave Mosher. 2016. "NASA Is Paying Russia More Than $70 Million to Bring an Astronaut Home in This Spaceship Tonight." *Business Insider*. https://www.businessinsider.com/space-travel-per-seat-cost-soyuz-2016-9.

30. Roser, Max and Esteban Ortiz-Ospina. 2013. "Literacy." *Our World in Data*. https://ourworldindata.org/literacy.

31. Tapscott, D., Tapscott, W. A. D. D., & Williams, A. D. 2011. *Wikinomics: How Mass Collaboration Changes Everything*. London: Atlantic Books Ltd.

32. Shutt, Sandra. 2017, "Artificial Intelligence. *Canadian Lawyer*. https://www.canadianlawyermag.com/news/general/artificial-intelligence/270447.

33. IBM Watson Health. "Artificial Intelligence in Medicine." IBM. https://www.ibm.com/watson-health/learn/artificial-intelligence-medicine.

34. Kinsella, Bret. 2017. "Google AI Improves 78% in Two Years, 2x Smarter than Siri According to Chinese Study. *Voicebot.ai*. https://voicebot.ai/2017/10/03/google-ai-improves-78-percent-two-years-2x-smarter-siri-according-chinese-study/.

35. Qi, Susan Ruyu. 2018. "AI in Medicine—Majority Decision Isn't Always Right." *Medium.com*. https://medium.com/health-ai/ai-2-0-in-ophthalmology-googles-second-publication-c3b5390c19ae.

36. Bansal, Manju. 2015. "Big Data: Creating the Power to Move Heaven and Earth." *MIT Technology Review*. https://www.technologyreview.com/s/530371/big-data-creating-the-power-to-move-heaven-and-earth/.

37. https://www.ibm.com/thought-leadership/summit-supercomputer/.

38. Caminiti, Susan. 2017. "Why Peter Thiel Believes in This 22-Year-Old's Dream to Clean Up the Oceans." *CNBC*. Retrieved 23 April 2017. https://www.cnbc.com/2017/04/20/thiel-benioff-backing-22-year-olds-dream-to-clean-up-worlds-oceans.html.

IMAGE CREDITS

For permission to reproduce copyrighted material, grateful acknowledgment is made to the following sources:

Images used under license from:

READY TO DISCOVER YOUR BIG IDEA?

FLIP THIS BOOK OVER FOR PART TWO:

HOW TO INNOVATE

THE INNOVATION HANDBOOK

JEREMY GUTSCHE, *NEW YORK TIMES BESTSELLING AUTHOR*
CEO OF TREND HUNTER

AXIOM BOOK AWARD WINNER

FAST COMPANY *Press*

Fast Company Press
New York, New York
www.fastcompanypress.com

The Innovation Handbook was previously published as Exploiting Chaos, 978-1592405077, Avery, September 2009.

This work is being published under the Fast Company Press imprint by an exclusive arrangement with Fast Company. Fast Company and the Fast Company logo are registered trademarks of Mansueto Ventures, LLC. The Fast Company Press logo is a wholly owned trademark of Mansueto Ventures, LLC.

Distributed by Greenleaf Book Group

For ordering information or special discounts for bulk purchases, please contact Greenleaf Book Group at PO Box 91869, Austin, TX 78709, 512.891.6100.

Design and composition by Greenleaf Book Group & Brian Phillips Design
Cover design by Greenleaf Book Group & Brian Phillips Design

Publisher's Cataloging-in-Publication data is available.

Print ISBN: 978-1-7324391-4-6

eBook ISBN: 978-1-7324391-5-3

Printed in the United States of America on acid-free paper

20 21 22 23 24 25   10 9 8 7 6 5 4 3 2 1

First Edition

WELCOME TO PART 2

This second side of the book contains fundamental lessons that have inspired more than 1 million people, taking the best parts of *Exploiting Chaos* and building on them with new insights, examples, workshop questions, and tactics.

The original edition won the Axiom International Book Award, was named one of *Inc.* magazine's Best Books for Business Owners, and was #1 on CEO Read for four months. So, on its 10th anniversary, I decided to refresh the content and bring it back!

To me, this book remains exciting and relevant because it contains some of my all-time favorite insights about business. It is structured to be a quick read with provocative titles to get you thinking about your potential. *Learn how to . . .*

1. **CREATE A CULTURE OF INNOVATION**
2. **IDENTIFY OPPORTUNITIES**
3. **METHODICALLY INNOVATE**
4. **INFECTIOUSLY COMMUNICATE YOUR GREAT NEW IDEA**

But first, a few words from some friends . . .

EARLY REVIEWS . . .

"Without a doubt, this is one of the best books on sparking ideas that I have ever read. I read it from cover to cover but believe that even a good skim will have you reaching for a blank piece of paper and pen or a fresh Word document."

JACK COVERT Founder of 800 CEO Read, author of
The 100 Best Business Books of All Time

"A rousing battle cry for the kind of creative, risky thinking that is most needed in times of change and disorder. Whether you're a CEO trying to stay ahead of the curve, a daydreaming teenager, or a wannabe trailblazer, this bold guide is the shake-up you need to check your assumptions, get inspired, and turn business-as-usual totally upside down."

DANIEL PINK bestselling author of *A Whole New Mind*

"A love potion for relentlessly creative souls looking to break boundaries, ignite customer passion, and start a revolution."

KEVIN ROBERTS Worldwide CEO of Saatchi and Saatchi

"Jeremy is a walking, talking, breathing trend, a living example of what happens when you take your own advice. With his ideas, you might catch an ideavirus."

SETH GODIN bestselling author of *This Is Marketing*

BY TONY HUNTER \\\\\\\\\\\\\\\\\\\\\\\\\\\\\|||||||||||||////////////////,

THIS BOOK MADE ME A BETTER LEADER

I know what it's like to be faced with CHAOS . . . And I'm experienced enough to know the CHAOS will continue. So what should you do? Curl up and assume the fetal position under your desk? Or find inspiration to capitalize on the opportunities afforded by disruption? Disrupt or be disrupted . . . by choosing to read Jeremy's book, you've already taken the first step to achieving success as a disruptor.

Which leads me to my story. In September 2008, I received a phone call that I wasn't expecting. The voice on the other end was asking me to be CEO of the *Chicago Tribune*. The catch was—the traditional publishing business model was imploding, and I'd have to eliminate many, many jobs and meet profit targets in a marketplace undergoing unprecedented change.

What a gut-wrenching offer—I couldn't resist. I said yes. In the years that followed, my team transformed the *Chicago Tribune* from bankruptcy to being one of the most profitable news organizations in America. In this book, you will uncover many of the tactics and techniques I used to transform the company in its time of chaos.

The first edition of this book became our manual for accelerating change and leading through unprecedented disruption. It was a visual, digestible handbook that I gave to all of my business leaders. Later, Jeremy and his team ran workshops and did a lot of research for us, but it all began with the insight from this book. You couldn't walk through the Tribune Tower offices without seeing posters from *Exploiting Chaos*.

If you're looking to extract better thinking from your team or to make change happen when change is hard, study and leverage the content in the pages that follow.

This made me a better leader, stretched my imagination, and created opportunities for our organization that were jumpstarted by Jeremy Gutsche.

Now, back to my story as CEO of the *Chicago Tribune*: I was a kid who loved Chicago and a man who loved working for the *Tribune*, a pillar of my community. I cared about

my job, I wanted Tribune to succeed, and frankly, Tribune was not simply a company to me. It was something I believed in so much that I'd dedicated my career to it, probably the same way many of you have dedicated your work life to the brands you work for.

So imagine you're me in 2008: I had a great start to my career at the Tribune Company; 15 years continuously moving up the ranks, record profits. All of a sudden the financial meltdown occurs, Great Recession begins, social media comes roaring into the scene, dollars are disappearing from the publishing industry . . . people are wondering if there will be newspapers in the future. Then, our corporate parent files for bankruptcy in late 2008—nice timing for a first-time CEO.

I was very humbled by the responsibility to lead a Chicago institution, and one of the best media brands. So what to do? Should I bring out the "standard" playbook of incremental actions, wish for better days ahead, assume I had all the answers?

In my case, it was clear we needed to make drastic changes, fast. I believe one of the key roles of a leader during disruptive times is to share the circumstances and details of the company's performance and context around the marketplace dynamics. Followed by a compelling vision, including the rationale for change.

We were clearly in a major transformation project. While innovation and new ideas would be helpful, it wouldn't be enough . . . so we set about transforming the company from a newspaper company to an innovative media and business services company that "happens to publish a newspaper." That proclamation shook the Tribune Tower and initiated a series of actions that would change our company, and position us to succeed.

In my experience, to transform a company you must be courageous enough to make proclamations and quickly follow with a number of actions that indicate big changes are required. You also have to explain why there's a need for change. Sometimes I think executives skip that step in the process, resulting in employees wondering, "Why change?"

Then, you must implement a business plan that provides employees with a road map and a reason to believe. While we made many mistakes in our journey, excelling in these five areas was critical to our success.

First, we simplified the plan and aligned the interests of our employees. That included real culture change, because our bureaucratic, slow-moving culture would not support the transformation plan.

Then we spent a significant amount of time on employee engagement and communication. We involved our team, and while it may have slowed us down at the beginning, it actually got us further, faster in the long run. Third, we put the customer at the forefront of all of our decisions. Next, we invested resources against the new opportunities we identified.

Finally, we forced discussions of competing alternatives rather than accepting the first "good idea." An example of how that paid dividends was instead of cutting the content in our product like everyone else was doing, our editor forced a discussion of what would happen if we added more content and asked people to pay more for it.

This idea, and plan, was totally against the grain of the industry. We knew the cycle of reducing content and raising prices would be short-lived. So despite concerns galore, we concluded that taking more risk to maintain our preeminent position in Chicago was the reason to go in the other direction. We doubled down and made investments in content to create a bigger, better *Chicago Tribune*.

That collaborative, innovative way of thinking ended up creating over $10 million of incremental profit, building brand equity, satisfying customers, and separating us from the competitors. It also gave us a rallying cry for the need for bigger, bolder ideas.

There's a narrow gap to get through as a leader operating in uncertain, disruptive circumstances—being proud of your past but hyper-focused on the future. Disruption might be viewed as challenging to your success . . . unless you view chaos as an opportunity to transform your company. The mantras "Culture eats strategy for breakfast," "Innovate often," and "Push the boundaries of the status quo" were facilitated through the use of Jeremy's tried-and-true handbook: *Exploiting Chaos*.

Enjoy the book and good luck on your journey!

—TONY HUNTER
Former CEO, the *Chicago Tribune*

DIFFICULTY CREATES OPPORTUNITY

Long before Twitter, Facebook, and the current financial crisis, Einstein proposed three rules of work:

- "Out of clutter, find simplicity."

- "From discord, find harmony."

- "In the middle of difficulty lies opportunity."

These rules are truer than ever before. We have encountered increasing media clutter (you could say I'm one of the causes of this!), organizational discord, and financial difficulty—in short, we are in an era of chaos.

The common reaction is to fear these conditions, but just as Einstein's rules profess, difficulty can spark extraordinary ideas.

This book is the quintessential road map for all those who seek opportunity in times of change. Gutsche vividly explores how remarkable companies have risen from chaos, and he provides a toolkit that managers can use to foster a culture of innovation, create great products and services, and change the world.

Read this book, or in the middle of your difficulty will lie more difficulty.

—GUY KAWASKI
bestselling author of 15 books

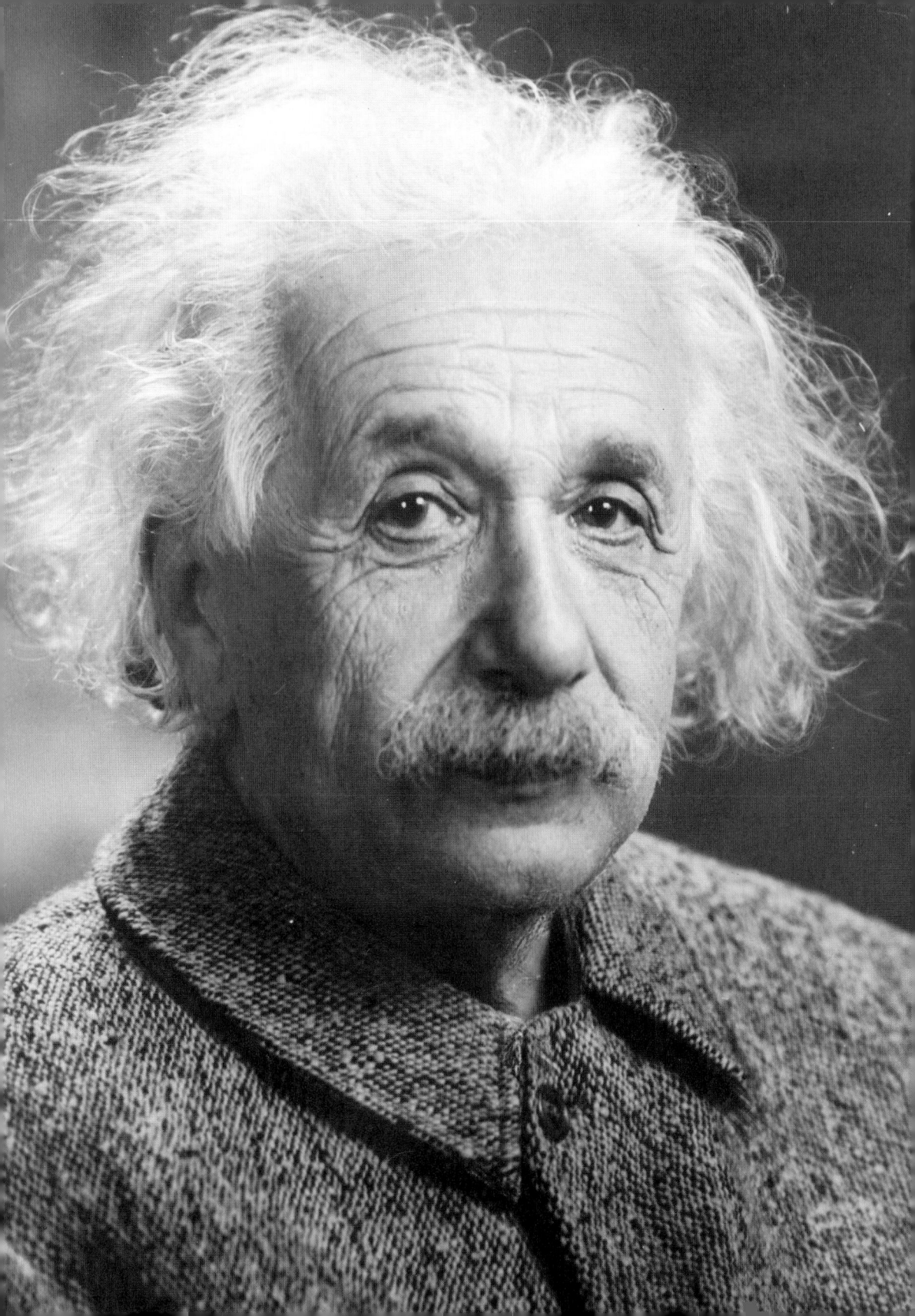

THIS BOOK WILL EQUIP YOU WITH BATTLE-TESTED METHODS TO CREATE THE FUTURE

After conducting more than 10,000 innovation workshops and custom futurism projects, my team has encountered almost every type of innovation problem. We have refined this framework with our clients to be our ultimate guide to the concepts you need to master to make innovation and change happen.

Create the Future Framework

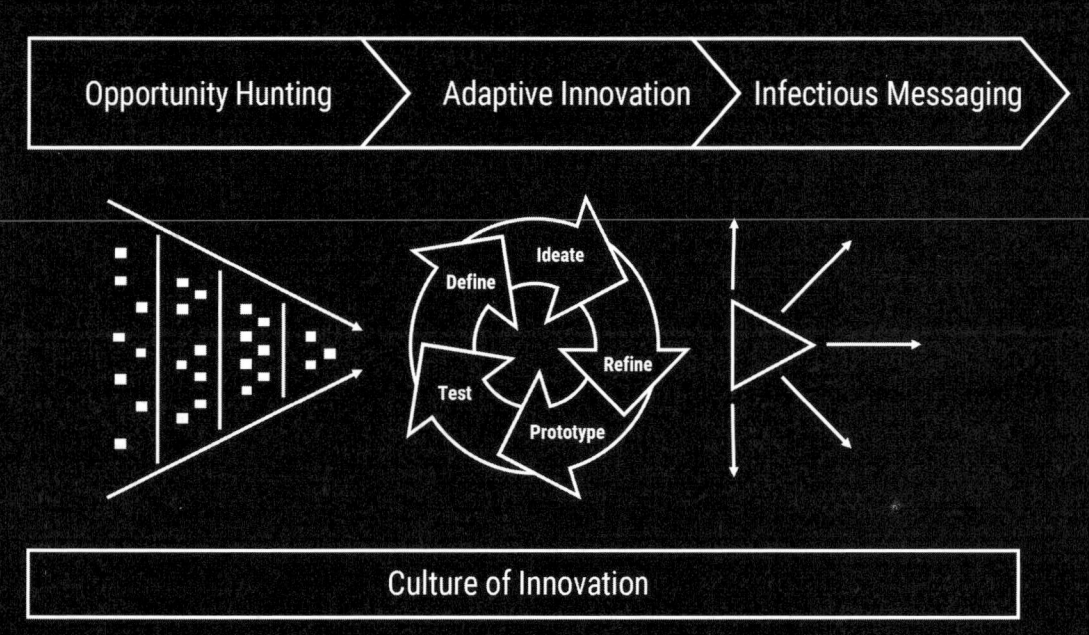

CONTENTS

Create the Future Framework

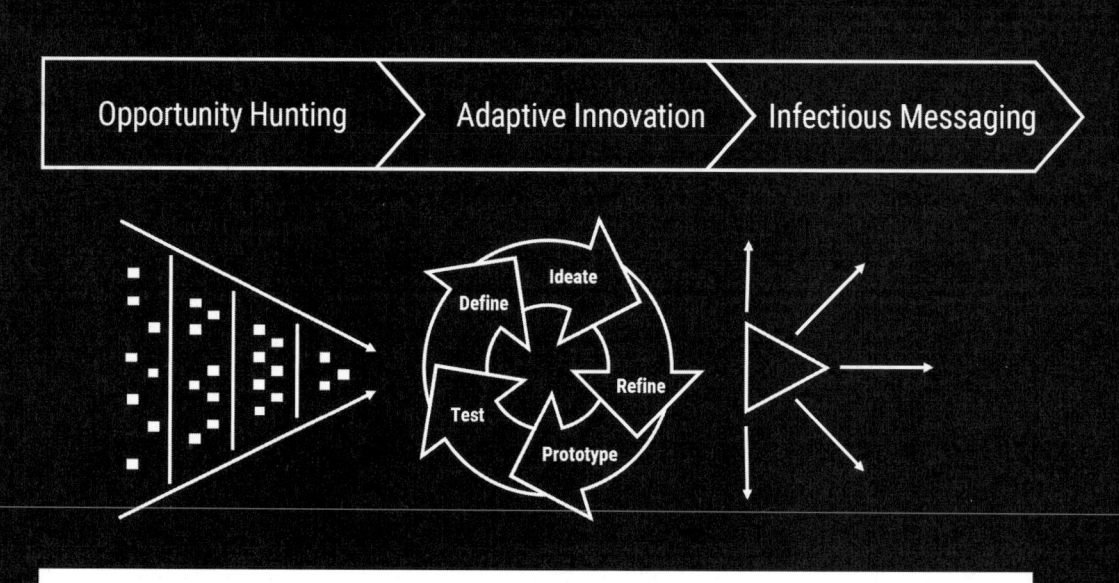

CULTURE OF INNOVATION

Peter Drucker, the father of management thinking, used to say, "Culture eats strategy for breakfast." The concept is that your great idea doesn't matter if you can't put that idea into action and make it happen. Your organization's culture can either enable disruptive thinking or lead to your company's total disruption and failure.

Culture of Innovation Framework

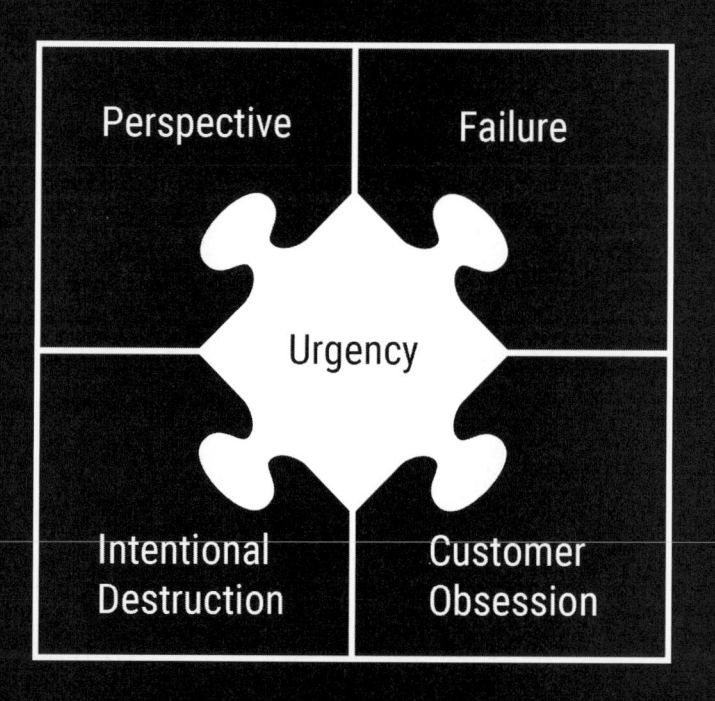

URGENCY

A culture of innovation requires five ingredients, with urgency at its core. Urgency—and an ability to act—is the fuel that enables a culture to achieve results in times of change.

YOU CANNOT ESCAPE DISRUPTIVE EVOLUTION

There are no industries or professions immune from the effects of disruptive change, the sort of change that enables new business models and topples corporate tycoons. Our generation is fundamentally reinventing the way human beings interact.

Broadcast Television	→ Viral Videos
Newspapers	→ Blogs
Album Sales	→ Concert Tours
Physical Stores	→ E-commerce
Advertising	→ Influencer Marketing
America	→ China
Japan	→ India
New York	→ Moscow
Men	→ Women
Email	→ Social Media
Phone Calls	→ Texts
Public Libraries	→ Wikipedia
Classroom Method	→ Virtual Learning
Recruiting	→ Offshore Outsourcing
Medical Doctors	→ Nurse Practitioners
Accountants	→ Online Filing
Lawyers	→ Online Legal Forms
Loan Officers	→ Automated Lending
Oil on Canvas	→ Digital Imagery
Studio Photography	→ Photoshopping

4

YOU MUST DISRUPT, OR BE DISRUPTED.

A STRONG CULTURE CAN MAKE IT DIFFICULT TO INTERNALIZE CHANGE

Viral videos, e-commerce, social media, crowdsourcing, influencer marketing, and a lack of self-censorship: these are the shifts toppling major corporations today.

The sneaky thing is that these shifts are not happening overnight; rather, they are slowly creeping up on us. It's kind of like boiling a frog.

If you place a frog into a pot of boiling water, he'll immediately hop out. And he'll be pissed off. If you place a frog into a pot of lukewarm water, though, and slowly dial up the heat, he will keep swimming until he's boiled alive.

Like us, the frog is more sensitive to shocking change. If change is moderate, urgency becomes less apparent. Before we know it—hey, what's that smell?—we're cooked.

Peter Drucker, regarded as the father of modern management, noted the following at age 94: "We now accept the fact that learning is a lifelong process of keeping abreast of change. And the most pressing task is to teach people how to learn."[1]

THE KEY TO ADAPTATION IS RECOGNIZING THE SUBTLE TRENDS SUGGESTING A NEED FOR CHANGE.

THE SMALLEST SHIFTS CAN DISRUPT A MARKET

The world of business is in a constant state of evolution. Great organizations fade. Fast-moving start-ups step into their place.

In *The Innovator's Dilemma*, Clay Christensen studied the evolution of the disk drive industry, where leaps in technology led to physically smaller hard drives.[2] This caused nerds around the world to rejoice. It also exemplified the difficulty of change.

In theory, the leap from one size to the next doesn't seem monumental. You might expect the same leaders to remain over time. However, when the world changed, leaders lost their places.

Leaders in the Disk Drive Market

1980	14" Drives	Control Data, IBM, Memorex
1984	8" Drives	Shugart, Micropolis, Priam
1988	6¼" Drives	Seagate, Miniscribe, Maxtor
1993	3½" Drives	Conner, Quantum, Maxtor
1995	2½" Drives	Prairetek, Quantum, Conner

"It is not the strongest of the species that survives, nor the most intelligent, but rather the one most adaptable to change."

—Charles Darwin

SMALL SHIFTS CAN DISRUPT THE MARKET.

EVEN THE CLEVER MUST ADAPT

If the disk drive industry is simple, the semiconductor market is complex. Semiconductors are so difficult to make that the leading players boast billion-dollar research budgets.

These budgets are supposed to create barriers to entry, barriers that protect the giants while preventing new companies from entering the market. However, just like in the simple disk drive market, shifts in technology cause new leaders to emerge.[3]

Leaders in the Computer Chip Market

1955	Vacuum Tubes	RCA, Sylvania, General Electric
1955	Transistors	Hughes, Transitron, Philco
1965	Semiconductors	Texas Instruments, Fairchild, Motorola
1975	Integrated Circuits	Texas Instruments, Fairchild, National
1985	VLSI Circuits	Motorola, Texas Instruments, NEC
1995	Submicron	Intel, NEC, Motorola

RCA, for example, was once double the size of IBM. They were rock stars in the vacuum tube market, but apparently people don't buy vacuum tubes anymore. RCA struggled with change, and eventually, the company was displaced. (Mental note: stop selling vacuum tubes.)

YOUR FOCUS SHOULD NOT BE ON PROTECTING WHAT YOU HAVE —— BUT RATHER ON ADAPTING TO THE NEXT BIG THING.

DISRUPTIVE IDEAS MOVE SLOWLY, UNTIL THE KNOCK-OUT PUNCH

When disruption happens, it is usually a surprise, but it doesn't have to be that way. In a *Harvard Business Review* article titled "Disruption Is a Moving Target," Scott Anthony reports that disruption is a three-step process:[4]

1. "Disruptors enter a market incumbents don't care about."

Protected by their unattractively small markets, entrants build skills and acquire market insight that big companies don't have. By servicing unwanted customers, they build maverick brands.

2. "Entrants grow as incumbents flee."

Growing in popularity and success, entrants begin to creep up the value chain. The "old school" incumbents respond by shifting focus away from their full customer base and instead toward "high-value customers."

3. "The incumbent hits a ceiling." (The knock-out surprise)

Once new entrants reach a critical mass, they create part-nerships that enable them to "go for the kill." The incumbents get pushed past their ability to compete and crisis ensues. *Sneaky.*

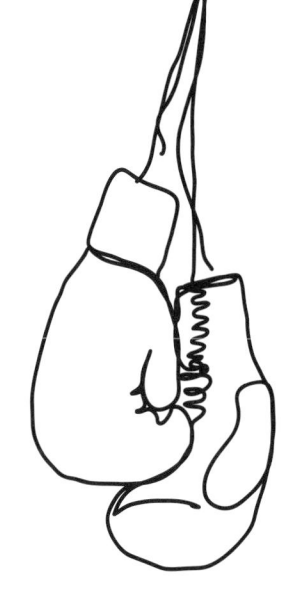

FOR BIG COMPANIES, THIS PATTERN OF DISRUPTION CAN BE USED TO CREATE STRATEGIES FOR SURVIVAL. FOR SMALL COMPANIES, THIS SHOULD INFLUENCE YOUR PLAN OF ATTACK.

BLUR YOUR DEFINITION OF THE MARKET YOU ARE IN

We live in a period of unbounded opportunity, but most business leaders have a tendency to look too closely at their current market. That can lead to disaster. Coke and Pepsi missed identifying Red Bull because their research firms closely studied the carbonated beverage category. Those same firms tracked Red Bull as a stimulant, in the same category as coffee. This oversight lasted for years, until the teams were blindsided by something outsiders watched all along.

This scenario happens in countless industries. People fail to act because they don't react to "different-looking" competitors. For example, Airbnb became the largest hotelier without owning hotels. Uber became the largest transportation company without owning vehicles. Facebook became the largest media company without writers. Amazon became the largest retailer without stores.

Be careful not to obsess about your closest competitor while missing out on the wide array of disruptors staring at your market. Here are just a few categories of disruptors:

1. DOMINANT INNOVATORS IN UNRELATED MARKETS—e.g., Amazon buying Whole Foods

2. FULLY-FUNDED START-UPS—e.g., automakers dismissing Tesla

3. FOREIGN COMPETITORS—e.g., TD Bank entering America

4. AMBITIOUS SUPPLIERS—e.g., Samsung supplies Apple

To make matters worse, sometimes the unrelated competitor enters your market without any intention of making a profit. They enter simply to expand their business with your key customer segment.

COMPANIES FAIL TO RECOGNIZE THE PACE OF CHANGE WITHIN THEIR OWN INDUSTRY, WHICH CAN LEAD TO DISRUPTION.

INTERNALIZE THAT CHAOS CREATES OPPORTUNITY

People often tell me that they cannot make change happen in their company because they lack buy-in, support, and funding. I usually point out that some of the greatest opportunities actually came about in periods of total crisis. How difficult could your challenges really be, in comparison?

For example, during the Great Depression, unemployment soared to 25%, 15,000 banks failed, and Wall Street was no longer a place of glamor.

Four dreadful months into this depression, Henry R. Luce launched a pricey magazine titled *Fortune*. At $1 an issue, the cover price surpassed the cost of a functional wool sweater. Seemingly bad timing.

Eight years later, *Fortune* had grown its subscriber base to 460,000 people. By 1937 the magazine reported an annual profit of $500,000. Scaled for inflation, that amounts to more than 7 million modern-day dollars. That's a lot of wool sweaters.

Luce successfully launched a luxurious publication during the Great Depression!

Kellogg professor Andrew J. Razeghi suggests, "*Fortune* worked for the very same reason that all great new products work: it made a uniquely relevant contribution to its customers' lives (period)."[5] *Fortune* was more than just a publication. It was a glimpse into the boardrooms of those that survived; *Fortune* was an answer. And it was an answer in a time where people felt the urgent need to adapt or collapse.

INNOVATION IS ABOUT CREATING AN IDEA THAT FULFILLS AN UNMET NEED, AND OFTEN PEOPLE NEED URGENCY TO SPOT THOSE NEEDS.

Disney, CNN, MTV, Hyatt, Burger King, FedEx, Microsoft, Apple, Gillette, AT&T, Texas Instruments, 20th Century Fox, IBM, Merck, Hershey's, IHOP, Eli Lilly, Coors, Bristol-Myers, Amgen, The Jim Henson Company, Sun, LexisNexis, Autodesk, Adobe, Symantec, Electronic Arts, Fortune, GE, and Hewlett-Packard.

These iconic companies were all founded during periods of economic recession.[6]

If such amazing success can happen out of recession, what greatness can emerge from periods of vast opportunity?

YOU CAN'T EXACTLY PREDICT
THE FUTURE . . .

Twenty years ago, I had the opportunity to learn how futurism works on a high-profile consulting case with Peter Schwartz, an early futurist and president of the Global Business Network (GBN). GBN was just acquired by the firm I worked for, the Monitor Group. This case was the first collaboration.

As a management consultant, I'd helped Fortune 500 companies to, well, make more money. As a futurist, Peter had done the same, but he had also helped Steven Spielberg design the future for *Minority Report*. He worked with the Department of Defense to interpret climate change as a risk to national security, and he regularly wrote for *Wired* magazine, including articles about hydrogen power, war, capitalism, and the future. I had a lot to learn.

My first lesson was the most important rule about predicting the future: you can't. What? If you try to predict the future, your vision will be guided by an extrapolation of the status quo. You will end up with a reasonable prediction and, at the same time, you will be completely wrong.

However, the act of actually predicting the future is quite possible. It's just more complex than outsiders first think.

SIMPLE PREDICTION WILL CAUSE YOU TO MISS UNEXPECTED EVENTS AND DISRUPTIVE CHANGE.

. . . BUT YOU CAN PREDICT SCENARIOS AND CREATE URGENCY

In the 1970s, Pierre Wack was planning for the future at Royal Dutch Shell. For nearly three decades, oil prices had been relatively steady, but now the world was changing. Demand for oil had increased, US oil reserves were drying up, Middle Eastern countries had grown stronger, and most of these countries resented the West, especially after the 1967 Arab-Israeli war.

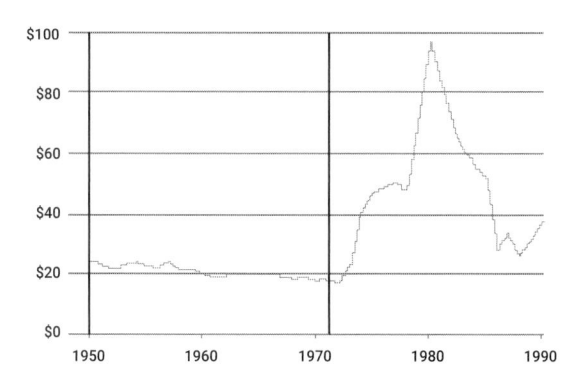

Retail Oil Prices
Before and After Pierre Wack's Scenarios

Weaving this information together, Wack realized that Middle Eastern countries could spark an energy crisis. That fear led him to develop two potential scenarios. The first scenario was based on the conventional wisdom that oil prices would remain relatively stable. The second assumed an oil crisis, which he conveyed in detail with vivid storytelling. The potential impact was so severe that Wack's managers were inspired to prepare for the worst.

In 1973 the world did encounter an oil price shock, but Royal Dutch Shell was ready. Once the weakest of the "big seven" oil empires, the company emerged as the most profitable and second in size. In *The Art of the Long View*, Peter Schwartz refers to Wack's example as one of the first modern uses of scenario analysis in business.[7]

BY DEVELOPING MULTIPLE SCENARIOS, YOU CAN AVOID THE CERTAINTY ——— *OF BEING INCORRECT AND INSTEAD PREPARE FOR DISRUPTIVE CHANGE.*

VISUALIZE DISASTER
AND OPPORTUNITY

World Cup ski racers, Formula 1 drivers, professional wrestlers, and astronauts all share one incredibly powerful tool: visualization. I spent a decade as a ski racer, a sport where 70 mph speed and icy inclines force action and reaction to coexist.

Picture yourself tearing down a mountain at a blood-curdling speed. You carve your razor-sharp skis from gate to gate, hoping to best your rivals by fractions of a second. The incline lures you faster and the world around you starts to blur. Your heart pounds. You cut each corner recklessly close, pushing the limits of personal safety. At this speed, a crash would send you tumbling past your dreams. But you only get one shot, and you're fully committed.

At some point, you will be thrown off balance. You are moving too fast to act with reverent caution. But when the unexpected happens, you'll know how to navigate because you've raced this exact track a dozen times in your head. You've thought about every corner, every bump, and every hairpin turn. You've visually rehearsed your reaction to every possible scenario.

In ski racing, visualization is not optional. It trains the human mind to react during unexpected situations.

A striking parallel exists between ski racing and innovating through chaos. In both situations, you navigate an unfamiliar course at uncomfortable speed. You'll make some mistakes, but how you react will make all the difference.

Chaos yields both risk and opportunity at the least convenient times. Projects will unexpectedly fall apart.

TEAMS THAT REHEARSE THEIR REACTION TO THE UNEXPECTED WILL BE MORE LIKELY TO SPARK URGENCY AND NAVIGATE THROUGH THE COURSE OF UNCERTAINTY.

- PEOPLE WILL QUIT WHEN YOU NEED THEM MOST.

- SUPERSTARS WILL BE AVAILABLE WHEN YOU CANNOT HIRE.

- COMPETITORS WILL FALTER.

- NEW CUSTOMERS WILL BECOME AVAILABLE.

How will you react to the urgent demands that prevail during both disaster and opportunity? How will you deal with sudden changes to customer needs?

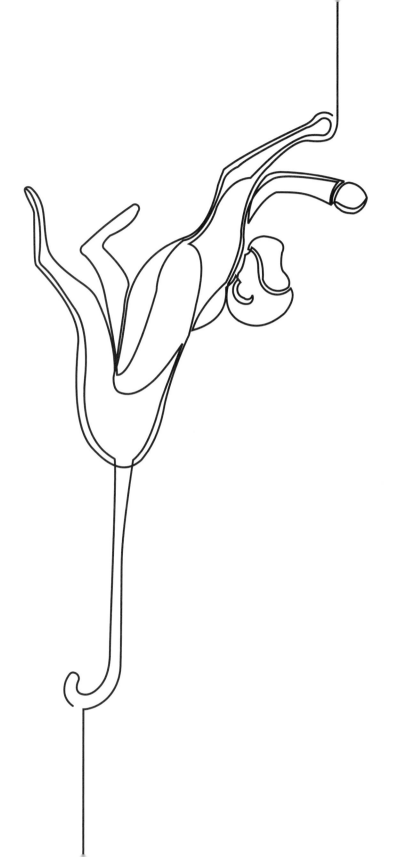

DON'T LET MONKEYS INHIBIT CHANGE

Long ago, five menacing monkeys were placed in a cage. In that cage was a ladder that led to a ripe bunch of bananas. The catch was that a powerful water hose was connected to the ladder.

When the first monkey raced up the ladder to reach for a banana, the entire cage was drenched with water. Another curious monkey made an attempt. She rushed up the ladder, greedy to grasp the yellow bundle, but she, too, triggered a shower on the cage. At this point, it became clear to the monkeys that if one of them reached for the bananas, they would all get soaked.

Each time one of the original monkeys was swapped out of the cage for a new monkey, the newcomer would immediately race toward the alluring fruit, but the group would beat him down before he made it up the ladder. This cycle repeated each time a new monkey was introduced to the cage.

Later the fire hose was removed, but it didn't matter. The monkeys already had their lesson hardwired: don't reach for the bananas. One by one, the monkeys were replaced until none of the original five were in the cage. The same behavior persisted.

Why? Because that's the way we do things around here.

THE "OLD WAY OF DOING THINGS" IS THE MOST POWERFUL ENEMY OF YOUR CULTURE, WHICH IS WHY PART 1, THE OTHER SIDE OF THIS BOOK, WAS FOCUSED ON THE ABILITY TO CHANGE.

- What external factors currently pose a threat to your business? How could you turn them into motivators of urgency?

- What actions, partnerships, or strategies could your largest competitors take that would seriously threaten your business?

- What if Amazon bought your largest competitor, just as they bought Whole Foods? How might they compete against you faster?

- What are 10 companies doing interesting things in your market, even if they are very small today? What if the largest competitor bought those companies to make them 100 times larger?

TACTICS ————————————————

1. Fear disruption and create scenarios for how disruption could happen.

2. Develop tactics for how you would react quickly to sudden market changes.

3. Invest in ideas that open up your future options.

4. Create a desire to compete with start-ups and large competitors alike.

5. Invent a fictitious competitor and create an ongoing story about actions they are taking (thanks to Josh Linkner, serial entrepreneur and author, for this idea).

CULTURE OF INNOVATION

Culture of Innovation Framework

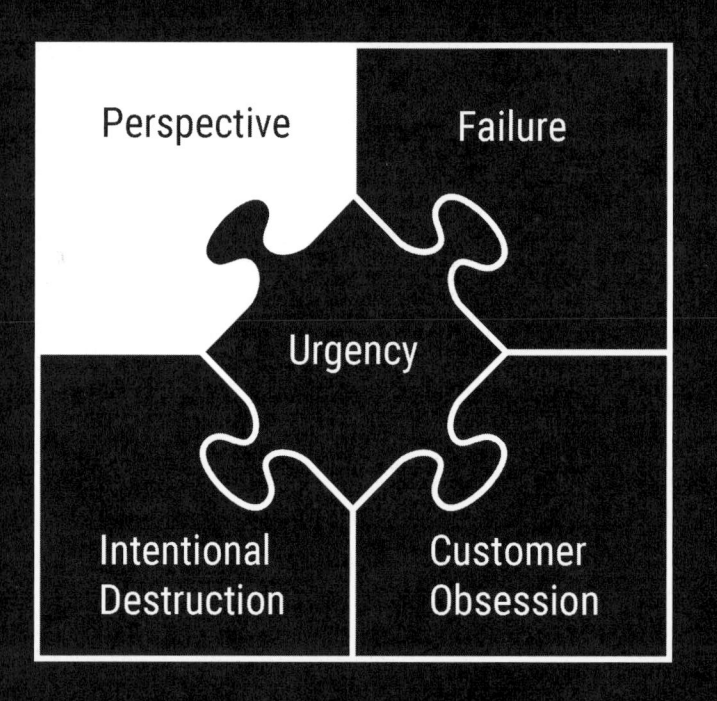

PERSPECTIVE

Your perspective is the way you look at the future and the problems that you are trying to solve. Your perspective determines your destiny.

WHAT *EXACTLY* ARE YOU TRYING TO DO?

When someone asks you to define your organization, what is your answer? How do you describe your role?

This might seem like a simple question, but it has a meaningful impact on your destiny. To really appreciate the importance of perspective, we begin with a quiz:

Can you identify this company?

- Their website boasts: "_____ has been turning creative ideas into breakthroughs for well over a century."

- They invented grammar checkers.

- They invented electronic dictionaries in 1985.

- They invented the laptop word processor in 1989.

- They started building PDAs in 1994.

Apple?

Microsoft?

Xerox?

Dell?

Hewlett-Packard?

Any guesses?

"SMITH CORONA—

THE **BEST** TYPEWRITER COMPANY IN THE WORLD!"

Not surprisingly, that's a title that they keep today. Smith Corona was once an innovation icon. So why didn't the typewriter experts get into the wonderful world of computing?

A closer look reveals the leaders were making rational decisions. In fact, the parallels to modern-day business problems are striking.

Diving deeper, the first step is to visit Smith Corona's website. It's funny because it actually exists. Also, one of the graphics illustrates a slogan you probably have not heard:

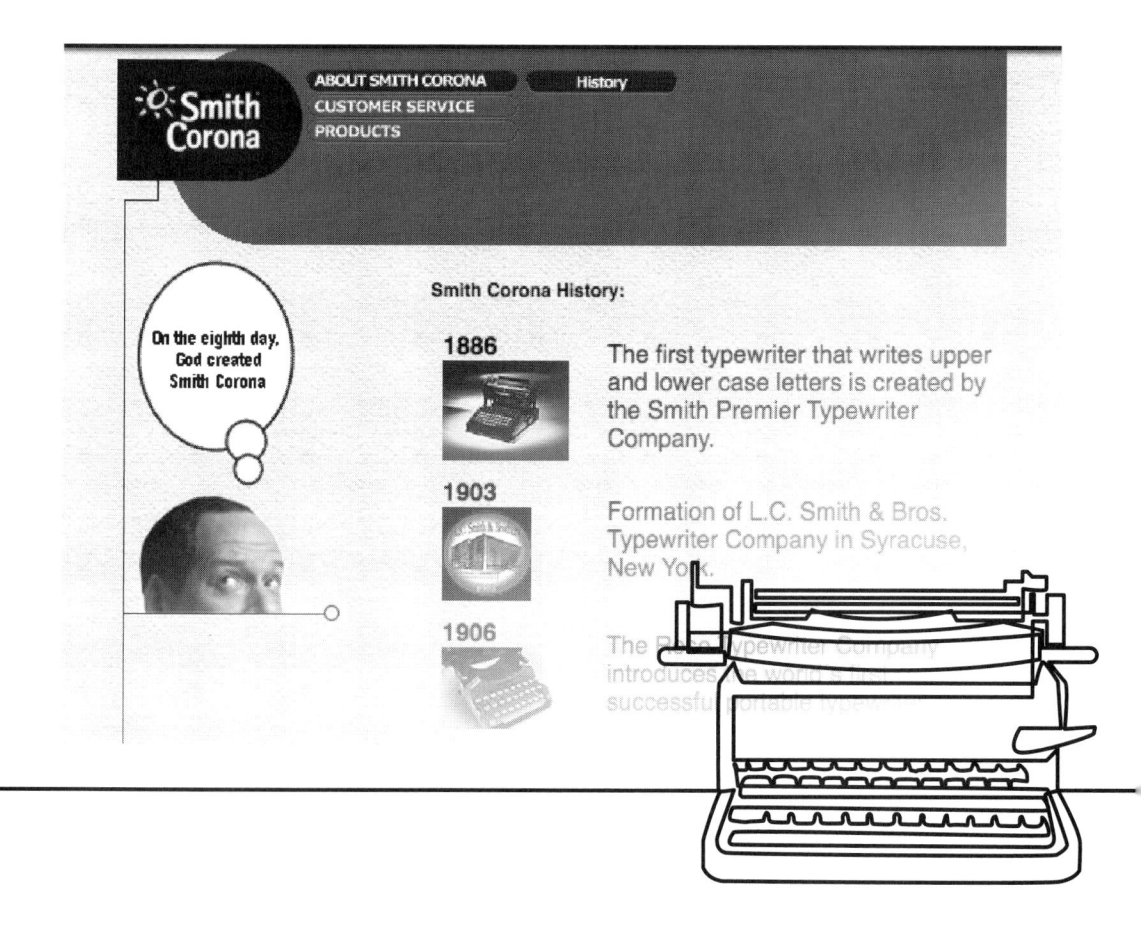

"On the eighth day, God created Smith Corona." Wow. I bet you didn't know that.

What would lead a company to put that graphic up on their website?

First, the company would basically have to be defunct, and not care. Second, Smith Corona had a 100-year history of reinventing itself:

- **1886**   FIRST TYPEWRITER WITH UPPER & LOWER CASE
- **1906**   FIRST PORTABLE TYPEWRITER
- **1957**   FIRST PORTABLE ELECTRIC TYPEWRITER
- **1960**   FIRST POWERED CARRIAGE RETURN
- **1973**   FIRST REMOVABLE CARTRIDGE
- **1984**   FIRST WORD ERASER
- **1985**   FIRST ELECTRONIC DICTIONARY
- **1985**   FIRST PERSONAL WORD PROCESSOR
- **1989**   FIRST LAPTOP PERSONAL WORD PROCESSOR

From the first electric typewriter to the first personal word processor, Smith Corona knew how to identify new trends and opportunities.

As an industry leader, Smith Corona could envision the big trends and competition. But what were they missing?

ACCOMPLISHMENT BLINDS US TO
THE URGENCY OF REINVENTION.

DON'T BE SEDUCED BY COMPLACENCY

Without the full story, Smith Corona's decline would seem to be rooted in careless decision-making; however, the missed opportunity was much less obvious. Smith Corona was making a ton of money as the world's best typewriter company.

No competitor could challenge that claim to fame. By 1989 revenues were at a record high:

$500 MILLION

Incidentally, that's a lot of money.

Yes, the world was changing, but there was not an urgent need to move into an unproven market. After all, if computer word processors became interesting, Smith Corona could easily just "buy their way in." Right?

UNFORTUNATELY, IT'S ALL TOO EASY TO REMAIN FOCUSED ON A GIANT, STAGNANT BUSINESS. IT'S TOO EASY TO BECOME COMPLACENT.

LOOK BEYOND THE FAILURE OF OTHERS

Remington was the first manufacturer of typewriters and one of Smith Corona's fierce rivals. In 1950 Remington did get into computing. But by 1975, the company started to falter. The computing division was sold off, and by 1981 Remington Rand declared bankruptcy. They would no longer be making giant computers like this bulky beast:

This catastrophic failure lingered in the minds of Smith Corona managers. Remington Rand had been an icon, an icon with a similar heritage. If Smith Corona expanded into new, uncertain markets, maybe they would inherit the same fate.

BE CAUTIOUS NOT TO LET THE FAILURE OF OTHERS REINFORCE INACTION.

ASSUME TREMENDOUS POTENTIAL IN RIVAL IDEAS

It's common to perceive rival ideas and new entrants as inferior. Sometimes these rivals are little start-ups that are disorganized and imperfect. Other times, the rivals are large, but only in their respective markets, hardly a threat to our own dominance. In short, large organizations often have the misconception that new entrants will fade away.

For Smith Corona, Commodore was one of these entrants. Computers were becoming popular, but not for word processing. Just take a look at the Commodore 128. Although it looks horrific by today's standards, in 1985 it was cutting edge. It came with an awkward set of boxes, lots of cables, and a big blue screen. Plus, it had two external floppy drives.

Yeah, baby!

By comparison, the Smith Corona PWP 40 was an ultra-compact typewriter. It could save to a disk, spell check, and perform "search and replace." It also had a built-in printer. In many ways, it was like an all-in-one laptop and printer 10 years ahead of its time.

Which product would Smith Corona's government and corporate clients want? The typewriter they knew and loved, or the computer box machine thing?

WHEN YOU EVALUATE NEW IDEAS, YOU NEED TO LOOK BEYOND INITIAL IMPERFECTIONS.

Commodore 128

Smith Corona PWP 40

- Spell check, "search and repla
- Save on a disk
- Laser-quality printing
- Essentially a laptop, 10 years

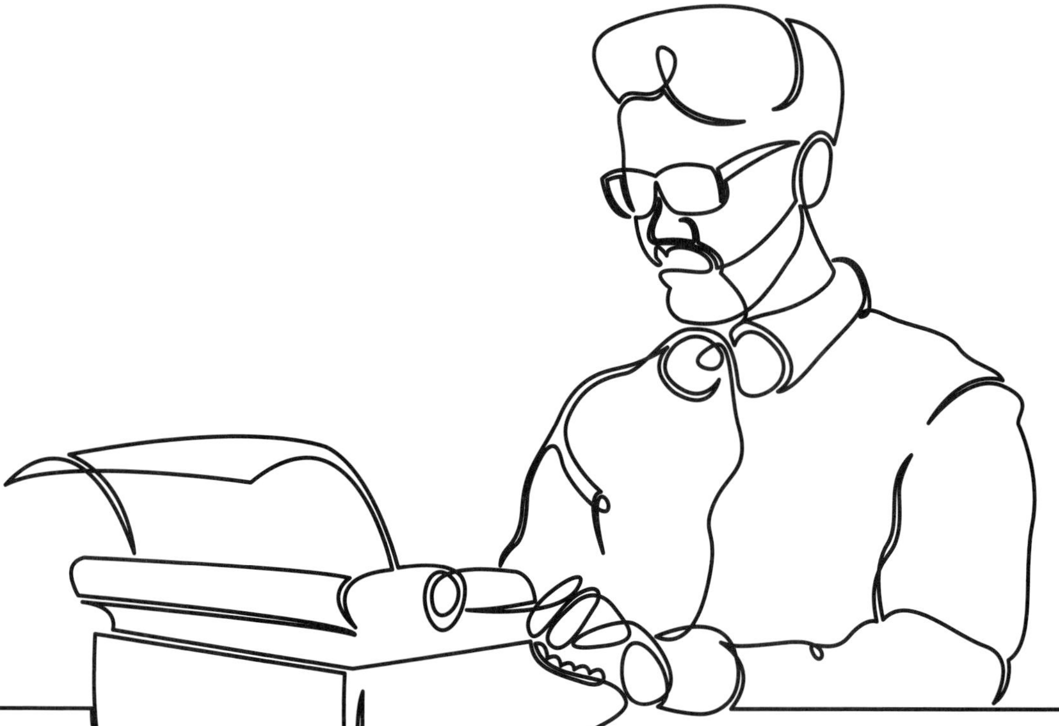

EMBRACE UNCERTAINTY

Smith Corona was not blind to emerging trends. The company had deep pockets, Ivy League–educated managers, a legacy of innovation, and an appetite for new ideas.

In 1990 the VP of marketing, Fred Feuerhake, observed that the industry was "in a period of transition between typewriters and word processors."

One year later, Smith Corona formed a partnership with the Acer computer company.[8] The Acer deal meant Smith Corona was cooking in the personal computer kitchen.

The partners concocted a recipe for a new product line branded "Simply Smart." The machines were targeted at Smith Corona's less sophisticated customers. They featured easy-to-use software and a low price point.

The partnership was a reasonably good strategy.

Although he dismissed the significance, CEO G. Lee Thompson noticed the progress: " [Computers] are a logical extension of our line."

AS A BIG PLAYER, IT IS NEVER TOO LATE
TO GET INTO THE GAME.

AVOID RETREATING TO YOUR COMFORT ZONE

"Computer machines" were worth exploring—until the typewriter business got in the way.

In 1992 Smith Corona decided to relocate production to Mexico. This sort of project created a sense of urgency and distraction. The organization was entering a period of chaos, and it seemed uncertain that computer word processors could save the company.

To a $500 million organization, the decision to move became the single biggest project. The relocation was expected to slash the company's costs by nearly 12%.

To a $500 million organization, a little venture making awkward computers seemed inconsequential.

Nothing, they believed, not even investing in computers, would have a bigger payoff. To make that payoff happen, Smith Corona needed organizational alignment and focus. Quite simply, they saw the computing projects as adding noise and distraction.

When the world became chaotic, Smith Corona did what most organizations do: they retreated to their comfort zone. Prudent managers ignore smaller opportunities and Smith Corona became a victim of rational decision-making. Question rational thought.

It had only been one year, but the board killed the Acer partnership. In a trade interview, the CEO defended his dying industry:

"Many people believe that the typewriter and word-processor business is a buggy-whip industry, which is far from true. There is still a strong market for our products in the United States and the world."

—G. Lee Thompson, CEO of Smith Corona, 1992

As a side note, Thompson's quote reinforces one of my personal philosophies: if you use the words "buggy-whip" to describe your company, you are predestined for failure . . .

Three years later, Smith Corona declared bankruptcy. Acer went on to become the fourth-largest PC company in the world. Snap. Mike Chernago, former VP of operations, noted, "People screamed like crazy when they killed that deal. But at the time, the executives thought that Smith Corona was never going to be put out of business. It was hard to imagine that the typewriter would be annihilated . . ."[9]

Smith Corona wanted to be the best typewriter company in the world, and they still are today. What if Smith Corona's strategy had been to develop tools for recording human thought? Better yet, what if they hadn't used a typewriter to write their strategy?

Luckily, there is a happy ending. In 2000, after a second bankruptcy, Smith Corona was acquired by a private investor, Robert Kanner, who saw potential where others did not. Kanner and his team, who I've had the pleasure of meeting several times, saw the potential of exiting the typewriter business and leveraging Smith Corona's expertise in ribbons and thermal technology. Today, the company has become one of the world's largest players in the market for thermal labels. Amazing!

BREAKTHROUGH REQUIRES COMMITMENT TO NEW FRONTIERS
AND QUESTIONING RATIONAL THOUGHT.

IF YOU'RE BIG, ACT SMALL

Liberate entrepreneurial thinking, invest in disruptive companies, and seek ways to break down structure.

Most importantly, feel threatened by little new entrants.

IF YOU'RE SMALL, ACT BIG

Steal customers from big companies, create partnerships that build scale, and exploit your superior understanding of the customer.

Take advantage of slow-moving incumbents.

CHASE THE RIGHT DREAM

In 1999, a talented teenager named Shawn Fanning created a disruptive opportunity: Napster. By February 2001, more than 25 million unique users were using Napster to illegally file share, a term denounced by the Recording Industry Association of America (RIAA). By July, an RIAA lawsuit forced Napster to "turn down the music."[10]

Next, the RIAA decided to sue 35,000 potential customers.[11] Among those subpoenaed: a dead grandmother,[12] families with no computers at all,[13] and children as young as 12.[14] As a general rule of thumb, never sue 12-year-old kids.

The RIAA also sued XM Satellite Radio,[15] several internet radio stations,[16] and a discounted Russian pay site (for $1.7 trillion).[17] Essentially, they sued anyone with a cutting-edge approach.

Consumers were so upset that there was even toilet paper made and sold with the RIAA logo on it.

The first legal solution to downloading music was iTunes in 2003. But in the four years "without an answer," Napster alternatives became so "useful" that illegal downloads still exceed paid downloads by 20 to 1.[18]

The music industry was forever changed, but the major players couldn't move past the death of their "typewriter." The RIAA was laser-focused on protecting CD sales, but what if they had instead focused on the future of music?

THE PROBLEM YOU ARE TRYING TO SOLVE CAN BECOME ALL-CONSUMING. DEFINE THE RIGHT GOAL.

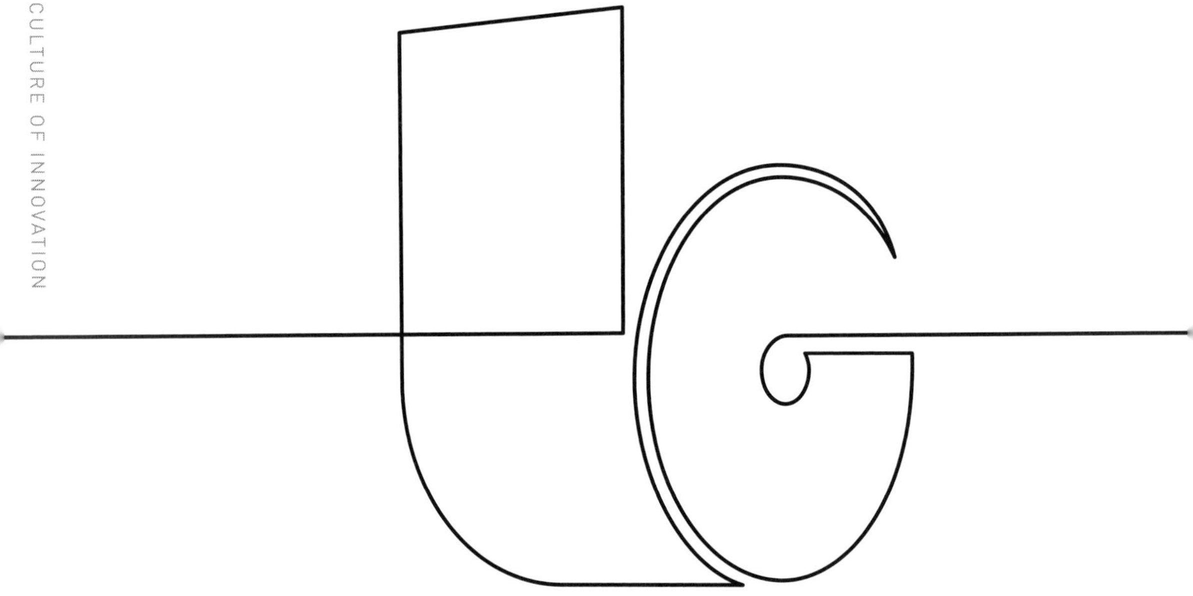

EXPLOIT CHAOS TO ACCELERATE CHANGE

The Boston Consulting Group and *BusinessWeek* surveyed 1,000 influential managers and determined the following enemies of innovation: lengthy development, lack of coordination, risk-averse culture, and limited customer insight.[19]

Top Enemies of Innovation

1,000 Respondents, Boston Consulting Group

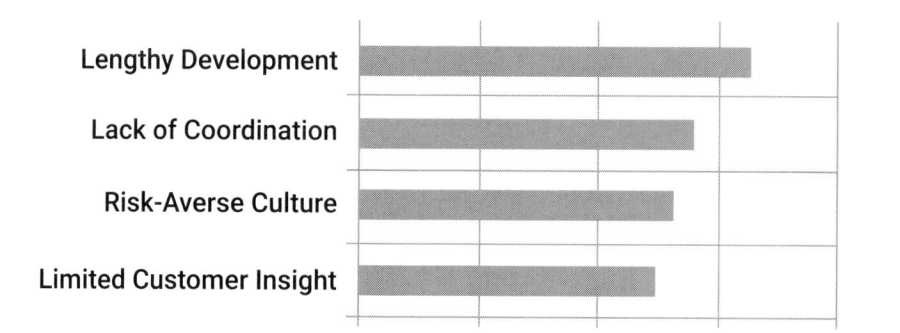

(As an aside, I was going to update this chart, which is from 2006, and then I realized the irony is that the world may have changed, but the people problems that inhibit change have remained the same.)

You can exploit crisis to accelerate change in each of these areas. At age 28, I was promoted to a new role as the head of Capital One Canada's high-end business: Upmarket Lending. At the time we had just one product, a 5.99% credit card.

In a market dominated by an oligopoly of five aging Canadian banks, our card was the best. Unfortunately, funding costs skyrocketed, and our product was no longer profitable. It was dead.

Worse yet, we couldn't increase our interest rate. Anything above 5.99% caused demand to plummet. I was given the following goal: don't let profits decline by more than 20%. Super. I could already imagine my future. I'd get to tell my friends, "I shrank the business by only 20% . . . Yeah, I'm that good." Fortunately, crisis creates opportunity:

1. Crisis reduced our time to market: we no longer had to spend a year proving that our ideas were perfect; we only had to prove they were better than the alternative—which was nothing.

2. Crisis let our team coordinate and cut through red tape: approvals were faster, and cooperation was greater.

3. Crisis enhanced our tolerance for risk: without a product, we were forced to push traditional boundaries.

4. Crisis forced us to relearn what our customers wanted: we used to be complacent knowing our 5.99% card was the lowest rate in the country. But crisis forced us to rethink what customers wanted. Why did Canadians hate slightly higher rates, like 6.99%?

This led us to an important insight. Our Canadian customers didn't think about their rates as numbers; they thought about whether or not their rates were fair. Numeric pricing like "5.99%" makes it difficult to understand how much the bank is actually making. But relative pricing, like "prime + 2," is easier to evaluate. (In Canada, prime is a base rate used to price mortgages.) By repositioning our card with "prime + 2" pricing, our card was essentially the same, but demand increased. Instead of declining by 20%, monthly bookings tripled, and the business grew to a $1 billion portfolio.

YOU CAN USE CRISIS TO DEFEAT

THE ENEMIES OF INNOVATION.

SHIFT PERSPECTIVE, SPARK REVOLUTION

In 1993, IBM was caught in a downward spiral, losing nearly a billion dollars a month. Demise seemed imminent. Then Louis Gerstner took over the role of CEO. Along the way, he realized that the key to change rested in culture: "If I could have chosen not to tackle the IBM culture head-on, I probably wouldn't have. . . . [C]hanging the attitude and behaviors of hundreds of thousands of people is very, very hard. [Yet] I came to see in my time at IBM that culture isn't just one aspect of the game—it is the game."[20]

One of the ways Gerstner changed IBM's culture was by shifting vernacular and ritual. He noted that "you can understand a lot about organizations by their word choice. . . . I choose my words very carefully."

Gerstner held a workshop with 420 company leaders. There, he introduced the adjacent chart that broke company lingo down into banned words and alternative vernacular. To inspire change, he read a quote from Larry Ellison, CEO of Oracle—one of IBM's largest rivals—who scoffed, "IBM? We don't even think about those guys anymore. They're not dead, but they're irrelevant."

In the six years that followed, IBM became a profit machine. Its shares skyrocketed more than tenfold. The change would be heralded as the greatest turnaround in corporate history.

REINVENTING PERSPECTIVE TRIGGERS AND SHAPES CHANGE.

IBM'S "REQUIRED BEHAVIORAL CHANGE"

Excerpt of memo sent by Louis Gerstner to all of IBM:

FROM	TO
Product (focus)	Customer (focus)
Do it my way	Do it the customer's way
Manage to morale	Manage to succeed
Decisions based on anecdotes and myths	Decisions based on facts and data
Relationship-driven	Performance-driven
Conformity (politically correct)	Diversity of ideas & opinions
Attack the people	Attack the process
Rule-driven	Principle-driven
Value me (the silo)	Value us (the whole)
Analysis paralysis (everything must be proven 100+%)	Make decisions & move forward with urgency (80% / 20%)
Fund everything	Prioritize

THE ONLY THINGS SLOWING YOU DOWN ARE THE RULES YOU NEED TO BREAK

The path to growth is full of obstacles, but it's not impenetrable. Your company could increase its innovation budgets, take risks, encourage failure, advertise, hire talent, invest in technology, and so on.

The problem with all this advice, you are saying, is that it seems unrealistic. At least, it seems unrealistic within my organization.

WE'RE TOO BIG.

WE'RE TOO SMALL.

WE CAN'T DO THAT.

WE TRIED THAT BEFORE.

I CAN'T MAKE A DECISION THAT SENIOR.

THAT'S OWNED BY ANOTHER DEPARTMENT.

WE'RE JUST STARTING OUT.

WE DON'T HAVE THAT MUCH MONEY.

OUR INVESTORS WOULD NEVER ALLOW THAT.

THE PURSUIT OF OPPORTUNITY WILL REQUIRE YOU TO THINK DIFFERENTLY AND BREAK THE RULES THAT PARALYZE CHANGE.

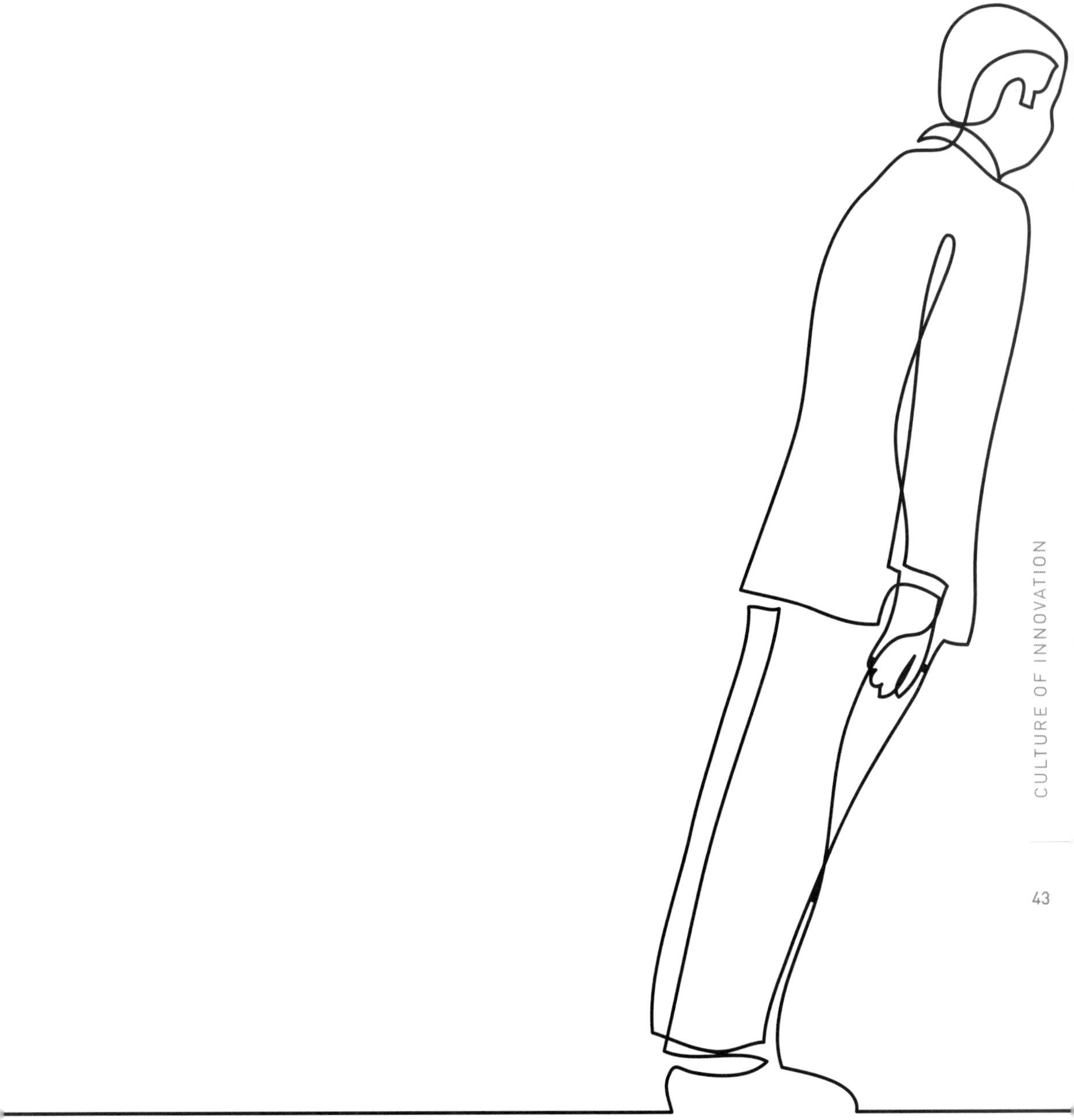

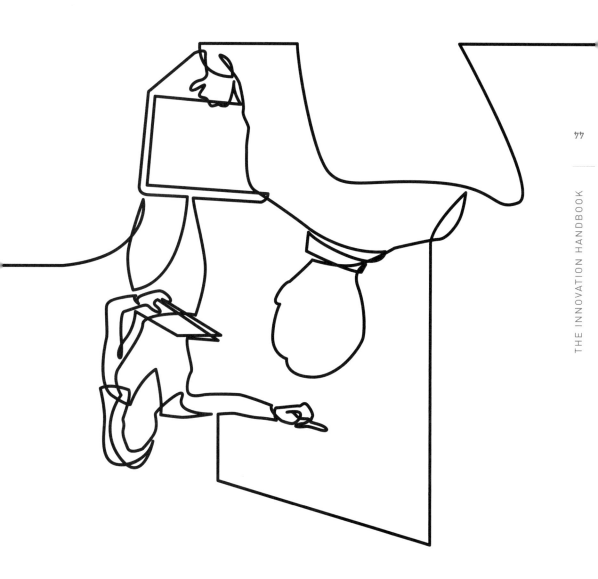

"THE RIGHT QUESTIONS DON'T CHANGE AS OFTEN AS THE ANSWERS DO"

This was the world according to Peter Drucker.

Drucker advised the world's most influential corporate leaders, including GE's Jack Welch, Procter & Gamble's A.G. Lafley, Intel's Andy Grove, Edward Jones's John Bachmann, and Toyota's Shoichiro Toyoda. He also wrote 39 acclaimed books.

Along the way, Drucker gained a reputation for the emphasis he placed on his three most important questions:

1. What is our business?

2. Who are the customers?

3. What does the customer value?

YOU WILL ONLY ANSWER THE PROBLEMS
YOU ARE TRYING TO SOLVE.

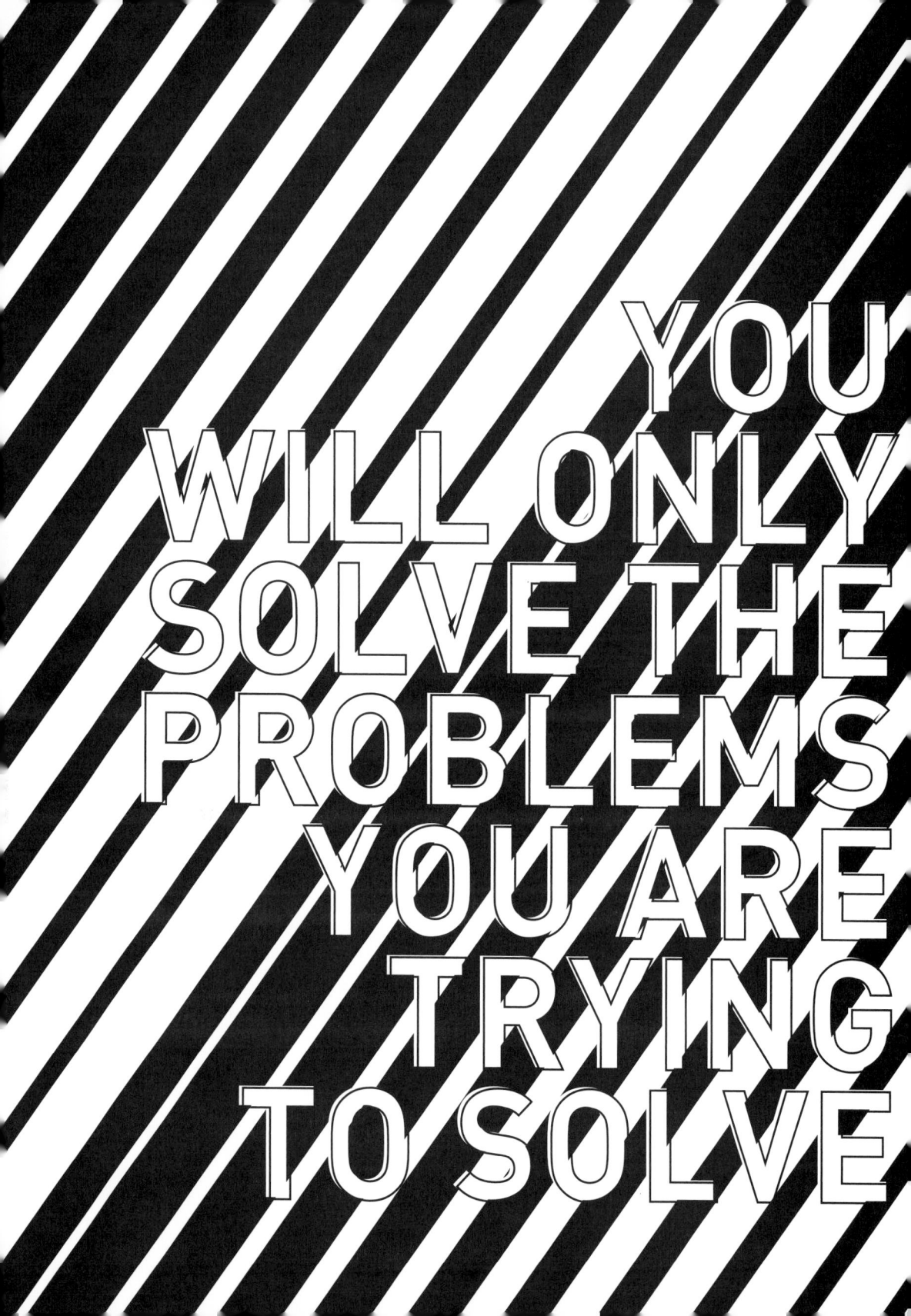

- Specifically what problem are you trying to solve?
  Explain WHY you are solving that problem. Okay, but WHY? Again, WHY?
  If you imagined a 10-year-old repeatedly asking you WHY, how different
  does your answer become?

- For your consumers, how might they interpret the problems you are solving?
  Consider breaking out your answer for each of your key market demographics.
  Also ask yourself how your future customers think about your relevance.

- How is your perspective different from the other competitors in the market?

- Would framing your problem differently lead you to a different outcome?

TACTICS

1. Understand the importance of your stated mission.

2. Interview your customers and ask them what problem you are solving. Then ask why that problem matters, and keep asking why until you get a deeper understanding.

3. Change your company's vernacular so that everything aligns to your purpose.

4. Adopt your customers' perspective about your purpose in all decisions about products, services, and brand.

CULTURE OF INNOVATION

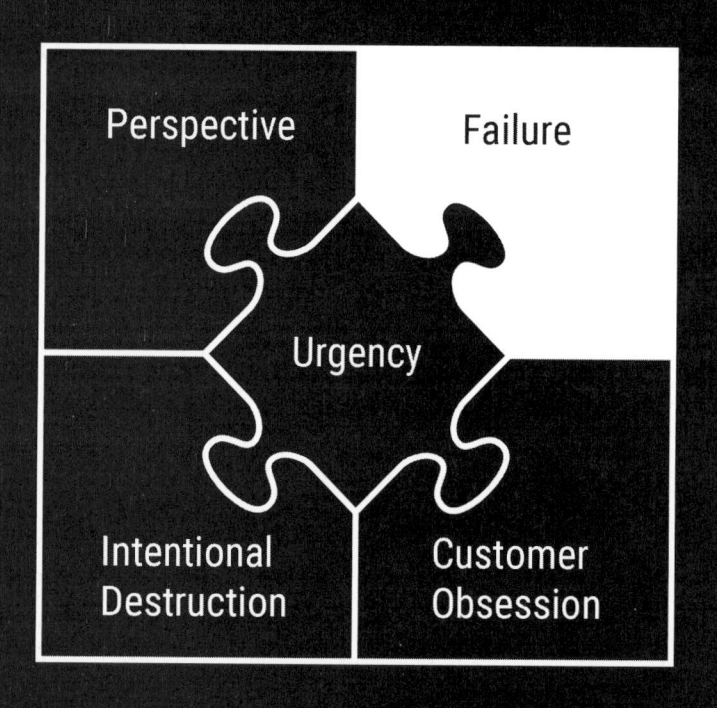

Culture of Innovation Framework

Perspective

Failure

Urgency

Intentional
Destruction

Customer
Obsession

FAILURE

Navigating through chaos requires your organization to adapt and change. This requires a culture that encourages testing and experimental failure.

MANY OF YOUR CREATIONS MUST FAIL

Expected failure sounds like a strange idea; after all, how many people want to be associated with a word like *fail*? If you don't fail, however, you will become the best typewriter company in the world. If you pursue your dreams, you will experience numerous failures. But you will be on the learning curve that leads to stardom. Take the following examples:

- TECHNOLOGY—During the tech boom of the late 1990s, Cisco was the largest company in the world. In its early days, the company was rejected by an astonishing 76 venture capital firms before receiving funding.

- SPORTS—Michael Jordan was the greatest basketball player of all time, but he was cut from his high school basketball team.

- FICTION—John Grisham is one of the most successful novelists of all time. He was rejected by a couple dozen publishers before getting his first big deal. He actually sold copies of his first book, *A Time to Kill*, out of the trunk of his car.

- FILM—In 2009 *Slumdog Millionaire* won eight Oscars. A year prior, the original producer, Warner Bros., lost confidence in the film. They sold half their investment to Fox Searchlight and later pulled the plug completely. If it wasn't for Fox Searchlight, *Slumdog* would not have made it to the big screen.[21]

- SCIENCE—Thomas Edison invented the light bulb, but he actually failed miserably along the way.

Navigating through chaos requires a deep understanding of what you can and cannot do. Failure is a part of this learning process. To accept failure, you need to find positive ways to interpret unexpected results. Here's how Edison looked at it:

SUCCESSFUL IDEAS FIRST REQUIRE
EXCESSIVE TESTING AND EXPERIMENTAL FAILURE.

BE WARY OF YOUR STRENGTHS.
SUCCESS LEADS TO COMPLACENCY.

Over time, we stop trying.

We own that market. He's been a client forever. She's already my girlfriend. He's already my boyfriend.

Even when the world is changing, individuals within big companies feel safe from the desperate pressure to adapt. The social repercussions of failure exacerbate this problem. In almost all situations, failure is both socially and managerially intolerable.

If a big project fails, will I miss my promotion? Will someone on my team lose his or her job?

IT'S EASIER NOT TO TAKE BIG RISKS, SO WE END UP TWEAKING AND OPTIMIZING WHEN WE SHOULD BE SEEKING BREAKTHROUGH IDEAS.

DON'T LET COMPLACENCY BE THE ARCHITECTURE OF YOUR DOWNFALL

Shortly after starting work as a management consultant, I was assigned my first client, in sunny Miami. Tough life, eh?

After checking into my hotel room, I journeyed to the lobby to meet my new colleague. He'd already been living in the hotel for a year when I asked him how everything was going.

"Horrible," he answered. "The hotel lost my laundry . . . I hope you like this outfit, because I'm going to wear these clothes all week."

Not sure how to react, I sputtered, "They gave me a fruit bowl."

"What!?" He marched across the lobby to the hotel manager. "I've spent $20,000 living in this hotel. You lose my laundry and do nothing about it." He turned and pointed to me. "This guy shows up and gets a fruit bowl on day one? Where's my fruit bowl?"

"I'm only going to say this once, and then I'm going to leave. Complacency will be the architecture of your downfall!"

Wow. That's intense.

BE CAREFUL NOT TO TAKE YOUR CUSTOMERS FOR GRANTED.

IT'S EASY TO FIND THE PEAK
OF A HILL . . .

When you find something you're good at, it's like ending up on the top of a hill. At whatever it is that you do, you become the best in the world. At any given point, it's easier to stay on top of your hill than to find a new place to climb.

For Smith Corona, their hill was the world of typewriters. At any point in time, the company's innovation teams could make a better typewriter. But any other project would seem like a failure by comparison.

In retrospect, the computing opportunity seems obvious, but making kickass typewriters prevented Smith Corona from seeing any other opportunity.

BE CAREFUL TO LOOK BEYOND YOUR OWN HILL OF COMPETENCY.

. . . BUT TO FIND A LARGER HILL, YOU HAVE TO WALK THROUGH A VALLEY

Finding new opportunities will force you to experiment in areas of uncertainty. To discover a new hill, you'll need to fail, and you'll need to fail a lot. The key is to stay committed to the pursuit of something new.

"Many of life's failures are people who did not realize how close they were to success when they gave up."

—Thomas Edison

FAIL YOUR WAY TO NEW SUCCESS.

DON'T CELEBRATE REACHING THE SUMMIT, CELEBRATE THE STYLE OF CLIMB

Cult brand Patagonia is a sporting goods company with a conscience. In their 1974 catalogue, cofounders Yvon Chouinard and Tom Frost published a surprising essay suggesting that people should buy fewer of their products.[22] Specifically, they asked hikers to carry less gear to reduce adverse impacts on the environment. This is not the advice you'd expect from a profit-centered company.

The essay contained a statement that serves as a reflection of their culture: "It is the style of the climb, not the attainment of the summit, which is the measure of personal success." Years later, Chouinard's hiking philosophy would become a metaphor for the way that Patagonia was managed.

More recently, he stated perhaps the boldest, most counterintuitive thing you'd expect a CEO to say, explaining, "Think twice before you buy a product from us. Do you really need it or are you just bored and want to buy something." Along with this statement, he launched Worn Wear, an initiative whereby the company will repair your old Patagonia clothing for free so you don't have to purchase a new product.

All of this has resulted in a cult-like following among Patagonia consumers.

CELEBRATING THE "JOURNEY" FUELS MORALE AND PASSION.

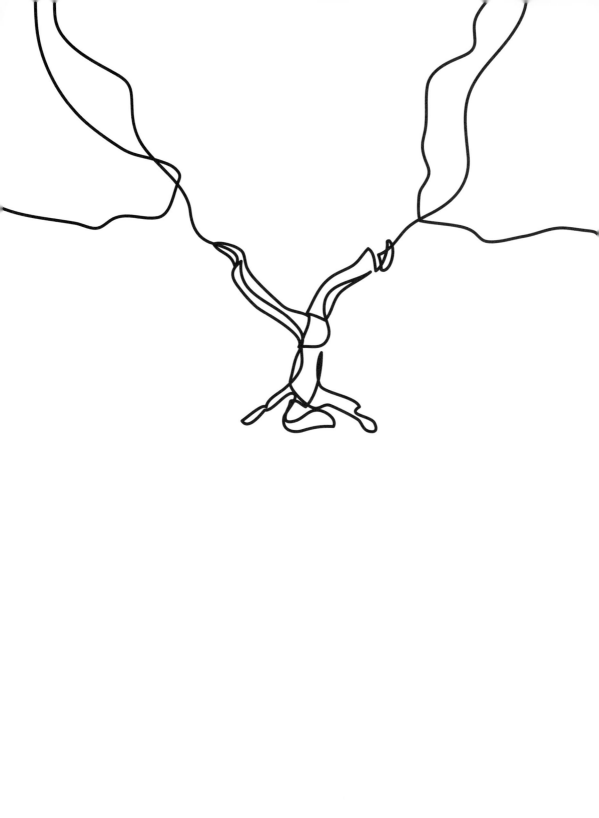

1. **CREATE A GAMBLING FUND.** At BBC Television, innovation means coming up with new show ideas. In the late 1990s, BBC's lineup was lackluster, and their market share started to fall. Desperate to improve, the CEO and CFO implemented rigid controls around the innovation process. They wanted to gain more control and consistency. Under the restraint, innovation narrowed. Market share went down even further. When that sort of thing happens, the upside is that you get a new CEO and CFO. Scandalous! The new leaders perceived BBC as a big bureaucratic organization. They wanted to make changes but were wary of sending ripples throughout the organization, so they made just one notable change: they created a gambling fund. Ideas expected to fail could still qualify for gambling fund money. The first big idea to win gambling fund money was *The Office*. It failed the normal screening process but went on to become the biggest hit in the BBC's history.

2. **BREAK DOWN MANAGERIAL CONFIDENCE AND ASK QUESTIONS.** When fresh new hires start at an organization, they are wide-eyed and full of questions. When people become more skilled, there is a natural tendency to stop asking as many questions. It's a way of proving that we've become confident and skilled. But this confidence prevents us from seeing that the world has changed. True leaders keep asking questions. They constantly push to get a deeper answer to the basic question: "Specifically what is it that you are trying to do?"

3. **DON'T ASK, "DO YOU LIKE IT?" ASK, "WHAT'S WRONG WITH IT?"** My favorite book in the world is Paul Arden's *It's Not How Good You Are, It's How Good You Want to Be*. The title itself is sage advice. Arden was the former executive creative director at Saatchi & Saatchi. His job was one of the most creative in the world. To cultivate an environment that accepted failure, he noted: "[People] will say nice things rather than be too critical. Also, we tend to edit out the bad so that we hear only what we want to hear. . . . If, instead of seeking approval, you ask, 'what's wrong with it? How can I make it better?' You are more likely to get a truthful, critical answer."[23]

4. **MAKE FAILURE A PART OF EVERY DAY.** *Pushing Tin*, the 1999 comedy about air traffic controllers, opened with the following line: "You land a million planes safely, then you have one little midair [collision] and you never hear the end of it." Most business situations do not involve landing airplanes, but the quote does a reasonable job of parodying the impact associated with failure: you never hear the end of it. Little jokes about failure are demoralizing, which leads to a crippling aversion to risk. Unless you are landing an airplane, encourage experimental failure as a path to thinking big. Here's how NBA legend Michael Jordan thinks about it: "I've missed more than 9,000 shots in my career. I've lost almost 300 games. 26 times I've been trusted to take the game-winning shot and missed. I've failed over and over and over again in my life, and that is why I succeed."

5. **WIN LIKE YOU'RE USED TO IT AND LOSE LIKE YOU ENJOY IT.** We are inclined to praise success and punish failure. In organizations, this manifests in performance appraisals, hallway conversations, and team dynamics. The unintentional impact is that individuals become less willing to pursue change. For example, at Smith Corona, which team do you think received the most praise, the team that failed to get into computing or the team that relocated operations to Mexico? No doubt the relocation team; however, relocating to reduce costs was strategically obvious. It was the computing team that could have reinvented the company. If there is no love for the people trying to fail their way into a new industry, why would anyone clever ever want to be on that team? If you want to encourage me to create breakthrough innovation, I need to feel protected. I need to know that I am better off trying new ideas and possibly failing than taking on riskless projects.

6. **FIRE PEOPLE WHO AREN'T BRAVE ENOUGH TO FAIL.** When people are not failing, they are not innovating. Accordingly, the most successful leaders look at failure as a beacon of success. In *Weird Ideas That Work*, Robert Sutton talks about the early days of MTV, a Warner subsidiary. At the time, Warner was trying to break free of its more traditional programming. To get people to think differently, chairman Steven Ross would fire people for not making mistakes.[24]

7. **INTERPRET FAILURE AS A TRAINING COST.** Using the same concept, but in a more positive way, Microsoft waits for people to have one large public failure before promoting them. IBM founder Thomas Watson Sr. also shared this philosophy when he received a resignation call from a manager who had made a $10 million mistake. Watson rejected the resignation, saying, "You can't be serious. We just spent $10 million educating you."

8. **USE FAILURE AS A BENCHMARK FOR THINKING BIG.** Even Michelangelo understood the importance of pushing limits to create something magnificent: "The greatest danger for most of us is not that our aim is too high and we miss it, but that it is too low and we reach it."

9. **HOST PROJECT FUNERALS.** In the earlier section on optionality, we already covered that our client Mic Lussier from adidas will host project funerals for a big failure. This enables the team to celebrate risk-taking while putting an idea to rest.

10. **GIVE WRITTEN PERMISSION SLIPS TO FAIL.** Also in the earlier section, we profiled how our client Brian Coupland from Staples will give written permission slips to fail. In addition, at the end of the year, he hosts a Penguin Award ceremony. The Penguin Awards are for the brave penguins who take the first leap, which is difficult but necessary to keep the flock alive.

- What is your last major work failure, and what did you learn from it?

- If you held project funerals, what are five failed projects worth celebrating?

- What tactical things could you do to make failure less intimidating?

- When in your childhood did failure lead to greater success?

- When did you last avoid doing something out of fear you'd fail?

Culture of Innovation Framework

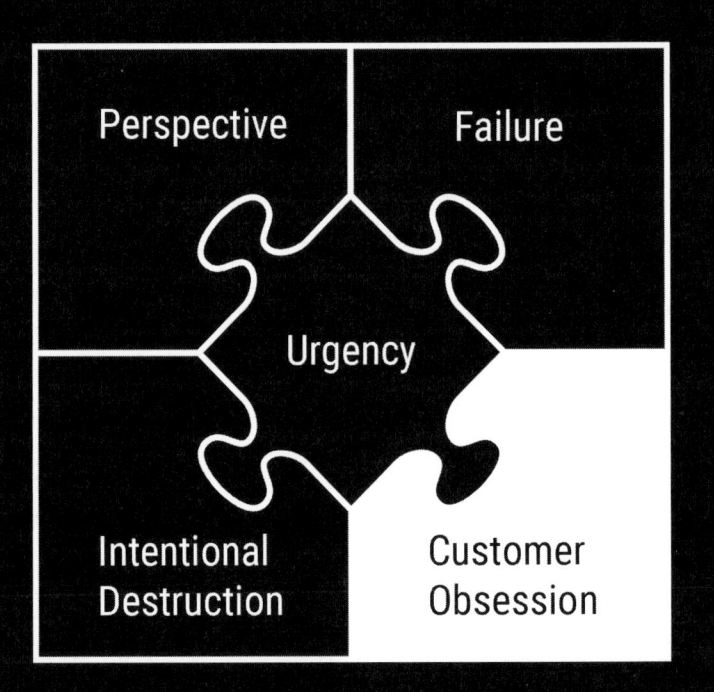

Breakthrough ideas and disruptive innovation stem from a deep understanding of the customer.

IF YOU WANT TO BE REMEMBERED, INVOKE AN EMOTIONAL CONNECTION

Do you recognize this photo? For many, the image of Iron Eyes Cody evokes a sharp memory of the Keep America Beautiful ad campaign.

The ads featured Iron Eyes Cody shedding a tear after a motorist throws trash from a speeding car.

Although the image dates back to 1971, people remember Iron Eyes Cody because he makes an emotional connection.

Ironically, Cody was actually an Italian actor named Espera de Corti, but that's not really the point.

BY CREATING AN EMOTIONAL CONNECTION, THE MEMORY OF YOUR MESSAGE CAN BECOME TIMELESS.

IF YOU WANT TO INSPIRE ACTION, INVOKE A CULTURAL CONNECTION

Regardless of what you are trying to communicate, there is a continuum of impact based on how you convey your message.

The Continuum of Persuasion

FUNCTIONAL   INCENTIVE   EMOTIONAL   CULTURAL

IMPACT

At a functional level, you could simply tell people not to litter. Going a step further, you could provide a reward or penalty. Create an emotional connection, and you could be remembered.

But being remembered is not actually the goal. In *Made to Stick*, Chip and Dan Heath suggest that Iron Eyes Cody failed because he only evoked an emotional memory. To really create an impact, you'd need to make a cultural connection.[25]

WHEN A CULTURAL CONNECTION IS MADE, YOUR PRODUCT OR SERVICE BECOMES A REFLECTION OF YOUR CUSTOMER'S LIFESTYLE.

OBSESS ABOUT YOUR CUSTOMER

A cultural connection is empowering. It aligns with the soul of one's identity and beliefs. It's the reason people tattoo Harley-Davidson's corporate logo onto their arms. When you make a cultural connection, people don't think of your creation as a product; they think of your creation as a part of their identity. To create this type of connection, you need to understand your customer.

Getting back to our case, who litters? Men or women? The young or the old?

Do they drive cars or trucks?

If you're like most people, you are probably thinking young males who drive trucks. And based on their research, the Texas-based marketing firm GSD&M learned . . . you're absolutely right![26]

70% of these litterbugs are males. They are young. They drive trucks. They drink beer. They have shotgun racks. And most importantly, they have a "King of the World" attitude.

Now, pretend you're one of those males, put yourself in that truck, and ask yourself if the crying actor stops you from throwing a beer can out of your truck window.

Probably not.

Instead, the following page reveals GSD&M's approach. When you see the campaign, you'll recognize the slogan. What you might not know is that the phrase is actually a trademarked ad slogan specifically created to stop young males from littering . . .

. . . BUT THE CATCH IS THAT IT DIDN'T HAVE A MEANINGFUL IMPACT ON LITTER.

DON'T
MESS
— WITH —
TEXAS™

DON'T SPEAK TO YOUR CUSTOMERS, SPEAK *WITH* THEM

In 1986, actors, sports heroes, and other icons appeared in TV commercials and shouted, "Don't mess with Texas!" My favorite part is that it's trademarked. This term was invented!

One of the first commercials featured two Dallas Cowboys football players, Ed Jones and Randy White, picking up trash on the side of the road. Ed Jones grabs a can and bellows with anger, "Did you see the guy who threw this out of his window? You tell him I got a message for him!" He then crushes the can on the side of his head and says, "Don't mess with Texas."

Wow.

Tim McClure, GSD&M's executive creative director, noted, "It was an attempt to get away from the 'Crying Indian' and look at things from the consumer's view." Today the phrase can be found on bumper stickers, T-shirts, and in the vernacular of Texans across the state. Yet this is a trademarked slogan, used for the first time as part of an ad campaign.

The Institute of Applied Research suggested that a reduction in littering of 10% would be above average; a reduction of 15% would be remarkable. In the five years that followed the launch (1986–1990), litter was reduced by 72%.[27]

"DON'T MESS WITH TEXAS" was so effective that it became part of Texan culture, and the challenge became keeping the slogan connected to its original purpose. To ensure this, the litter campaign relies on celebrity endorsements from Texan stars like Matthew McConaughey, Jennifer Love Hewitt, George Foreman, Owen Wilson, the rapper Chamillionaire, and Chuck Norris.

MARKET FROM THE PERSPECTIVE OF THE CUSTOMER,
NOT THE ADVERTISER.

IN ALL INDUSTRIES, INNOVATION STARTS BY OBSERVING THE **CUSTOMER**

Designers

Entrepreneurs

Artists

Marketers

Retailers

Strategists

CUSTOMER OBSERVING IS IMPORTANT FOR ALL LEVELS, FROM THE NEWEST HIRE TO THE **CEO**

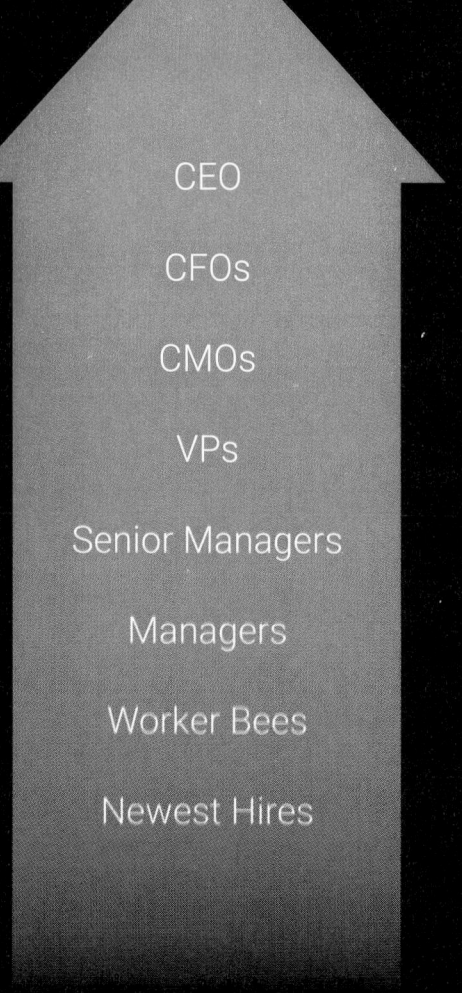

CEO

CFOs

CMOs

VPs

Senior Managers

Managers

Worker Bees

Newest Hires

OBSERVE IN THE ZONE

Observing the customer used to mean conducting focus groups, surveys, and interviews. There is still a place for this sort of research, but it will not help you connect. To connect, you need to observe your customers in their zone. This means interacting, watching purchase behavior, and engaging in conversation.

I interviewed Cadillac's head of external design, John Manoogian, about the Escalade, which was the bestselling full-size SUV for several years.

The Escalade was successful because it became an icon for hip-hop culture. Eagerly, I asked him, "How did you make this all happen? Product placement in rap videos?" Manoogian explained that the success was a surprise. The vehicle was targeted toward older affluent males.

John knew that the customer who would drive the Escalade's success was a customer he knew nothing about. Accordingly, he went to one of the most dangerous neighborhoods in Detroit and waited for an Escalade to drive by.

Who do you think drives the Escalade in such a neighborhood? I'll give you one guess.

He then introduced himself to the driver in a way that probably sounded like this: "Excuse me, young man, but may I accompany you for a ride as you conduct your business?"

Wow.

WHEN YOUR WORLD CHANGES UNEXPECTEDLY, OR WHEN YOUR CUSTOMER IS VERY DIFFERENT FROM YOU . . .

CUSTOMER OBSESSION CAN BE THE

FASTEST WAY TO GAIN PERSPECTIVE.

CHALLENGE THE BELIEF THAT YOU KNOW YOUR CUSTOMER

In 2006, I was part of Stanford Executive Education's very first Customer-Focused Innovation program, led by Bob Sutton and Hayagreeva "Huggy" Rao. I was privileged to learn alongside a group of colleagues that included CEOs and innovation heads from the world's hottest companies.

Our team was working on a project to optimize a gas station store. (Today, I drive an electric car, but I digress.)

If you challenge me to make a gas station better, I am ready to go. I feel like I don't even need to research the project. Just put me in the game and let me begin. Despite the fact my entire team shared the same enthusiasm, we decided to spend six hours in a gas station.

Seriously? That six hours seemed excessive.

In the first hour, my observations were as expected. But then a pattern emerged. An interesting beast: the teenage boy!

When a teenage boy drives up in his (parents') Honda Civic, not one, not two, not three, but four hormonal boys pop out to descend upon the store. Teenage boys group-shop at gas stations!

As they examine products, they say things like, "Hey, is that the new Red Bull? How much? Five bucks? What a rip-off! Yeah, get me one too . . ."

They are price-insensitive (because they are shopping with your money) and are therefore a marketer's dream.

But what do teenage boys like? Is there anything that gets their attention? I think we all know a few easy answers to that.

The challenge then evolves into how you attract teenage boys without alienating every other market segment. So, we decided to specifically test the limits of what we could do by building a prototype store called Rock Star Fuel.

We asked ourselves, "What would make my mom upset if she knew I'd created it?" We launched a line of combo packs aimed at teenage boys, like a six-pack of beer with a box of condoms. If that doesn't upset my mom, I really don't know what would.

As people went through our store, I'll never forget the reaction of one 50-year-old female. When I asked her if she liked our store, she said, "Yes!" Surprised, I inquired further, and she explained, "Yes, it's dirty, but . . . in a different way. Normally, the bottle of water I buy is next to motor oil and a fan belt. This is at least physically cleaner. It's not for me specifically, but it's cleaner."

In contrast, our teenage boys would never leave the store.

Customer obsession can drive insight, but getting to breakthrough ideas will require you to push your comfort limits.

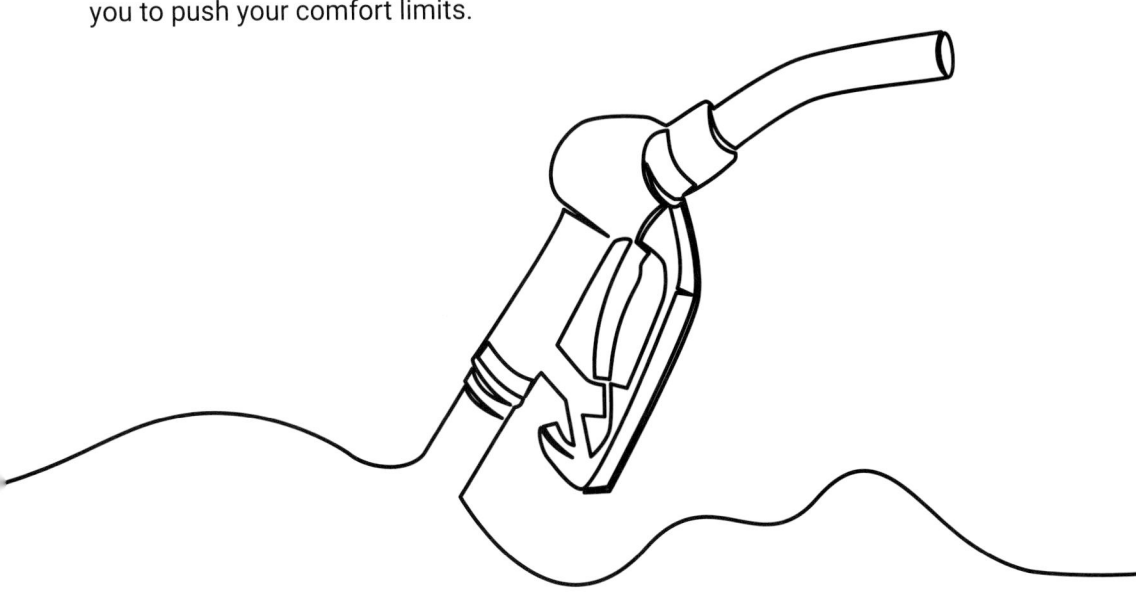

ONE OF THE MOST DIFFICULT BARRIERS TO CUSTOMER OBSERVATION ———— *IS THE BELIEF THAT YOU ALREADY UNDERSTAND YOUR CUSTOMER.*

SEEK AUTHENTICITY

There are many reasons to obsess over your customer, but the most important is the simple concept of authenticity. If you want to create a cultural connection, then quite simply, you need to take an authentic interest in your customer.

I had a chance to "hang out" with Shaheen Sadeghi, cofounder of Quiksilver. Shaheen lets the concept of cultural authenticity rule everything he does. He loves to describe the way Nike struggled and failed to build their way into the surfing market.

Basketball, tennis, running, soccer, hockey, football, and golf: these are just a few of the areas in which Nike merchandise reigns supreme. But after countless attempts, Nike was never able to penetrate surf culture.

Shaheen attributes this to Nike's lack of an authentic cultural connection. Surf culture is grassroots. It is less about the individual superstar and more about the lifestyle. Nike didn't get it.

In the end, Nike bought Hurley to capture part of the market, but the Nike swoosh remains absent from the rip curl.

Shaheen explained, "People are starting to really be a lot more connected to what is important to them. Nike is a great example because if you don't have a cultural connection, you can't make it."

He summed it up like this:

*"AUTHENTICITY IS BIG,
AND YOU CAN'T BUY IT.
YOU HAVE TO EARN IT."*

MAKE AN IMPACT

It's no secret that people are becoming increasingly more conscious of their impact on the planet, particularly those in the younger generations, Z and Y. As a result, we are observing many brands, like adidas, focus on new socially good product lines, like the adidas and Parley line, made from recycled ocean plastic. Other brands, such as Patagonia and Lululemon, are taking the concept of impact a step further by entirely anchoring their brands on cause, purpose, and the goal of helping their consumers live the positive-impact lives they desire.

Our desire to support products with a purpose is not too dissimilar to the psychology that drives us to be interested in influencers instead of brands. We seek realness and purpose. Having said that, the current state of influencer marketing is in flux. Influencers have appeal because they are *more* authentic, but ironically, if they are promoting the product of a brand, they are potentially less authentic than if they were introducing us to their own product or cause. Entrepreneur Taylor Klick created a business model to tackle this disconnect.

Instead of getting influencers to hype whatever product a marketer wants promoted, her company, Influence for Impact, took a different approach. The company creates custom product lines and e-commerce shops for the personal brands of the influencers themselves. A typical influencer shop might feature half a dozen custom shirts and sweaters, each adorned with the influencer's slogans and designs. The products are made from recycled plastic, sustainable hemp, or bamboo. Each purchase results in a planted tree and 10% of the revenue going to the influencer's charity of choice.

The result of these purpose-driven stores is that the influencer entrepreneurs are able to make deep connections with their fans while making the world a better place. That drive fuels fan support, creating a virtuous circle that any entrepreneur would aspire to attain.

An additional lesson would be that influencers don't actually think about their fans as customers. The people buying their socially good products are fans who support the same mission, aligned to the same cause.

TACTICS

1. **ANSWER PHONES.** At Capital One, we trained senior executives to spend a day in the call center speaking to customers.

2. **WORK THE KIOSK.** Also at Capital One, I took my entire product design team across the country to work kiosk booths. We weren't taking product applications. Instead, we were simply talking to prospective customers.

3. **INTERVIEW LOST CUSTOMERS.** Editors of *Fast Company* called those who had canceled their subscriptions, hoping to better understand their discontent.

4. **HANG IN THE STORE.** Michelle Gass, former senior vice president at Starbucks, took her category team to Paris, Düsseldorf, and London to spend time in Starbucks locations and local restaurants. The goal was to better understand the cultural differences in each city.[28] Her CEO, Howard Schultz, visits 25 shops a week. Since publishing the original version of this book, Michelle has become CEO of Kohl's, where she continues to be a beacon for customer-driven innovation.

PEOPLE SEEK AUTHENTICITY AND PURPOSE FROM THE BRANDS OR INDIVIDUALS WHO HELP THEM LIVE LIVES THAT HAVE A MORE POSITIVE IMPACT ON OUR WORLD AND THE PEOPLE LIVING IN IT.

5. **HELP CUSTOMERS PLAN EVENTS.** At the Lavin Agency, the speaking bureau that represents me, agents get involved with clients at the conference-planning stage and even attend client events. This helps Lavin better understand client needs and helps the agents book more business.

6. **HIRE YOUR CUSTOMER.** At Trend Hunter, we decided to hire one of our favorite clients, Kareth Middlemass, who had been an innovation leader and brand manager at companies like Loblaw, Nestlé, Pfizer, and Unilever. We wanted someone to help develop our products and client strategies and figured, Who would know more about what our client wants than our actual client?

Customer interaction results in a profoundly deeper understanding of customer needs and desires.

WORKSHOP QUESTIONS

- Describe your ideal customer in a story about their typical day.

- If you were to spend a day accompanying your customer, what activities would you want to observe?

- What are the largest uncertainties you have about your customer's preferences and purpose?

- Why specifically does your customer want to purchase from you? What is their actual end objective?

Culture of Innovation Framework

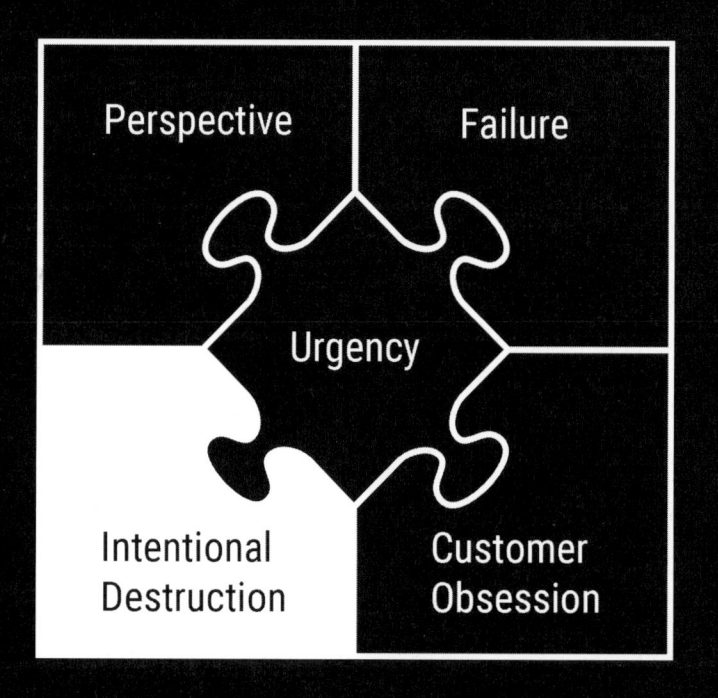

INTENTIONAL DESTRUCTION

In order to adapt, we must intentionally destroy. We need to break down the structure and hierarchy that prevents us from seeing the realities of market change.

TEAR APART STRUCTURE

Most animals behave instinctively. Fish know how to swim. Birds know how to build a nest. But for primates, including humans, behavior is learned within a social structure. We follow organizational patterns and rules unless those rules are dramatically changed.

Stanford neuroscientist Robert Sapolsky studies the social structure of baboons.[29] More than 20 years ago, Sapolsky observed a baboon troop with multiple layers of structural rank. Socially senior baboons would beat on middle-ranking baboons, who would in turn beat on lower-ranking baboons. Those bastards.

But then something happened. The senior-ranked males started fighting a neighboring troop over tourist garbage. Eating trash exposed the aggressive males to tuberculosis-tainted meat. Instant karma.

Over the next three years, the elders died off, leaving the troop absent of structure. Instead of re-creating multiple levels of aggressive hierarchy, the young baboons created a culture of pacifism. Acts of friendship replaced aggression.

Instead of struggling, the community flourished. Hormone samples indicated lower stress, and the same culture remains 20 years later.

ORGANIZATIONAL STRUCTURE GUIDES THE WAY WE GROW AND THE WAY WE THINK. TO SPARK A REVOLUTION, STRUCTURE NEEDS TO BE BROKEN DOWN.

EMPOWER WITH IDEOLOGY INSTEAD OF WITH RULES

Rod Beckstrom, an entrepreneur and Silicon Valley CFO, was on a jetliner waiting to leave New York's LaGuardia Airport. On that very day, two planes smashed into the Twin Towers, where Rod often held his meetings.

From then on, Rod dedicated himself to understanding the dynamics behind such devastation. He studied terrorist networks and started to identify patterns between the structure of Al-Qaeda, P2P file sharing, and Alcoholics Anonymous.

In *The Starfish and the Spider*, Rod and his coauthor, Ori Brafman, explore what they call the "unstoppable power of leaderless organizations," using the metaphor of the starfish. When you pull off the arms of a spider, it dies. In contrast, if you rip off the five arms of a starfish, you'll get five new starfish. This happens because starfish have decentralized nervous systems.

Like a starfish, a terrorist network is decentralized, united only by ideology. If you attack one arm, it grows back even stronger. Similarly, when the recording industry attacked Napster, unstoppable replacements stepped into Napster's place.

If we apply these lessons for good, remarkable movements can be created.

For example, in 1934 Bill Wilson was a talented individual who drowned his Wall Street career by being perpetually intoxicated. In the years that followed, he created a support group that would later be known as Alcoholics Anonymous (AA). In their most recent Fact File, AA reported more than 100,000 support groups totaling nearly 2 million members.

"We are constantly amazed by how much people will do when they are not told what to do by management."

—Jack Welch, CEO of GE

Despite its success, the AA Fact File describes its structure as follows: "Alcoholics Anonymous is not organized in the formal or political sense. There are no governing officers, no rules or regulations, no fees or dues."[30] Instead, the organization thrives based on a universal ideology.

Inspired by this, Beckstrom and Brafman created Global Peace Networks, an underground ring of CEOs united by a common ideology for peace (and business). In 2003, these CEOs initiated Track II diplomacy between India and Pakistan. Specifically, the actions opened the borders, enabled trade, and contributed to the end of the latest Indo-Pak war.

The authors summarized their view toward innovation using a rule they call The Power of Chaos: "Starfish systems are wonderful incubators for creative, destructive, innovative or crazy ideas. Anything goes. Good ideas will attract more people, and in a circle, they'll execute the plan. Institute order and rigid structure, and while you may achieve standardization, you'll also squelch creativity. Where creativity is valuable, learning to accept chaos is a must."[31]

TO NAVIGATE CHAOS, ORGANIZATIONS REQUIRE THE REACTION SPEED AND CAPABILITIES THAT ONLY EXIST WHEN EMPLOYEES ARE EMPOWERED.

INTENTIONALLY DESTROY IN ORDER TO CREATE

In the late 1980s, Bill Gates dreamed about a future where learning would be digital. He took his dream to the Benton Foundation, which owned Britannica, the leading encyclopedia.

Benton turned Gates down, worried about cannibalizing their printed book sales.

Years later, Gates bought the rights to the Funk & Wagnalls Encyclopedia, a third-tier brand available in grocery stores. In 1993 the content was digitally relaunched under a new brand, Encarta.

By 1996, Encarta had become the most recognized, bestselling brand of encyclopedias. The Benton Foundation was forced to sell Britannica below book value.

Had Benton been willing to destroy value, they could have thrived. But it's not that easy. Later on, even Microsoft was unable to destroy value. Instead of moving to the web, Microsoft held on to its CD-based Encarta.

This opened the door for Wikipedia, which stepped into the limelight and grew to become one of the world's 10 most popular websites.

DESTROYING VALUE MAY SEEM NEARLY IMPOSSIBLE, BUT RESISTANCE WILL CAUSE YOUR ORGANIZATION TO BE DISPLACED.

THROW AWAY YOUR BEST IDEAS

Peter Lynch is an award-winning documentary director. He directed many of the Trend Hunter TV episodes and, along the way, provided some paradoxically remarkable advice: **throw out your best idea.**

When creating documentary films, Peter shoots a lot of footage. During the process, patterns emerge, and certain ideas resonate. The danger is that these ideas become points of fixation.

In the 1980s, Peter was making an unusual film, titled *Project Grizzly*. The documentary features an eclectic man whose life mission has been the creation of a grizzly bear–proof suit of armor. The man's goal was to build the suit and put it to the ultimate life-thrilling test: to see if a bear could kill him or if the suit would offer enough protection.

Within a week, Peter recorded footage of the man tumbling down a cliff, setting himself on fire, getting hit by a speeding truck, and getting his friends to beat him with baseball bats. Bizarre. The footage was leading Peter to focus on just how crazy this man had become. However, Peter removed the most bizarre footage. This forced him to look beyond the concept of insanity to unlock a deeper plot: the man's search for meaning.

Peter told me, "If I used the most bizarre footage, the audience would have lost empathy for the character, and the overall story would have become less engaging." His concept is that your best idea can blind you to breakthrough creativity.

BY REMOVING YOUR BEST IDEA, YOU'RE FORCED TO RAISE THE BAR ON EVERYTHING ELSE.

BUILD A CREATIVE WORK ENVIRONMENT

In the early 1980s, New York City was riddled with crime. A decade later, however, instead of cracking down on the murder and gang warfare, Mayor Rudolph Giuliani ordered police to crack down on petty crime.

Individuals who dodged paying for subway tokens were handcuffed and fined. The streets were swept clean of litter. Graffiti was covered with fresh paint on a daily basis.

Within a couple of years, New York's crime rate fell dramatically. The city went from being one of the most dangerous to one of the safest cities in America. Many attributed New York's metamorphosis to the "Broken Window Theory," which suggests that the presence of disorder and petty crime triggers more disorder and petty crime.

This theory was popularized by Malcolm Gladwell in *The Tipping Point*, but critics initially suggested that there was no psychological proof.

In a 2008 article titled "The Spreading of Disorder," Kees Keizer and his colleagues created dozens of real-world experiments to prove or disprove the "Broken Window Theory."

For example, if you walk past a mailbox and notice $10 sticking out of an envelope, would you push the envelope back into the box? Or would you steal the money? Would your answer change if the mailbox was covered in graffiti?

The results were astounding.

Without graffiti, 13% of people would steal the cash. With the presence of graffiti, stealing doubled to 27%. With the presence of litter, stealing increased to 25%.

In another experiment, Keizer placed fake flyers on the handlebars of bicycles. When the adjacent wall was clean and orderly, 33% of bike owners threw the flyer on the ground. When the wall was laden with graffiti, the proportion of litterbugs jumped to 69%.[32]

A traditional and boring work environment will result in traditional and boring ideas. Knowing that environmental context is so powerful, what can you change to make your office a place for creativity?

CREATING AN ENVIRONMENT OF INNOVATION CAN ENCOURAGE PEOPLE TO BREAK ROUTINE AND PURSUE REVOLUTIONARY IDEAS.

1. TOLERATE CRAZY IDEAS AND BOUNDARY PUSHING

The role of a leader is not to suggest great ideas but rather to create an atmosphere that fosters the ideas of others. At the Stanford Institute of Design (d.school), we were brainstorming to come up with ways to improve a women's fashion store. The most influential person in the group was the COO of a major company. To kick things off, he boldly stated his first idea, "Free nachos when they enter the store!"

What?! Free nachos? It sounded like a crazy idea, but around the room, people got the point: if he says that, I can say anything. Not only did he spark creativity, but he also encouraged free thought. In fact, his wild suggestions even inspired realistic ideas from others: "Free nachos to welcome people? Okay, how about a customized welcome experience . . . a tailored entrance to the store."

2. CELEBRATE THAT NOTHING IS PRECIOUS

One of the principles at the d.school was the mantra: "Nothing is precious." I remember watching a student tediously present his idea for an eco-product. His idea was carefully sketched out on a big piece of paper, but it was difficult to understand. I still don't know what he was trying to create. When someone said, "Nothing is precious," he laughed, ripped up the paper, and everyone cheered.

In most office cultures, people lack the support to jokingly dismiss their failure. Here, "nothing is precious" enabled a cultural celebration of both good and bad ideas. People felt comfortable sharing undeveloped thoughts. If your culture requires people to refine ideas before sharing, people spend weeks crafting their ideas. Then, two things happen: First, people become resistant to feedback. Second, feedback providers cushion their input.

In contrast, if your culture enables someone to share an idea scribbled on a napkin, he or she won't get upset if somebody rips that napkin apart. Imagine trying to

say, "Why did you do that? I spent five minutes of my life working on that napkin!" Embrace diversity.

You cannot expand your perspective and think differently if you are not exposed to a broad perspective. In the 1980s, "diversity" simply meant gender and culture. Today, diversity also means nontraditional thought. Long ago, my team was running a scenario-planning workshop for one of the world's top five tech companies. To broaden our perspective, we had gender diversity, racial diversity, and people with very different ways of thinking. I remember one of our brainstorming helpers was Jaron Lanier. In a group of clean-cut consultants, Jaron stood out not only because he was wearing a T-shirt but also because his bio explained that he was a goat herder, an assistant midwife, an artist whose work had been shown at the Museum of Modern Art of the City of Paris, a Polygram-published musician, a Stanford lecturer, a high school dropout, and the inventor of virtual reality.[33] Adding nontraditional thinkers to your group will challenge your organization to look at alternate perspectives and develop in more creative ways.

3. HIRE FREAKS (I.E., NONTRADITIONAL THINKERS)

Nontraditional thinkers offer the maverick ideas and the personality required to adapt. Tom Peters likes to use the term *freaks*, noting that he loves freaks for many reasons. In his "Re-imagine" presentation slides, Tom notes the following key points: When interesting things happen, they were done by a freak. "Freaks are more fun," and "We need freaks. Especially in freaky times."[34]

(Side note: my team loves that I put this in the book.)

4. ENCOURAGE INFORMALITY

To be creative, individuals need to feel that their environment allows change. In large organizations where structure and process define so many rituals, it can be difficult to foster this kind of creative flexibility. Jack Welch, who made GE a nimble powerhouse, recognized this dilemma: "Send handwritten notes instead of memos, keep

meetings conversational, and encourage dialogue up and down the corporate ladder."[35] Even the most bureaucratic organizations can spark creativity by creating the perception of openness to change.

5. LET REASON TRIUMPH OVER HIERARCHY

In 1975, Ray Dalio was fired from his job at a stock brokerage. From his point of view, he couldn't fit into a corporate culture where hierarchy was more important than logic. So, he started his own firm, Bridgewater Associates, where conflict and reasoning are more important than seniority.[36] At Bridgewater, a superior cannot overrule a subordinate. Disagreements need to be solved through reasoning or reviewed by a third party. His concepts seem to be working. Today, the firm manages $160 billion of assets, making Dalio worth $18 billion.

6. PISS PEOPLE OFF

Chaos requires organizations to make bold changes. Pursue the welfare of the group by making difficult decisions. As Colin Powell puts it: "Being responsible sometimes means pissing people off. Good leadership involves responsibility to the welfare of the group, which means that some people will get angry at your actions and decisions. It's inevitable, if you're honorable. Trying to get everyone to like you is a sign of mediocrity."[37] When leaders avoid making these bold changes, the organization fails to adapt.

7. DESTROY THE PERKS OF SENIORITY

Elements of status create both hierarchical distance and physical separation, which prevent agility and teamwork. Executive parking spots, dining rooms, separate floors, and hierarchical power are just a few examples of the perks that cripple agility. In 1989 Marcel Telles became the CEO of Brahma, the struggling #2 player in the Brazilian beer market. A market trader, Telles was accustomed to the high-paced

open environment of the trading floor. With this background, he made two powerful changes: First, he ramped up Brahma's analytics. Second, he knocked down office walls, created an open work environment, and removed all of the executive perks that might lead to a sense of entitlement. In the two decades that followed, Brahma grew from #2 in Brazil to #1 in the world. Brahma is now an agile, growth-hungry beer monster.

WORKSHOP QUESTIONS

- What would your business look like if you threw away your top product line?

- If you were starting from scratch, with the same team and resources, what business would you actually get into?

- If you were restarting your career, what three industries currently have the most appeal?

- How might you reposition your company's future potential to better align to market opportunities that are predictable today?

- For creativity's sake, how would you re-imagine Amazon, Facebook, Uber, Walmart, Tesla, or Google if you took away their top product or feature?

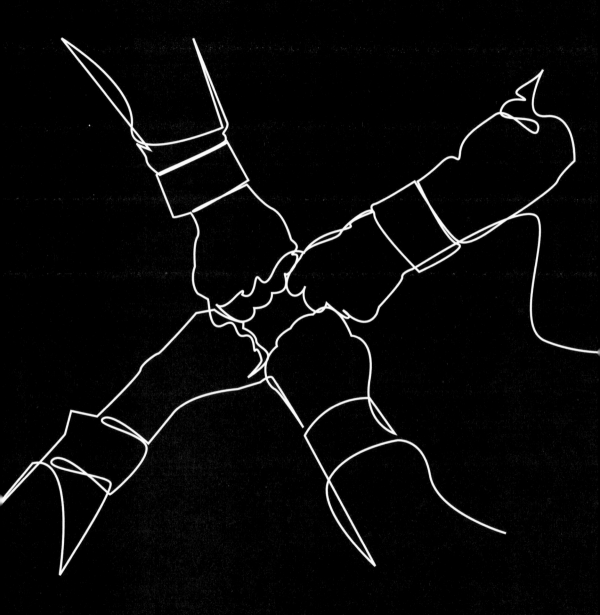

FOUR PROVOCATIVE QUESTIONS ABOUT YOUR CULTURE

A truth that is too often overlooked in today's business world is the interdependence between innovation and your organization's culture. What many people fail to recognize is that culture can either be your company's biggest asset or your company's biggest liability. Unfortunately, too many employers, managers, and leaders suffer from a false sense of really understanding their teams.

Thanks to Trend Hunter's Innovation Assessment, we've studied tens of thousands of employees all across the world, spanning dozens of industries and roles. The assessment is a unique tool that not only evaluates how an individual approaches creativity and innovation but also measures how employees really feel about their company's culture.

While our Culture of Innovation Framework certainly gives you five areas to focus on, we realize that many of our clients want to more broadly benchmark their culture along base characteristics—the characteristics that more broadly describe the day-to-day aspects of your culture. This bonus interlude conveys our learnings.

Since launching in 2016, our assessment has produced some incredibly telling results and insights. At a glance, 53% of employees don't think their organization has a strong innovation strategy; 51% feel they are not provided with the time or resources to pursue new ideas; and 27% feel their ideas aren't listened to.[38] This paints a rather grim picture for the state of work culture today. How can you, as an innovator or employer, overcome this challenge?

Let's start by defining work culture. At Trend Hunter, we like to look at work culture as the character, personality, and energy of your organization; it is the ethos that drives your employees. But more importantly, it's the way your employees feel every single

day when they walk through the door. And the thing about culture is that it's going to exist no matter what—no matter how little or how much you choose to prioritize it. The sooner we can see the connection between culture and innovation, culture and growth, culture and success—the better we'll all be.

Beyond our research done through the assessment, 88% of employees surveyed by Deloitte believe a strong culture is a competitive advantage in today's market, while 94% of executives believe a distinct culture is key to overall business success.[39] A "distinct workplace culture" is not characterized by unlimited salad bars for employees, in-office yoga classes, or bring-your-dog-to-work days. A distinct work culture consists of things you can't necessarily see or touch, but they contribute to a thriving environment for you and your team. Things like deliberate collaboration, open communication, opportunity for growth, aligned values, and a consistently supportive environment for all employees.

After working with 700 of the world's most powerful brands and assessing innovators from every corner of the workplace, we've identified the four *E*s of modern work culture: Evolution, Engagement, Experiential, and Excellence.

1. HOW IS YOUR CULTURE SET TO EVOLVE?

It's safe to say today's workplace is incredibly different than it was 5, 10, 20, 50 years ago. From the furniture we put in our offices to the idea of trading in a pension for a job with a purpose, the technologies we use, how we interact with colleagues and clients, and even the benefits we've come to expect from employers—so much has changed.

The most influential shift taking place in the workplace today relates to its demographic landscape. It's estimated that 50% of the workplace will be made up of Millennials by the year 2020, while Gen Z will account for 20%.[40] In other words, a new type of employee will soon occupy 70% of the workplace. Understanding the different behaviors, motivations, values, and mindsets of these generations is critical to the success of your organization.

To say that technology has also undergone a drastic transformation in the workplace might be an understatement. From the way we communicate and share information to how we manage our time, how we interact with one another, and even how we turn our ideas into products—so much has changed. Where we're seeing increasing change like never before is in AI, robotics, and automation. We know how this type of technology impacts the consumer experience, but how is it altering the world of the modern employee? Over the next few years, organizations can expect to have 10 to 10,000 times more data than they do today.[41] Simply put, data is good for innovation, but you probably already know that. At work, it enables employees to make more informed decisions, do their jobs more effectively, and ultimately make a bigger and more profound impact within their role.

When it comes to AI, according to a study by McKinsey, 49% of work across 800 jobs today can already be automated.[42] While our instinct is to internalize this shift as negative, it means your employees can spend more time and energy tackling your most complex challenges.

Google is a great example of a company leveraging AI to make day-to-day work easier for its employees. Its most recent product, Hire by Google, uses AI to take care of recruiting-related tasks, including scanning résumés and booking interviews.[43] Other companies are using AI for training purposes and engagement tracking.

Technology is regularly rewriting the rules of the workplace and the jobs people can do. Not only are new roles emerging, but the type of employee is changing as well. Dell estimates that 85% of future jobs don't exist yet or are currently unknown to us.[44] While that seems like a staggering number, there have been some very interesting predictions of what jobs might start popping up on LinkedIn. Jobs like personal reality designer, digital archaeologist, ethical technology advisor, robot liaison officer, nostalgist, cloud cleaner, and freelance relationships officer are roles we can expect to see in the future.[45] That last one on the list is particularly interesting, as the gig economy continues to take center stage. Studies suggest that 50% of workers in the US will be freelancing in 10 years if the current pace continues.[46] For many people, the perks of a flexible schedule, autonomy, control, and new career experience outweigh the traditional benefits of full-time employment, including steady income, paid vacation, and health care.

This aligns with a changing preference in people's preferred work style. According to the assessment, 52% prefer variety within their work versus focusing on one main role or project.

2. HOW ARE YOU FOSTERING ENGAGEMENT?

There is an overwhelming amount of research that draws a correlation between an engaged group of employees and a high-performing team. Sadly, there's also a lot of research that points to a disengaged workforce. Nearly 70% of employees today identify as being disengaged in the office.[47]

To make matters worse, so many employers simply accept the fact that their employees are disengaged and unhappy. But what happens when clients are upset or dissatisfied? Companies spend millions of dollars every single year gathering consumer data to better understand their customers and to make more informed decisions. So why not invest the same in our employees?

From those who have taken the assessment so far, we know that 48% feel they aren't provided with the resources or time to pursue new ideas, while nearly 70% of people would prefer variety in their work in favor of consistently achieving a high performance. The stereotypes and the assumptions we make about our employees are holding us captive. Leveraging data that we get from tools like the assessment is much more powerful than relying on our gut instinct, guessing, or simply not knowing.

Communication is another effective avenue through which we can engage our employees, but this, too, has drastically changed. Thanks to technology, employees can communicate with one another quicker than ever before, but this doesn't necessarily make more effective communication. One study found that 81% of Millennial employees actually prefer an open communication policy over fancy work perks.[48] According to our assessment, 21% of people aren't sharing their ideas with managers, and a whopping 43% don't even know who is responsible for their company's innovation strategy. While tech-driven communication accommodates more flexibility and remote working, it leads employees to feel disconnected and confused about what's going on within their organization and how they fit into it.

Putting a communication strategy in place that fosters face-to-face time, one-on-one check-ins, transparency, and a process for sharing ideas is critical in today's world.

3. WHAT ARE YOU DOING TO MAKE WORK EXPERIENTIAL?

In today's world, the employee experience begins the moment a recruiter reaches out and lasts well beyond an employee's final day in office. Much of the employee experience is rooted in the relationships people have in the office. Many people actually enjoy spending time with their colleagues and would even consider some of them close friends.

It turns out, though, that having a work best friend offers many benefits to employers. Employees with work friends are more loyal to their company, seven times more engaged in what they're doing, 57% more productive, less stressed overall, and more likely to enjoy work on a day-to-day basis.[49] Younger employees also want to have a closer relationship with their managers, often turning to them as coaches and mentors. The fact is we spend one-third of our lives at work.[50] Because of this, employees are looking for meaningful relationships in the office, characterized by trust, openness, understanding, a space for growth, and acceptance of failure. This is key in establishing employee loyalty. In fact, studies show that employees who feel they can be their true selves at work will be 46% more likely to stay at a company for longer than five years.[51]

Also connected to employee loyalty is the way we recognize and reward employees. Many employers today are recognizing employees by paying back some of their student loans and debt. Not only does this show how much they care about their staff, but it also drastically improves the quality of life for these employees, which is directly tied to work-life balance. 66% of full-time employees today believe they don't currently have work-life balance,[52] and the United States ranks in the bottom 20% of countries in this area.[53]

While we're seeing employers start to be more flexible with things like scheduling, much of today's work force is looking for general flexibility in their working environment. With four different generations in the workplace today, there is going to be a wide range of demands and needs.

Employers that allow employees to create their own work-life balance structure will come out on top in the long run.

4. HOW ARE YOU PURSUING EXCELLENCE?

Employees today not only expect excellence from themselves but look for it from within their organizations as well. According to the assessment, 87% of people prioritize working with an innovative group of people, and 60% will be influenced to stay or leave based on their company's approach to innovation. In the same way that consumers shop mindfully, employees want to work for companies with a purpose beyond profit. Studies show that companies with a clear, strong sense of purpose will attract top talent.[54]

Studies also suggest that organizations with more diversity will retain employees longer. But diversity, especially at the executive level, is an ongoing challenge for many companies. A recent study by Ernst & Young found that there are more men named John, Robert, William, and James on executive boards than there are women.[55] Companies can no longer deprioritize diversity across race, gender, education, religion, experience, and background. Younger employees especially value inclusivity and diversity, seeking both when looking for a new job.

A phenomenon known as job-hopping is very common among younger people today, most notably Millennials.[56] While many like to point fingers at Millennials for being lazy as the root cause of this, it's not fair or truly representative of the entire story. Many young people are ambitiously looking for new opportunities and roles that are more fulfilling and meaningful. According to the assessment, 51% view experimenting within their role as the most satisfying part of their job, and 70% stop enjoying work as soon as it becomes routine. Young people today want careers in which their professional development is prioritized and valued. 87% say professional development is most important to them in a job. If a company can't offer that, employees will have no problem leaving to find it elsewhere.[57]

Despite the increasingly rapid pace at which technology is evolving, the true horsepower behind any successful company is its people. Work culture can no longer be an afterthought in today's business world.

Create the Future Framework

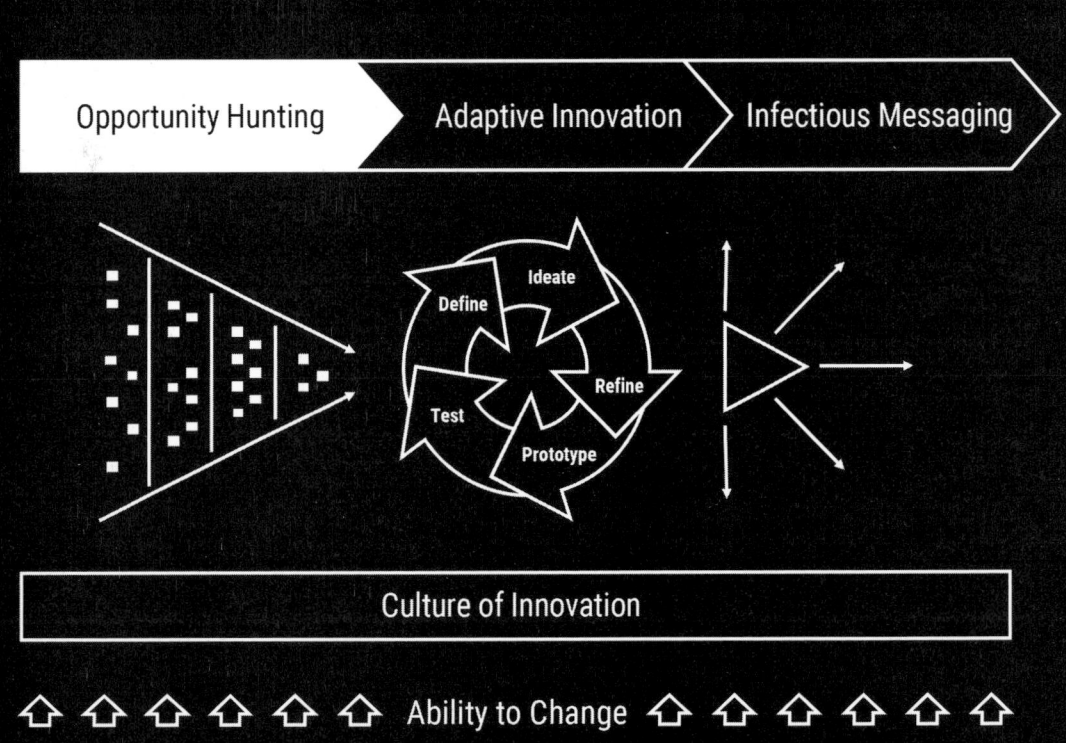

Opportunity Hunting | Adaptive Innovation | Infectious Messaging

Define | Ideate | Refine | Prototype | Test

Culture of Innovation

Ability to Change

OPPORTUNITY HUNTING

Innovation and strategic advantage hinge on the ability to anticipate trends and identify the next big thing. By casting a wide net and clustering ideas, you can filter through chaos to identify patterns of opportunity.

This section breaks opportunity hunting into a number of key steps we've learned in our work on more than 10,000 custom trend projects and over 400,000 published articles.

THERE'S NO POINT INNOVATING IF YOU THINK YOU ALREADY KNOW THE ANSWER

Brainstorming meetings are supposed to generate killer strategies and smoking-hot ideas. The problem is that we enter those meetings with a few ideas that we already want to incorporate. We then work those ideas into the mix and let everything else convince us that our original ideas were really good. Tragic.

I interviewed Marco Morrossini, a designer for Ferrari. I asked him how he spots trends. He said he spends half his time designing handbags, scarecrow fashion, and temples for dogs (yes, dog architecture). He explained, "You need to be more open to the complete possibility of what could be."

In his mind, there is no way that he could keep his work at Ferrari on the cutting edge of macho automotive design if he wasn't also on the cutting edge of experimental women's fashion.

It doesn't matter if you are a bureaucrat or a bartender; the concept of trend hunting applies to your role. But it requires an open mind and a willingness to explore seemingly random innovation.

BEFORE TREND SPOTTING, RESET YOUR EXPECTATIONS.

ACTIVELY SEEK INSPIRATION

Iconic fashion designers don't craft their ideas around a boardroom table. Despite being tremendously creative, they actively seek inspiration. They look for ideas in other industries, like design, architecture, pop culture, music, and art.

They can't get ideas by observing their customers, because their customers are kids in suburban shopping malls—trend followers. Instead, these designers look for bizarre and unique ideas.

They look for the kids in metropolitan cities who walk around making fringe fashion statements in gas masks, homemade clothing, and peculiar shoes. Too cool for school, these kids cringe at mainstream fashion, but by being unique, they inadvertently drive the pulse of fashion culture.

In any industry, it is not difficult to find unique ideas. Micro-trends and viral innovations surround us. But the world has become saturated with chaos. Thus, when we hunt for cool, we find bizarre trends like baby toupees, terror fashion, tattoos for the blind, Twitter, and co-ed matching haircuts.

If you layer on your customers, competitors, and corporate strategies, the act of inspiration becomes distracting.

HOW DO WE MAKE SENSE OF ALL THE NOISE?

DEVELOP A TOOLKIT
TO FILTER IDEAS

Whether you're an entrepreneur, artist, bureaucrat, or marketer, your goal probably involves creating something that "connects" with other human beings.

In the pursuit of something that connects, your creativity and effectiveness are likely hindered by organizational structure, uncertainty, and unexploited opportunity.

To break free of these constraints, you need a trend-spotting toolkit, a plan of attack that will help you filter through the noise and increase your likelihood of "connecting" new products and services with your customers.

Part of this toolkit involves your personal commitment to seeking inspiration pro-actively. Try saying it out loud: "I will relentlessly pursue new ideas. I will feed my insatiable hunger for innovation. I will expose myself to the fringe. I will be cutting edge and spectacular."

Nice.

The other tools discussed in this section include the techniques that will help you to hunt ideas and identify opportunity.

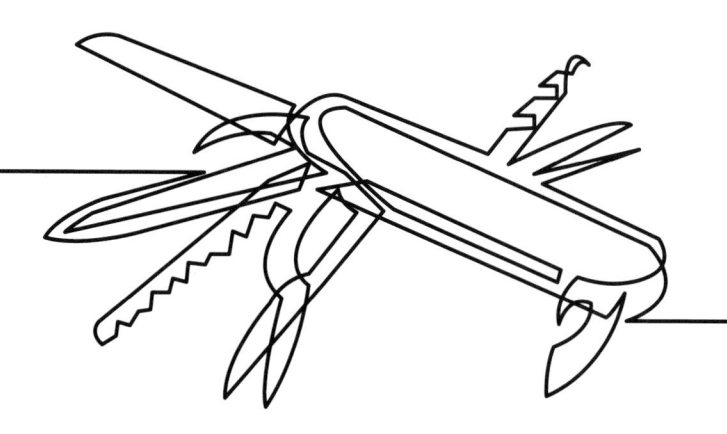

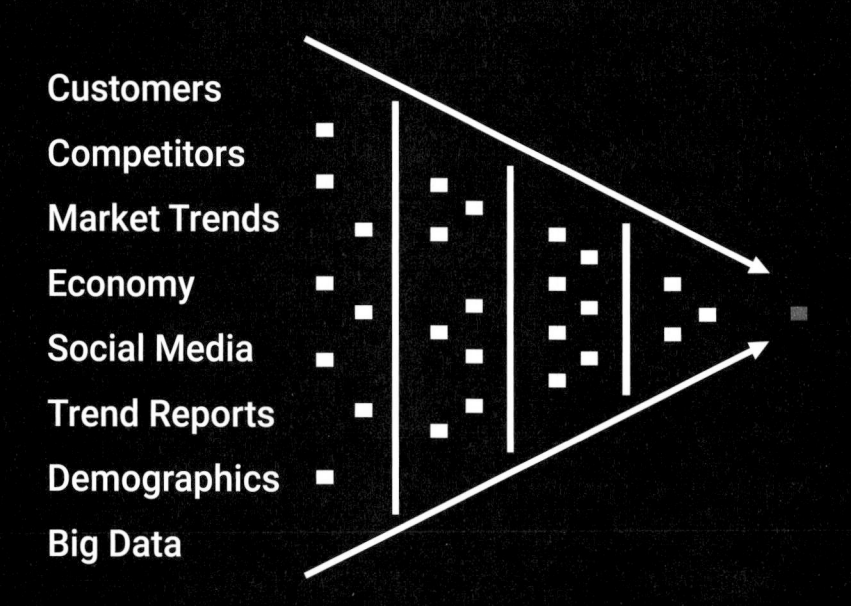

Customers
Competitors
Market Trends
Economy
Social Media
Trend Reports
Demographics
Big Data

IN TIMES OF GLOBAL CRISIS AND INCREASING MEDIA CLUTTER, A TOOLKIT MATTERS MORE THAN EVER BEFORE.

LEARN FOUR LEVELS
OF OPPORTUNITY

- **LEVEL 1—IDEAS:** You might get inspired by a single great idea. At Trend Hunter, we've published roughly 400,000 articles about individual ideas. Seeing something inspiring can be an insightful way to come up with a new idea. The caveat is that the world is overwhelmingly full of individual ideas, so it can be difficult to discern which idea is right for you, and one single example could be fleeting. A single idea would be something like the first caffeinated soft drink, Red Bull.

- **LEVEL 2—CLUSTERS/CONSUMER INSIGHTS (THE SWEET SPOT):** If you can identify a group of several ideas that are very appealing and similar, you are likely identifying a cluster of opportunity, or as professionals call it, a consumer insight. At Trend Hunter, our 400,000 Ideas have resulted in just 10,000 Consumer Insights. An example would be caffeinated beverages, caffeinated potato chips, caffeine pills, and caffeinated chocolate bars. When these four started spiking in popularity, your consumer insight might have been called "alternative caffeination." Based on the momentum behind these alternatives, you could predict new products and services that would probably trend positively for one to five years.

- **LEVEL 3—MEGATRENDS:** If you look at everything impacting our future, there are probably just 50 megatrends that explain every major change in consumer demand. Instead of predicting what's hip next year, megatrends explain how our world changes in the next 3 to 10 years. At Trend Hunter, we are constantly reevaluating which megatrends are the most important and publicly reveal just 18 Megatrends that we believe have the most sway.

- **LEVEL 4—PATTERNS OF OPPORTUNITY:** Every new innovation is like a splash in water. Each splash creates ripples of opportunity. These are the Six Patterns of Opportunity, and you can use them to classify every major innovation or to predict what innovations will happen next. There are only six possible patterns, which never change.

IF YOU WISH TO FULLY EXPLORE EACH LEVEL,
VISIT TRENDHUNTER.COM/MEGATRENDS.

AWAKEN YOUR INNER TREND HUNTER

No doubt there's a rebelliously creative Trend Hunter spirit inside you. It just needs to be called into duty. Like any soldier, it needs discipline and methodology.

Hunting for new ideas can be exciting, but the constant need to focus can also become tedious. It's not challenging to find a random idea, but it's tremendously difficult to narrow in on something spectacular. To get inspired, actively hunt in three places:

- **CUSTOMERS:** Above all, innovation starts with the customer. In times of chaos, your customer will be looking for dramatic change. So obsess about your customers! Who are they? What do they need? What are they eating for dinner right now? (Too far? Sorry.) In short, customer obsession is so critical to trend spotting that it was given its own section in this book.

- **COMPETITORS:** Closely observing your competitors can be a helpful way to understand the market. The trick is to have the right definition of who your competitors are. Looking more broadly for competitors can trigger more stellar ideas.

- **ADJACENT MARKETS & POP CULTURE:** Breakthrough innovation blends an intimate knowledge of the customer with culture and emerging technology.

IF YOU WANT TO SPARK INSPIRATION, YOU NEED TO HUNT IDEAS THAT SEEM "COOL." BUT WHAT EXACTLY IS COOL?

LEVEL 1: INDIVIDUAL IDEAS

Constantly seek to be unique. Individual ideas can inspire your breakthrough, but you have to filter through the noise.

Ugg boots, Von Dutch hats, Hush Puppies, iPods, 7 For All Mankind jeans, Crocs, and Mini Coopers. Breakthrough products become viral because they are unique.

- **UGG BOOTS:** Traditionally worn by Australian farmers, these hideous boots get their name from the reaction they invoke: "Ugh," as in "ugly." Despite their appearance, the boots started appearing on celebrities like Madonna, Britney Spears, Sarah Jessica Parker, and Cameron Diaz in the mid-2000s. By 2008, the brand had $580 million in revenue.[58] Whose boots are ugly now?

- **HUSH PUPPIES:** In *The Tipping Point*, Malcolm Gladwell popularized the case study of Hush Puppies. Just when the ugly shoe brand was ready to fold, trendsetters in New York's East Village started wearing Hush Puppies precisely because they were rare and unique. Soon afterward, the shoes appeared on runways and celebrities. Sales exploded from 30,000 pairs in 1994 to 1.7 million pairs by 1996.

- **CROCS FOOTWEAR:** At the 2002 Miami Boat Show, Crocs sold out of their first inventory of just 200 pairs. The plastic shoes were so ugly that they inspired a website called ihatecrocs.com, where people glamorize the destruction of the hideous shoes. And thousands have joined Facebook groups dedicated to hating Crocs. Despite the hate, Crocs sales grew from $6,000 at the boat show to a peak of $850 million in 2007.[59]

TRULY UNIQUE IDEAS CAN DRIVE VIRAL BEHAVIOR.

Popular is not cool.

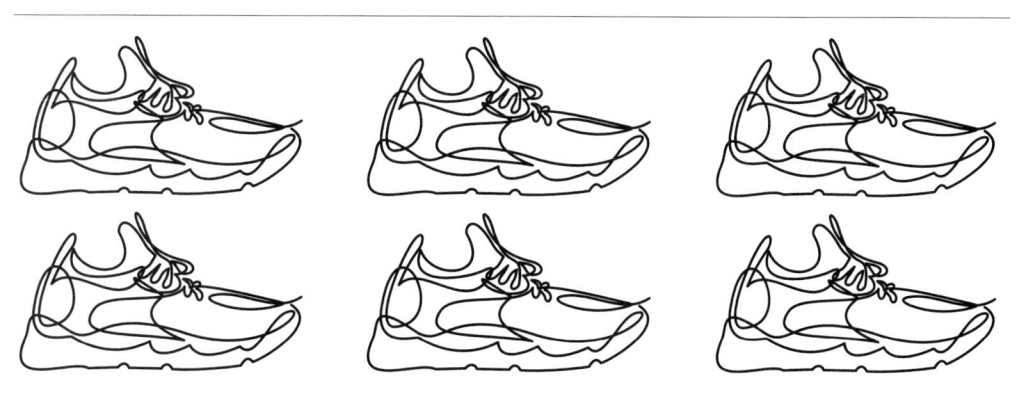

Cool is unique and cutting edge,

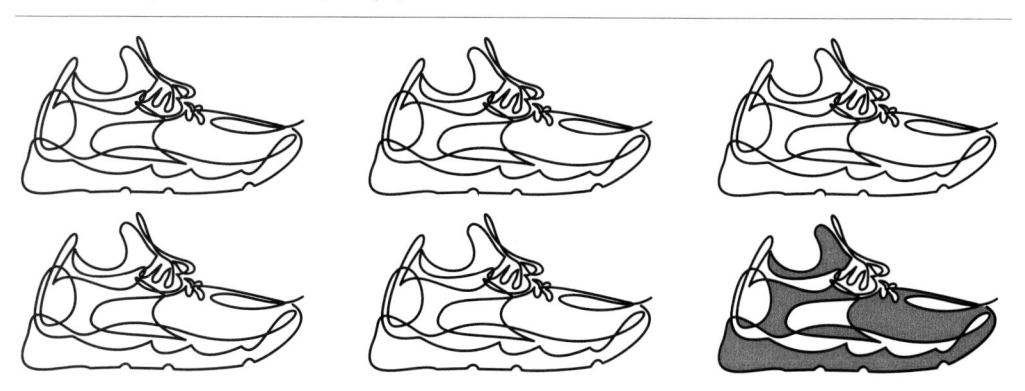

and cool is viral, which is why marketers and product designers seek to attain it.

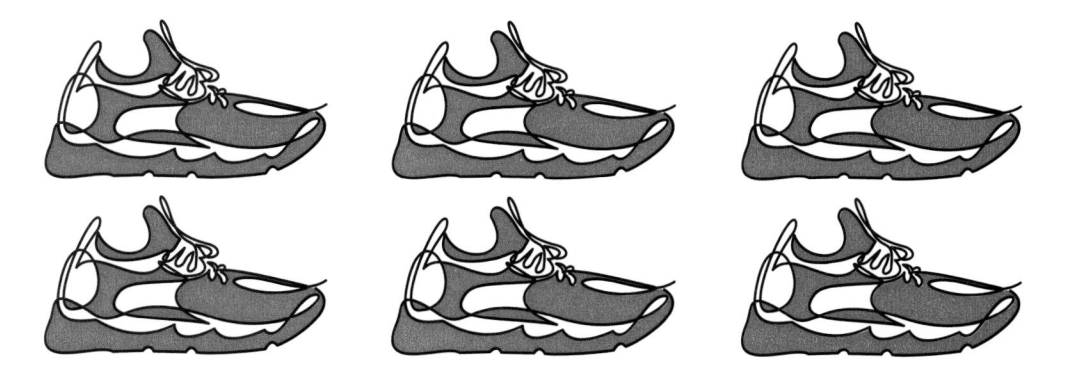

LEVEL 2: CLUSTERS/INSIGHTS

Hunt for meaningful clusters of opportunity. This is the sweet spot for most great opportunities, so we'll dive in a lot more.

First of all, why would the Trend Hunter guy use a word like *cluster* instead of *trend*? Quite simply, the word *trend* is too broad. It can refer to next fall's fashionable color or to macro-trends like the green movement, female buyers, consolidation, outsourcing, Web 2.0, and aging Boomers. These trends are somewhat useful but too generic to enable breakthrough thinking.

Clustering is the art of identifying insights that are meaningful to your customer. To create clusters, you'll need to collect your observations from trend hunting and filter through the noise.

THE CLUSTERS YOU IDENTIFY WILL BECOME THE FOCUS OF YOUR INNOVATION.

KEEP REGROUPING YOUR BEST IDEAS TO UNLOCK INSIGHT

The human mind is great at identifying patterns . . . by creating shortcuts! We create stereotypes, heuristics, and schemas to make our thought process more efficient. In the innovation process, this means our natural tendency is to identify trends we were already aware of and reinforce those trends with examples. This is bad.

*FORCING YOURSELF TO RECLUSTER WILL ENABLE YOU TO
ESCAPE YOUR BIAS AND UNLOCK TRULY UNIQUE PATTERNS.*

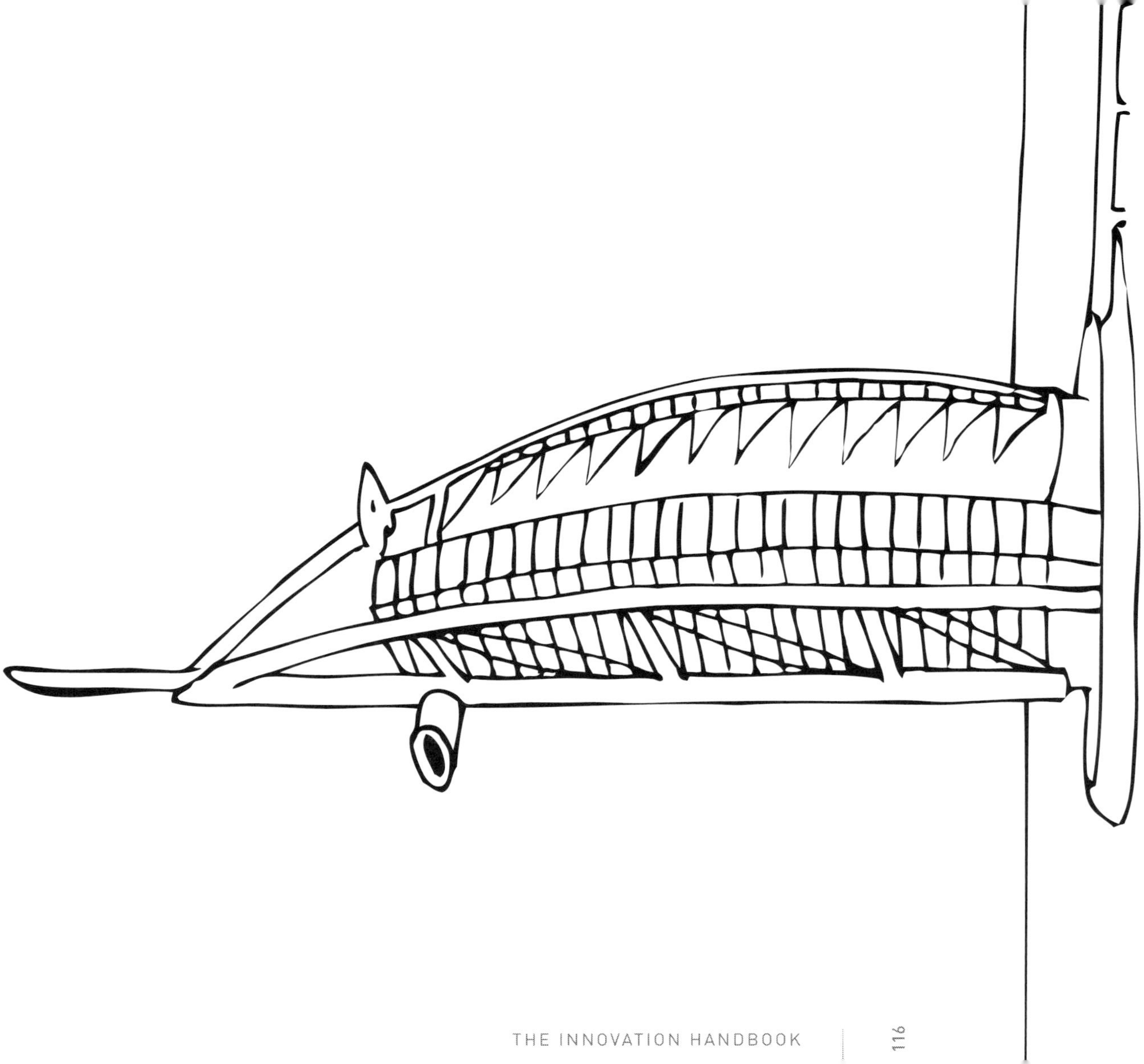

EXAMPLE: DESIGN A HIP HOTEL

No doubt you will end up being incredibly successful. But then what will you do? You're far too creative to retire, so you'll need a hobby.

To illustrate the trend-hunting process, let's pretend that you've decided to launch a hip hotel. As a first step, how would you design a hotel if you had to make it today?

- What would it look like?

- Would it be in a city or a beach town?

- Would you tailor it to a specific demographic?

- What would be your theme?

- What type of music would play in the elevator?

- What would make the rooms unique?

- How awesome would it be?

TAKE A BREAK TO IMAGINE YOUR HOTEL.

First step: Reset

Now that you have your hotel idea, it's time to throw it away. Snap. Remember that "nothing is precious." The first step is to erase your expectations and start with a blank slate. Getting you to come up with an idea only to throw it away was not a trick. Rather, it illustrates that it can be difficult to let go of your initial idea.

Prepare to hunt

Innovation starts with your customer. Hypothetically, let's pretend you've uncovered the following: the world has become saturated with hotels. When the global economy started to collapse, vacancies skyrocketed, and it became all too easy to book an affordable room at a luxury chain hotel. The market has become tilted. On the low end, budget hotels are thriving. But in the high-medium to high end, where you would like to compete, there is abundant choice. It's not an easy market.

While hanging out in hotel lounge bars, you interview a dozen travelers and identify an opportunity: young urban professionals. They have money to spend and they want to travel, but most hotels don't fit their needs. In one interview, a 28-year-old woman explains, "These days, there are always hotel deals. I can afford to stay anywhere, but I'm looking for something unique and creative, somewhere I can tell my friends about."

Urban travelers don't want a hotel; they want an experience. Market Dynamics: Since 2000 there has been a surge in niche hotels, but the market is still relatively underserved. Most "hip hotels" are privately owned, although some of the larger chains are getting into the market.

For example, in 2005 Starwood launched Aloft, an affordable version of their hip "W Hotels" brand. This makes Starwood one of your biggest competitors. In 2009 Hilton announced the launch of Denizen, their own line of hip hotels. However, chain hip hotels like Aloft and Denizen fit a certain mold. Opportunities still exist for truly unique ideas.

To find unique ideas, it will be important to hunt for trends on the fringe of pop culture: in addition to looking at hip hotels, you'll also want to look at adjacent industries and random examples of innovation. As you look for ideas, remember the advice of Marco Morrossini: "You need to be more open to the complete possibility of what could be."

NEXT, YOU DECIDE TO GO TO TRENDHUNTER.COM TO BROWSE —— —— *HUNDREDS OF UNIQUE HOTELS, SERVICES, AND RANDOM TRENDS . . .*

HUNT IN YOUR MARKET

When you begin a hunt for inspiration, always start by fully exploring your own market. You might discover something new, somewhere in the world, that inspires your next level. In this case, we would begin by looking at all the hip hotels getting attention.

EXAMPLE: Hip hotels featured on Trend Hunter

PRISON HOTEL

19872

COFFIN HOTEL

34985/3

LITTLE SLUM INN (RIO)

608

PIPE HOTEL

4010

DOCKSIDE CRANE HOTEL

5206

CELEBRITY B&B (TORI SPELLING)

5380

LUXURY BLIMP HOTEL

531

EXTREME HOTEL (CLIMB IT!)

3426/5

UNDERWATER HOTEL

14403/1

PORTABLE HOTEL

11242

CAVE HOTEL

3965

ROLLS ROYCE HOTEL

3679

OPPORTUNITY HUNTING

121

HUNT ADJACENT MARKETS

After examining your own market, the next step is to look at the adjacent market. What are the products and services being enjoyed by your consumer when they experience your offering? In this case, we would look at unique hotel services.

EXAMPLE: Hotel services—ideas from the fringe

IN-ROOM MASSAGE

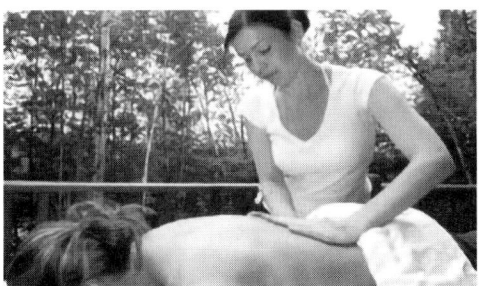

4673

GRAFFITI ARCHITECTURE

4954

PRO-RUN SLEEPOVER PARTIES

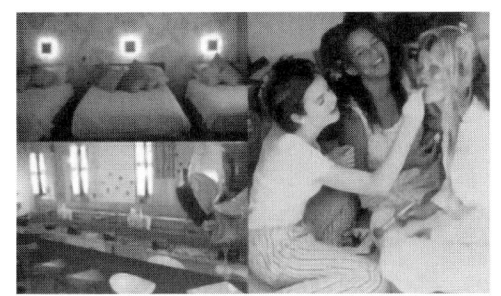

1579

GLOWING BATH TUBS

102

RAINSKY SHOWERS

3994

ARTIST-DESIGNED ROOMS

3234

122

WINE SPAS

2835

PRECOOKED GOURMET MEALS

4673

PET SPAS

8583

IN-ROOM CHEFS

4673

BEER SPAS

2835

BUBBLE ARCHITECTURE

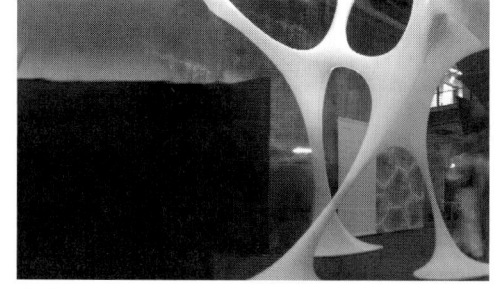

2541

OPPORTUNITY HUNTING

123

HUNT WHAT'S IMPORTANT TO YOUR TARGET

Finally, we would look at all of the interesting and innovative things that your target demographic is experiencing. In the case of hip hotels, we can look at other innovations being shared and enjoyed by young urban professionals.

EXAMPLE: Trending concepts in this market

SKATEBOARD PARK IN MUSEUM

5456

LUXURY CAR TIMESHARES

556

DOG HELMETS

102

URINALS FOR DOGS

3234

ORTHODOX JEWISH BARBIE

3234

MUSLIM BARBIE

3234

TETRIS TOWERS

102

FREE VENDING MACHINE

102

SPRAY-ON MAKEUP AT HOME

40626

NYC GARBAGE AS ART

1260

BIZARCHITECTURE

14364

BARBIE COSMETICS (CO-BRAND)

4183

OPPORTUNITY HUNTING

125

IDENTIFY CLUSTERS/INSIGHTS

After you finish hunting trends (and booking your next stay at the prison hotel), the next step is to identify clusters. Certain patterns will jump out immediately. For example, you might have noticed the following two clusters:

- **ULTRA-LUXURY**: The Rolls Royce Hotel, in-room massage, and luxury car rentals all reinforce this pattern.

- **SENSATIONALISM**: The beer spa, slum hotel, and urinals for dogs all reflect an outrageous pattern.

As warned, you need to be careful with your first round of clusters. Your first patterns will always reflect your initial bias.

In this exercise, if you were asked to brainstorm hip hotel trends before looking at the examples, you probably could have come up with Ultra-Luxury and Sensationalism. That means anyone in the world could have the same clusters. You need to seek originality.

WHEN IDENTIFYING CLUSTERS, IT IS IMPORTANT TO LOOK BEYOND YOUR INITIAL PRESUMPTIONS AND SEEK UNIQUE CLUSTERS OF OPPORTUNITY.

IN-ROOM CHEFS

ROLLS ROYCE HOTEL

EXTREME HOTEL (CLIMB IT!)

COFFIN HOTEL

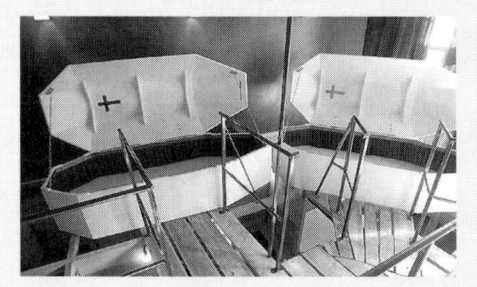

PIPE HOTEL

BEER SPAS

THROW AWAY YOUR CLUSTERS
AND LOOK HARDER

Force yourself to create more clusters. From the same group of ideas, you might identify the following clusters:

- **IN-ROOM LUXURY**: in-room massage, precooked gourmet meals

- **NOSTALGIA CO-BRANDING**: Barbie cosmetics, Muslim Barbie, Orthodox Jewish Barbie

- **THE HUMANIZATION OF PETS**: urinals for dogs, pet spa, motorcycle helmets for dogs

- **VIRAL YOUTH TARGETING**: professionally run sleepover parties, skateboard park in a museum

- **RENTING CULTURAL EXPERIENCE**: Little Slum Inn, prison hotel, luxury car timeshares

If you focused your hotel idea on any one of these specific clusters, you could develop something spectacular. For example, pick just one of the clusters above and take another break to imagine a new hip hotel.

If you were to focus on creating the best hotel for "renting cultural experience," what would it be like? Where would it be? What type of cultural experience would your clients get to encounter?

WHEN YOU FORCE YOURSELF TO FIND NEW CLUSTERS,
YOU WILL UNLOCK UNIQUE INSIGHT.

IN-ROOM LUXURY

IN-ROOM CHEFS

PRECOOKED GOURMET MEALS

IN-ROOM MASSAGE
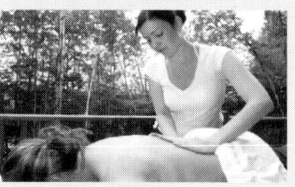

NOSTALGIA CO-BRANDING

ORTHODOX JEWISH BARBIE

MUSLIM BARBIE

BARBIE COSMETICS (CO-BRAND)

THE HUMANIZATION OF PETS

DOG HELMETS

URINALS FOR DOGS

PET SPAS
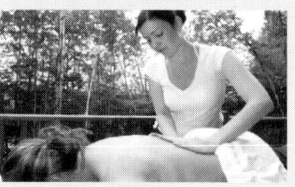

VIRAL YOUTH TARGETING

SKATEBOARD PARK IN MUSEUM

PRO-RUN SLEEPOVER PARTIES

EXTREME HOTEL (CLIMB IT!)

RENTING CULTURAL EXPERIENCE

LITTLE SLUM INN (RIO)

LUXURY CAR TIMESHARES

ROLLS ROYCE HOTEL

BRAINSTORM IDEAS BASED ON EACH CLUSTER

When you identify a new opportunity, keep in mind it can feel awkward and unfamiliar because you have discovered something new. That's why it is helpful to focus your brainstorming efforts on each of the specific clusters you discovered.

When you focus your creativity, two things happen: The first is that your idea will reflect the pulse of the trends you found meaningful. The second is that you will end up with an idea that is more focused.

For example, if you had picked "renting cultural experience," you might come up with an idea for an "African Hut Hotel in America." Guests could stay in mud huts and experience the life of African poverty. A stay could be accompanied by educational lectures and films. Perhaps after the first night or two, your guests could finish their stay at a local 4-star hotel.

Building mud huts wouldn't cost much (certainly less than the 7-star Burj Al Arab Hotel pictured on page 116). Despite the low cost of building a hut, your guests would never forget their eye-opening experience.

Finally, the idea could attract international media attention. For any "hip hotel," international attention is the Holy Grail.

BY CREATING UNIQUE CLUSTERS, YOU CREATE A LEVEL OF FOCUS THAT GENERATES POWERFUL IDEAS.

Personalization

Many-to-Many

Co-Creation

Authenticity

Hybridization

Gamification

Multisensation

Experience

Curation

Tribalism

Simplicity

Youthfulness

Instant Entre-
preneurship

Naturality

Catalyzation

Nostalgia

AI

Prosumerism

LEVEL 3: MEGATRENDS

Megatrends are larger-impact trends that continually sway consumer desire. They are more readily known than clusters, because they typically consist of at least 100+ examples with an impact of 3 to 10 years. Examples include Personalization, our desire for Authenticity, and Many-to-Many. The latter refers to the proliferation of individual creators versus large brands.

The following chart shows our current top 18 Megatrends, described in just a few more pages, but first, here are some factors to consider when using megatrends to develop a long-term strategy:

1. CURRENT ALIGNMENT—Which megatrends are you currently aligning to? This is not an exercise of checking the box. It is a challenge to deeply think about which three or four megatrends currently have the most impact on your business. Has your alignment to these trends been intentional or accidental?

2. FUTURE POTENTIAL—Which megatrends align to future markets where you *could* compete? Perhaps there are simple changes you could make to align to certain megatrends, providing you a North Star that will continually propel your innovation efforts to greater success.

3. FUTURE MISALIGNMENT—Do you have products or initiatives that do not align to a megatrend? For example, if you work at a beverage company and your products come in plastic bottles, your business is imminently under threat from the megatrend of Naturality and the next generation's desire to be more eco-friendly and sustainable. This would need to be fixed or it will lead to your disruption.

MEGATRENDS ARE LARGER-IMPACT TRENDS THAT CAN GUIDE YOUR LONGER-TERM STRATEGY AND GOALS.

LEVEL 4: PATTERNS OF OPPORTUNITY

When you see a big splash in water, it creates ripples of opportunity. If you study the ripples, you know which way the water will flow. Similarly, competitor actions, disruptive innovation, and changes to your consumer's life ALSO create patterns of opportunity. By using patterns, you can predict where your competitor is headed.

My last book, *Better and Faster*, was mostly devoted to the art and science of understanding the six most impactful patterns. For example, Divergence is a pattern suggesting that products that are the opposite of the mainstream can enjoy remarkable success. As humans, we tend to gravitate toward things that are unique, different, or customized just for us. Accordingly, Divergence teaches us that we can be successful in certain markets by employing a strategy of being counter to the mainstream, like Red Bull, Virgin Airlines, and other brands that challenge the status quo.

You can use the patterns in two ways. On one hand, patterns can be used to classify trends and explain why some ideas are propelled by culture. On the other hand, you can use patterns to predict opportunities in a given market.

For example, if I were looking to create an idea for a new hotel, I could go pattern by pattern and host six brainstorming sessions with my team. In the Divergence category, I might think about all the things that currently annoy people about hotels, and then I would try to create a hotel that did everything in an opposite way. In the hotel world, I know that people hate the slow check-in process, lack of customization, small menus, and being treated like a number. I might instead be divergent with a hotel where you are checked in before you get there, with a customized menu and personalized greeting.

PATTERNS ARE TOOLS THAT HELP PREDICT HOW OUR WORLD IS EVOLVING.

THE 6 PATTERNS OF OPPORTUNITY & 18 MEGATRENDS

Acceleration
1. Perfecting One Thing
2. Aspirational Icon
3. Exaggerated Feature
4. Reimagined Solution

Prosumerism
From user-generated content to maker culture, today's consumers expect professional tools & services.

Catalyzation
Brands have taken a role of accelerating the personal development of consumers.

AI
We are entering a transformative new era, denoted by an exponential growth in data, robotics, and intelligence.

Reduction
1. Specialization
2. Fewer Layers + Efficiency
3. Crowdsourcing
4. Subscription

Instant Entreprenuership
New services make it easier than ever to conceptualize, fund, and launch companies.

Curation
Hyper-targeted offerings, services, subscriptions, and recommendations to simplify lives with better things.

Simplicity
In a fast-paced, cluttered world, simplicity stands out, resulting in focused businesses & clean design.

Convergence
1. Combining + Layering
2. Adding Value
3. Co-Branding + Aligning
4. Physical + Digital

Multisensation
Tech, AR, VR, and interactive experiences are raising our expectations in the realms of entertainment, retail, and even food.

Co-Creation
Brands, products, services, and customers are increasingly co-creating an interdependent world.

Hybridization
Lines are blurring as business models, products, and services merge to create unique concepts and experiences.

If you want to extend your depth of knowledge in trends, explore 400,000 examples at Trend Hunter to discover YOUR inspiration.

If you create a free account, you can track your favorite categories.
Visit TrendHunter.com/PRO.

 ## Cyclicality
1. Retro + Nostalgia
2. Generational
3. Economic + Seasonal
4. Repetitive Cycles

 ## Nostalgia
Fond memories fuel a desire to bring the past into the present, especially with respect to one's formative years.

 ## Naturality
The desire for sustainable products, including local, organic, recyclable, and pronounceable ingredients.

 ## Youthfulness
The world is becoming more playful, driven by generations not ready to grow up, including Boomers who desire a more active, enriched life.

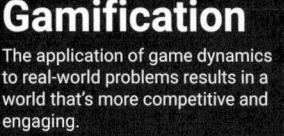 ## Redirection
1. Refocusing
2. Reversing
3. Surprising
4. Gamifying

 ## Tribalism
Allegiant groups are more readily formed around specific interests, causes, and even brands.

Gamification
The application of game dynamics to real-world problems results in a world that's more competitive and engaging.

 ## Experience
In a world abundant with "stuff," experience becomes a more important currency and life priority.

Divergence
1. Personalization, Customization
2. Status + Belonging
3. Style + Fashioning
4. Generational Rebellion

 ## Authenticity
Social media and a resistance to traditional advertising have created a desire for authenticity and reality.

 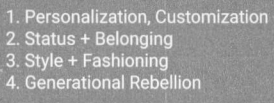 ## Personalization
Small batch production technologies and more personalized media are creating an expectation for personalization.

 ## Many-to-Many
A mass proliferation of sellers and media creators has shifted the world to a many-to-many economy.

1. **TRAVEL:** "I look for subcultures of cool and emerging cool. To find this, travel is the #1 thing for me. Connecting with different cultures and subcultures is important." —Shaheen Sadeghi, Cofounder of Quiksilver, Awesome Dude

2. **PURSUE CURIOSITIES:** "Create something that you would use and answers the question, 'Wouldn't it be cool if . . . ?' Do not depend on focus groups and market research. That's for losers." —Guy Kawasaki, Venture Capitalist, Author, Honorary Trend Hunter

3. **CARE:** "Innovation has no agenda, no plan, no rigid structure. It's about doing something you care about. I've found that people who truly care are the ones that are most likely to be innovators." —Seth Godin, Bestselling Author

4. **REBEL:** "You need a culture of rebellion, an elastic-sided sandbox, a mindset that rules are made to be tested . . . Inevitably you do need process and planning elements to create a culture of innovation . . . But if you're not stretching the boundaries with spontaneous ideas, you're going nowhere quick." —Kevin Roberts, CEO of Saatchi & Saatchi, Funny as Hell

5. **RANDOMIZE:** "Focus on what you love, but don't limit yourself to only things that you love. Subscribe to new magazines, download podcasts on a topic that has nothing to do with your current life, go to lectures by people at the top of their field—even if you've never heard of their field. Get books on tape, and follow websites that gather interesting information. (I get *Cool News of the Day* from Reveries.com and *Trend Candy* from TrendHunter.com)."[60] —Tom Kelley, General Manager of IDEO, World's Leading Design Firm

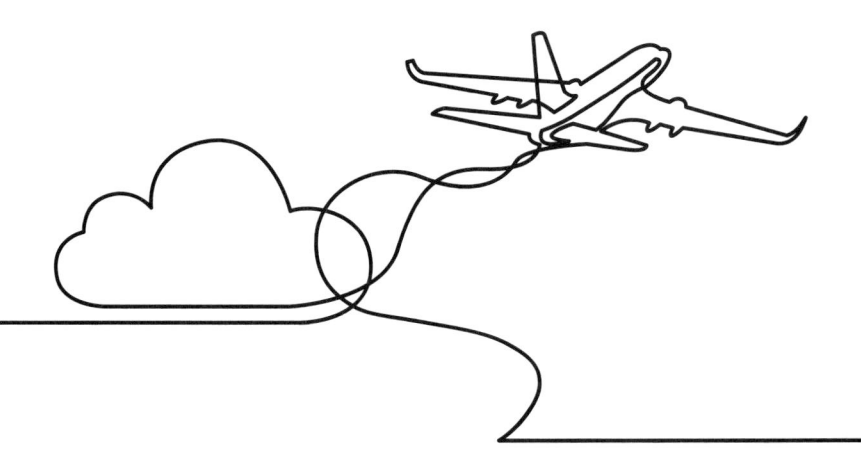

6. **SHARE IDEAS:** "I try to act on as many of my ideas as possible, from a simple blog post to starting a company. Simply writing them down, usually in public, is a great discipline, and once they're out there they tend to improve." —Chris Anderson, Former Editor-in-Chief of *Wired*

7. **FORM AN IDEOLOGY:** "The principle is that you find a common point of pain or passion and you get people organized around that." —Rod Beckstrom, Coauthor of *The Starfish and the Spider*, Inspirational Guy

8. **HUNT FOR COOL:** "Through cool hunting, marketers are able to identify the cultural meaning of trends ahead of competitors. . . . Traditional product positioning has been based on physical attributes. . . . Cultural branding is based on positioning the product on the cultural meanings to consumers. This makes cool hunting the new source of product positioning." —Jay Handleman, Queen's University Professor, Teacher Who Inspired Me to Start TrendHunter.com by Showcasing Malcolm Gladwell's Article "The Coolhunt"

9. **TALK TO STRANGE PEOPLE:** "It's also important, I think, to communicate, whether by email, in person, or on the phone, to a wide variety of people. Talking with only the usual suspects can become an echo chamber." —Dan Pink, Only Guy I Know to Make a Manga Cartoon Business Book

10. **CONSUME POP CULTURE:** "I am a voracious consumer of pop culture, whether it's books, magazines, art, blogs, websites, or serialized television. A key to being creative is to pay attention to what's going on around you. Constant stimulation and being open to new ideas are musts." —Marian Salzman, CMO of Porter Novelli, Renowned Futurist

11. **SEEK POSITIVITY:** "Consciously seek positivity. Often the media is abuzz about something negative, like Iran, for example. I hunt specifically for a unique angle that offers a positive twist, such as fashion in Iran, the underground music scene in Tehran, or the efforts of eco-bloggers in that part of the world." —Bianca Bartz, Original Editor of TrendHunter.com (4,000 Published Articles)

12. **SOCIALIZE AND CONNECT:** Find colleagues and friends who will keep you challenged in the quest for new ideas.

13. **SPEND A DAY:** "Spend a day immersed in your target consumer's life and environment—true ethnography!" —Marianne McLaughlin, Senior Manager of Global Consumer Insights, New Balance

14. **GO ON A TREND SAFARI:** "Real life experiences, like safaris (to experience other industries and cultures), inspire me. Try different geographies, like comparing businesses in Shanghai versus London." —Maria Åkerlund, Macro Insights Manager, Ikea

15. **CREATE A PERCEPTUAL MAP OF COMPETITORS:** What needs do your competitor products satisfy? "Create a perceptual mapping of competitive products to identify white space. Repeat the exercise thinking of micro to macro metrics." Also consider, "Move further up the continuum of your product category. Being in consumer packaged goods, I'll tour restaurants, bars, and food trucks." —Lisa Tirino, Director of Innovation, Ocean Spray

16. **SHOP ALONGSIDE YOUR CUSTOMER:** "I host monthly 'Shop Alongs,' where we shop alongside our customers. Colleagues get a chance to experience shopping and study buying behaviors to help design and develop products." —David Dombrowski, Director of Industrial Design & Innovation, GSK/Pfizer

17. **PEOPLE WATCH:** "I visit competitors and smaller shops to study what customers are doing." —Lauren Simoneschi, Consumer and Sensory Specialist, Nestlé

18. **TEACH:** Surprisingly, one of the best ways to really challenge your presumptions is to teach or mentor. You'll form a clear perspective as you force yourself to articulate important answers.

19. **STUDY OTHER CATEGORIES:** "I get inspired looking to other categories of products and services and visualize how I can apply insights to my job and make it better." —Nikolaos Ananikas, Senior Brand Manager, Coca-Cola

20. **ASK QUESTIONS:** "Have a workshop where only questions can be asked. No answers can be presented. Then have a separate workshop where everyone brings solutions." —Tom Kneubuehl, Digital Strategy Consultant, American Family Insurance

21. **VISIT TREND HUNTER:** "At TrendHunter.com, find out what's cool before it's cool." —MTV Live

TrendHunter.com has more than 400,000 cutting-edge ideas, broken into 100+ categories, including design, pop culture, advertising, modern art, and innovation. You can explore ideas on the site, sign up for a free Weekly Trend Report, or start your own Trend Hunter portfolio to collect and publish your favorite ideas.

- What are the key innovations happening in YOUR industry?

- What are the innovations happening in ADJACENT markets?

- What innovations are happening in the world of your TARGET customer?

Create the Future Framework

| Opportunity Hunting | Adaptive Innovation | Infectious Messaging |

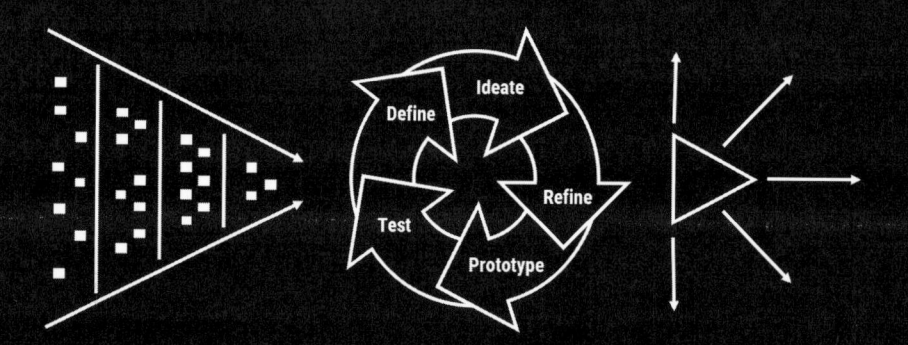

Culture of Innovation

⇧ ⇧ ⇧ ⇧ ⇧ ⇧ Ability to Change ⇧ ⇧ ⇧ ⇧ ⇧ ⇧

PART 4

ADAPTIVE INNOVATION

Chaotic markets and untamed creativity have the potential to take you dangerously off-course. To increase the consistency of winning, you need to manage your innovation and prototyping in a methodical, adaptive way.

This section breaks innovation down into two parts: a set of circular steps, and tactics to manage innovation like a stock portfolio.

BE METHODICAL AND SCIENTIFIC ABOUT INNOVATION

My Adaptive Innovation Framework is a simple process to help you think about innovation in a scientific way. It is important to develop a process that is your own, inserting the right checks and balances to ensure you find your new fields of opportunity. However, the simpler takeaway is that you want to increase your odds of success by approaching creativity with consistency.

Step 1   Define a clear customer need.

Step 2   Ideate like it matters.

Step 3   Refine in a smaller team.

Step 4   Create rapid prototypes.

Step 5   Test and optimize.

Repeat.

Innovation is circular. Like a dog chasing its own tail, you always need to be adapting, redefining the customer need you are trying to solve. Unlike a dog, you will become more intelligent with each spin.

At any given time, the process can be adjusted based on observations from your wonderful trend hunting.

ADAPTIVE INNOVATION IS METHODICAL AND CIRCULAR.

The Adaptive Innovation Framework

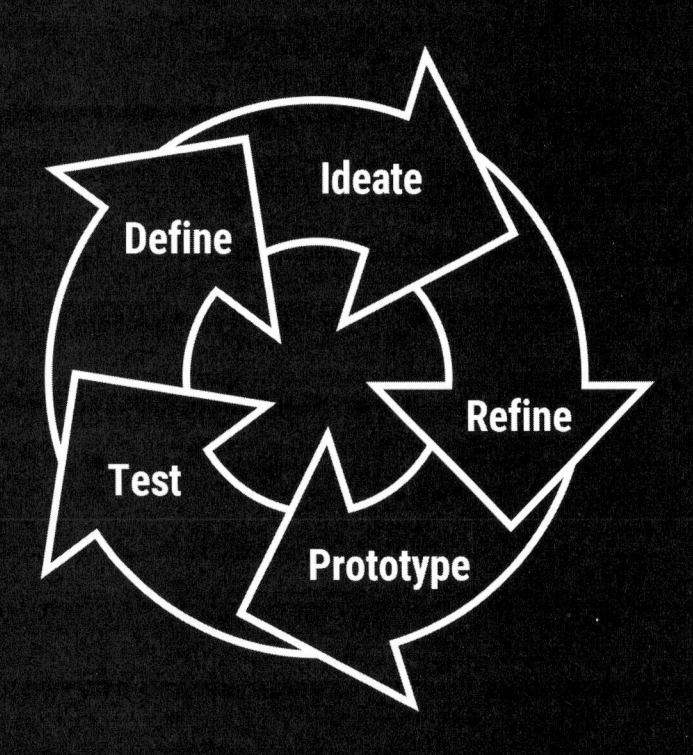

STEP 1: DEFINE A CLEAR CUSTOMER NEED

Adaptive innovation begins with a clearly defined customer insight. This should be the result of your trend-hunting process and past product testing.

A well-defined problem will dictate the outcome of your entire project, so you want to ensure that your insight is specific, or you will end up creating vanilla ice cream.

Here's what that means: if you study the dessert market, you'll learn that ice cream is exceptionally popular. Within the ice cream category, vanilla is the dominant flavor.

However, vanilla ice cream is a commoditized space. People do not really care about their vanilla ice cream brand, and it would be nearly impossible to capture and retain a vanilla ice cream customer.

Vanilla is boring.

DON'T PURSUE MEDIOCRITY.

FIND THE NEXT CHERRY GARCIA

To become a player in the delicious ice cream market, you need a cult following. You need to find the next "Cherry Garcia."

Cherry Garcia is a flavor of Ben & Jerry's ice cream that contains pieces of cherries and chunks of chocolate. It was launched in 1987 as a tribute to Jerry Garcia, lead guitarist for the Grateful Dead. Since its launch, it has become the most popular flavor offered by Ben & Jerry's.

In fact, despite being a luxury product, Cherry Garcia helped Ben & Jerry's to grow sales 400% during the 1990–91 recession.[61]

The whole world does not crave cherry and chocolate chunk ice cream, but for the millions who do, there is no substitute. This concept is epitomized by Jerry Garcia's assertion that:

"You do not merely want to be the best of the best. You want to be considered the only ones who do what you do."

WHEN SCREENING FOR OPPORTUNITY, LOOK DEEPER THAN THE BROADEST IDEA.
LOOK FOR UNDERSERVED NICHES OF OPPORTUNITY.

STEP 2: IDEATE LIKE IT MATTERS

Ideate is a better word for brainstorming. Why? First of all, there is no such thing as a storm in your brain. Ridiculous.

Second, people don't take brainstorming seriously because they mistake it as being relatively straightforward (and partially ineffective). I used to think this too until I experienced the caliber of "storming" that takes place at Stanford's d.school. At Stanford they obsess about these rules:

- DEFER JUDGMENT.
- ENCOURAGE WILD IDEAS.
- GO FOR VOLUME.
- HAVE ONE CONVERSATION AT A TIME.
- HEADLINE.
- SPRINGBOARD (BUILD UPON THE IDEAS OF OTHERS).

In particular, I use "springboarding" as a measure of good ideation. When someone is able to build upon the idea of someone else, it proves that your exercise is actually inspiring new ways of thinking.

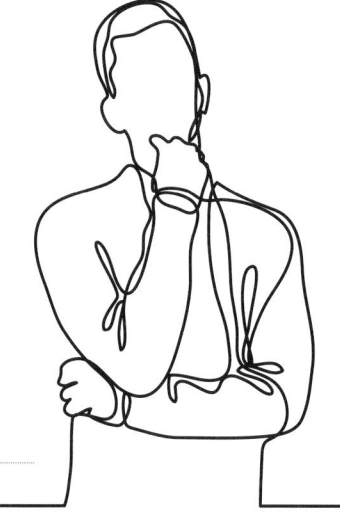

148

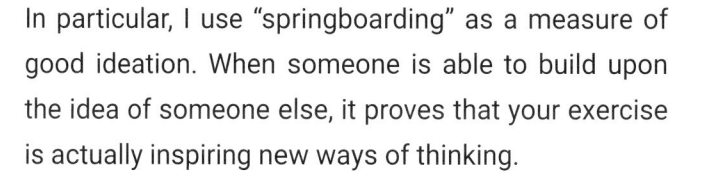

IDEATION RULES ARE SO IMPORTANT THAT EVEN STANFORD'S SUPERSTARS REVIEW THEIR RULES BEFORE EACH SESSION.

BRAINSTORMING BEST PRACTICES

Although i've spiced up the titles and details, the following set of steps generally reflects the structure we used at the d.school, where the goal for an hour of brainstorming was around 100 ideas.

- **SET THE STAGE**: Invite the best people, create a useful space, and break the ice.

- **FOCUS**: Create very specific questions and very specific rules. You can change the rules throughout the brainstorming, which I often do to mix it up.

- **SEEK FLEXIBILITY**: Push for range and variety in the ideas suggested.

- **KEEP IT FUN**: Create group energy and encourage humor.

- **ADD SOME SALT AND PEPPER**: Reshape the question. Take an idea and dive deep. Contribute a crazy idea. Encourage physical movement.

- **CHALLENGE WITH SPECIFIC PROBLEMS**: For example, if you are trying to sell more pantyhose to men, try to answer the question, "How do we rename the color 'pantyhose brown' to make it more masculine?"

- **WRAP IT**: Get people to vote for their favorite ideas. Circle the room to see if there are any important comments.

MAKE IDEATION THE BEST PART OF YOUR JOB, AND PASSION WILL TRANSLATE INTO BREAKTHROUGH IDEAS.

STEP 3: REFINE

After an ideation exercise, how do you filter down to the best ideas (without arguing and pulling hair)? Here's one example:

- **COLLECT (100 IDEAS):** Start with your results from Step 2.

- **FILTER (20 IDEAS):** Find the best nuggets! In a smaller team, create clusters or simply pick the best ideas.

- **REFINE (10 IDEAS):** Prepare "headlines" for your best 10 ideas as if you were selling them to a customer.

- **RANK ORDER (10 IDEAS, RANKED):** Quantitatively rank your 10 refined ideas. Ideally, perform an online survey with a sample of your actual customers.

- **FOCUS (3 IDEAS):** Select your three best ideas to move on to Step 4.

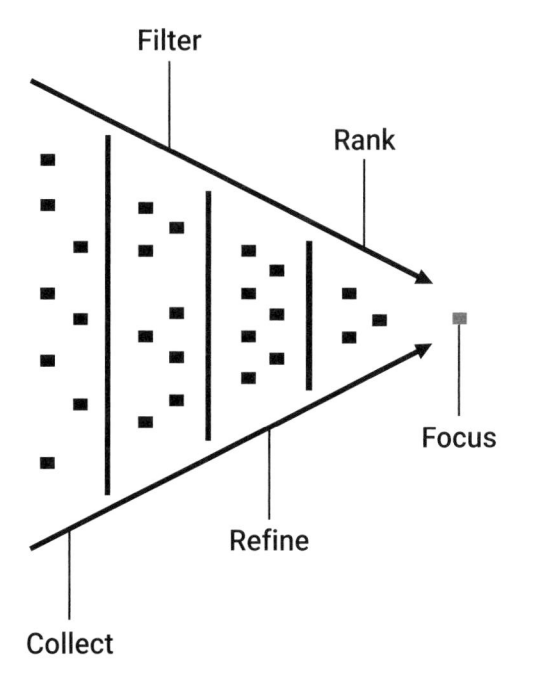

STEP 4: CREATE RAPID PROTOTYPES

Rapid Prototyping is a term that will make you sound like you really know what you're doing. Also, it's an enjoyable step in the innovation process. It involves creating pretend versions of your product or service. It's different from planning in that you are building something to simulate the experience. This could mean creating a skit to preview a new experience or spending a couple of hours building a model of a sample store.

> "The value of prototypes resides less in the modules themselves than in the interactions they invite."

—**Michael Schrage, author of** *Serious Play*[62]

By prototyping, you and your team will quickly uncover the factors that could enable or hinder the success of your idea.

Almost anything can be made into an effective prototype. Here are some examples:

Mock Products: diagrams, frameworks, physical mock-ups, slideshows, simple crafts, models, sample packaging, 3-D models, sample advertisements, and "photoshopped" designs. Mock Services: role-playing, skits, videos, and flow charts.

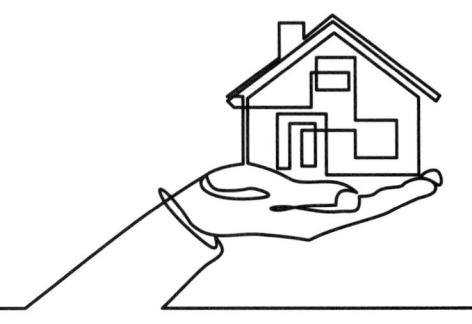

THE ACT OF CREATING A PHYSICAL PROTOTYPE ALLOWS YOU TO VISUALIZE THE CONCEPT AND OBTAIN USEFUL FEEDBACK.

STEP 5: TEST AND OPTIMIZE

Scientific method becomes important when you are in uncharted territory, testing new and cutting-edge ideas. Find ways to quantify the uncertainty, and each successive design will inch closer to breakthrough innovation:

- In our growth phase, Trend Hunter would test 10+ layouts a week, measuring the impact on page views per visitor, time of visit, and likelihood to return.

- Dell tests new products in real time, testing the price sensitivity and impact of special promotions.

- Capital One mails dozens of product tests each month, playing with price points, wording choice, and even envelope color.

The important caveat is that you need to test broadly in the areas where you are most uncertain. Typically, companies screw this up.

When companies are good at something, they make slight tweaks to improve—they climb to the peak of the hill they are already on. When finding a new hill, you cannot get caught up in testing small details. You need to explore broadly.

BY EXPLORING AND MEASURING AMBIGUITY, CHAOS BECOMES ORDER.

EXPLORE, TEST, GAMBLE, OPTIMIZE, AND BE SAFE

Manage innovation like a stock portfolio

This is the part of the book that you've been waiting for! The magical moment when I pull out my chartered financial analyst alter ego and seduce you into the wonderful world of portfolio management. At first glance, the term *stock portfolio* does not seem sexy and creative; however, there is no other industry where risks are more tolerated and studied. Here are just a few strategies that financial managers do to create a portfolio that can safely grow. Applied to your business, these tactics can help you to navigate chaos while pursuing innovation:

1. DIVERSIFY—Increase your odds of winning while limiting your likelihood of loss. Diversification improves your consistency while reducing risk. As the investment legend Peter Lynch once explained, "If you're good, you're right six times out of ten." You will never be perfect, but diversification means you don't have to be. For innovators, diversification means the following:

- **Work on Multiple Projects at Once**: In some ways, the number of successes you will have is a mathematical product of how many ideas you try. WD-40 was the 40th attempt. How much can you test?

- **Set Aside Exploration Time**: Whether you are an artist or a marketer, it's important to have specific time allocated to the pursuit of new styles, ideas, and techniques. Google and 3M both give employees 5% of their time to work on pet projects. How much time do you spend just coming up with new ideas?

- **Try Both High- and Low-Risk Projects**: Often organizations try multiple products, but all at the same risk level. Focusing on too many low-risk projects is just as bad as focusing on one high-risk project.

2. CONTROL THE SIZE OF YOUR BET—Innovate inside the box. Part of portfolio management means budgeting the size of each experiment and forcing yourself to be creative within that box. How horrible and boring does that sound? Surprisingly, the concept comes from Disney, one of the most creative organizations in the world. When Michael Eisner took over Disney, the company was losing money. One of his first mandates was to assign a strict financial box to each Disney project. Employees were then challenged to creatively fit their ideas inside the financial box. Unfamiliar with such intense control, the creative people at Disney were skeptical (if not angry). Years later, it worked. Eisner grew Disney from a $2 billion market capitalization to over $60 billion.

3. CREATE ARTIFICIAL CONSTRAINTS—Even artificial constraints can lead you to success. At Capital One, a typical experiment for my team involved a multimillion-dollar test. We kept wondering if there was a better way. Instead of allocating a couple million dollars to the next project, I challenged my team to see what we could do inside a $500,000 box. At first glance, that still sounds like a lot of money, but when you consider the price of media, half a million bucks means we couldn't use TV and everything else would have to be on a smaller scale. So we pushed ourselves: What if that money were our personal $500,000? How could we use that money to better understand our customers and lure them toward our wonderful products?

Within our box, we developed word-of-mouth campaigns, publicity stunts, charity sponsorships, and our first-ever referral program—an impressive list of projects, given the budget. The project led us to a revised view of just how much we could do with our money, making us more effective in all of our much more costly campaigns.

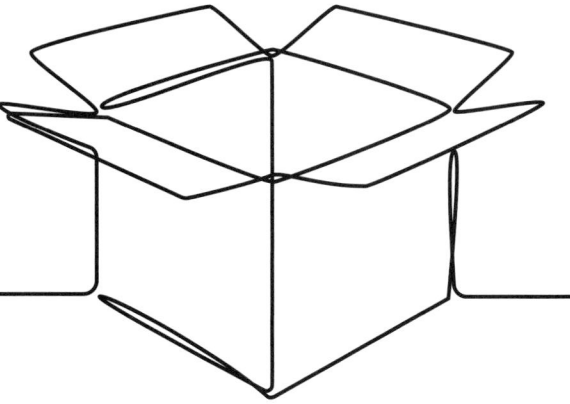

4. STAY STRONG AFTER A SNAKEBITE—Innovation budgets become the first places to scale back after a snakebite, but calculated risks still need to be taken. When gamblers suffer a big loss, the natural reaction is to become more conservative on the next bet. This is referred to as the snakebite effect. It stems from the concept that a real snakebite makes you want to curl up in fear afterward (kind of like a visit from your in-laws). In organizations, we receive "snakebites" when we fail, which basically happens everywhere that we explore dramatic change. Snakebites lead teams to become too conservative with their innovation. The danger in today's chaotic environment is that giant losses in the market will cause companies to be excessively cautious.

5. DON'T PLAY WITH THE HOUSE MONEY—The opposite effect of the snakebite is house money. When a gambler experiences a big win, there is a tendency to perceive the profits as the "house's money" (still belonging to the casino). It then becomes psychologically easier to gamble away that money. Even after big wins, it is important to keep a balance between calculated risk and playing it safe.

6. PULL WEEDS, GROW ROSES—If you had a garden, would you want to grow roses or weeds? When investing, you have the luxury of anonymity. Nobody can see your mistake, and you can pull out at any time. But it's still difficult. In organizations, there is no anonymity. People know which projects are failing, pride becomes involved, and jobs may be on the line. This makes the power of sunk costs paralyzing. Know when to give up. Nothing is precious.

- How might you add more of the scientific or portfolio management approach to your innovation process?

- If you looked at all of your offerings and new ideas, how would you classify them in terms of low risk, medium risk, and high risk? Do you feel like you have enough projects in each category? With the right buy-in and financial backing?

- If you evaluated new products not by the likelihood of winning but by the size of the bet, what ideas might suddenly be more appealing?

Create the Future Framework

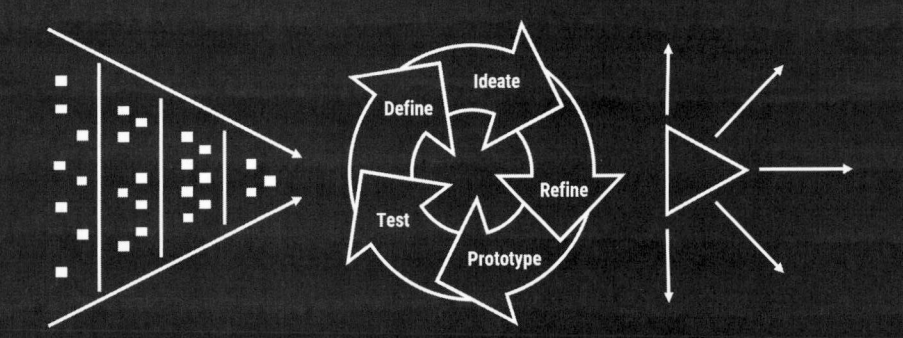

| Opportunity Hunting | Adaptive Innovation | Infectious Messaging |

Ideate
Define
Refine
Test
Prototype

Culture of Innovation

Ability to Change

PART 5

INFECTIOUS MESSAGING

We live in a world cluttered with chaos. If you want your innovative idea to break through all the noise, you need a well-packaged story. Fortunately, we've spent a lot of time studying this in our quest to attract billions of views to Trend Hunter's website.

By cultivating infection, your ideas will resonate, helping you leapfrog ahead of the competition.

WHEN YOU CREATE SOMETHING THAT FORMS A CONNECTION, YOUR MESSAGE TRAVELS FASTER THAN EVER BEFORE

I created Trend Hunter in 2005, before YouTube and before Facebook. In the early days of social media and the blogosphere, we were all like pioneers discovering how the internet could really work. My first example of something going viral seems awkwardly simple in today's pace of change, but at the time it was epic and educational. So here goes:

Do you ever work from home? If so, you know the joys of working in your boxer shorts (or pajamas). But sometimes you need to videoconference with your team. If so, you need a suit, but you don't need any suit, you need a half suit.

An actual product, known as the Business Bib, this little half suit is all business up top and all party down below.

When Trend Hunter wrote about the half suit in 2006, there were 180 sites that linked to our article. Thousands linked to those sites, and by our calculation, that little half suit was exposed to millions of free views.

Today the article no longer sits in our Top 100 list, but we love the half suit because it was our first experience at the epicenter of the viral blogosphere. Plus, I want one.

Your product won't be a half suit, but the lesson is that for the first time in history, you will have a viral platform.

CREATE SOMETHING THAT IS INTERESTING TO YOUR CUSTOMERS AND YOUR PRODUCT WILL HAVE THE POTENTIAL TO BECOME VIRAL.

PACKAGE YOUR PRODUCT LIKE IT'S THE BEST IN THE WORLD

Do you recognize the name Joshua Bell? Probably not. He plays a $4 million Stradivarius violin. He played the music in the movie *The Red Violin*. When he is onstage, he makes $1,000 per minute.

Josh Bell is quite simply one of the best violinists in the world. Accordingly, the *Washington Post* wanted to throw an unannounced concert.

They wanted to do this in the busiest public walkway they could find—the DC Metro corridor, which more than a thousand people pass through every hour.

The planners wanted to know how many people would stop, even for a moment, to watch him. Half? That would be roughly 500 people. Perhaps that's too many. 200? 100? Probably at least 50, right?

As it turns out, only seven people stopped.

In his category, Josh Bell is the best product in the world, but when he is packaged in the wrong way, he does not make $1,000 a minute.

He made just $35 in a whole hour (most of which was from one lady who actually recognized him).

THE MEDIUM CAN ENABLE OR RUIN YOUR MESSAGE.

SCREW LOGIC, TELL A STORY

The human mind is bafflingly bad at logic, but shockingly superb at understanding stories. Here's an example called the Wason Test.

Imagine the following four cards are placed on a table:

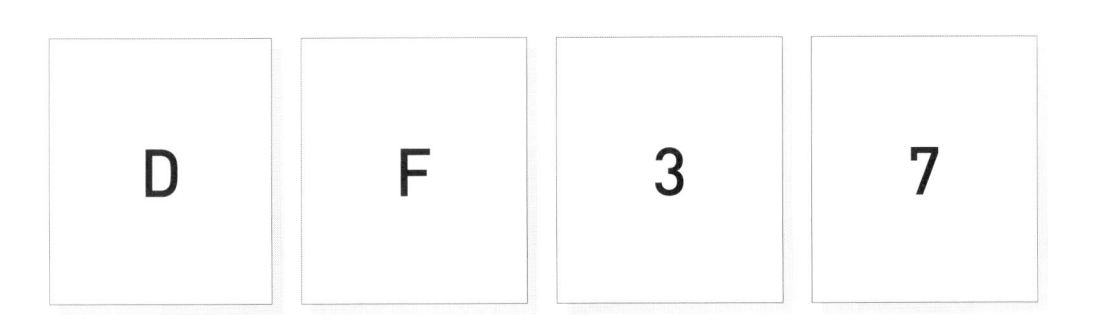

Each of these cards has a number on one side and a letter on the other. Which cards would you need to flip over in order to prove the following rule true or false:

Every card with **D** on one side has a **3** on the other. Which cards would you guess?

The correct answer is that you would need to turn around just the **D** and the **7**.

The **D** would prove that the rule is true, and the **7** could prove it if the rule is false. People typically suggest the **3**, but that is incorrect.

When Leda Cosmides conducted this test at Stanford University, less than 25% of the students answered correctly. The logic of numbers and letters is too abstract.

The beauty of the Wason Test is that you can ask the same logical question in a completely different way.

Imagine you work as a bartender and you have four patrons. One of them might be an underage drinker, which would cause you to lose your job.

Who would you need to investigate to enforce the law that "If a person is drinking beer, then he must be over 20 years old"?

Drinking Beer	Drinking Coke	25 Years Old	16 Years Old

This time the question is much easier. You would investigate the beer and the 16-year-old kid. When asked this way, correct response triples to 75 percent.

In *The Red Queen*, Matt Ridley attributes this phenomenon to the concept of social contracts:

"The human mind may not be much suited to logic at all . . . but is well suited to judging the fairness of social bargains and the sincerity of social offers."[65]

PEOPLE HAVE AN INNATE ABILITY TO
UNDERSTAND SOCIAL STORIES.

CONTEXTUALIZE YOUR MESSAGE WITH CULTURE AND EMOTION

Recall that with a cultural connection, you are not speaking to your customers, you are speaking *with* them, and that's empowering. The most powerful way to speak with your customers is to tie your message to a story or a lifestyle.

This principle is best described by the following quote from an executive at Harley-Davidson:

"What we sell is the ability for a 43-year-old accountant to dress in black leather, ride through small towns and have people be afraid of him."[66]

In a related example, P&G spent years struggling to break into the Japanese market. By 1985, losses had piled up to over $200 million. Their marketing tactics were not working.

As a last effort, they tried something bravely new, marketing a new skin care line, SK-II, with a story: "The fascinating story behind SK-II began at a sake brewery in Japan, where scientists noticed the elderly workers had wrinkled faces, but extraordinarily soft and youthful hands. These hands were in constant contact with the sake fermentation process. It took years of research for scientists to isolate the miracle ingredient Pitera®, a naturally-occurring liquid from the yeast fermentation process."[67]

SK-II became the star product, rocketing up to $150 million in revenue by 1999.

MYTHOLOGY AND CONTEXT CREATE A VIVID EMOTION THAT SURROUNDS YOUR BRAND.

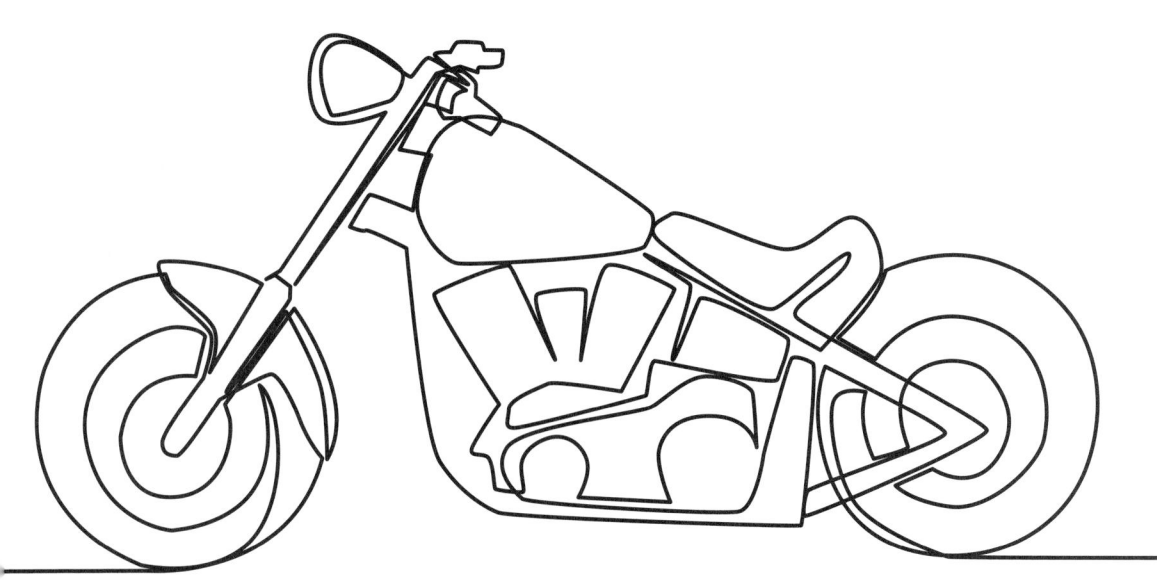

ARTICULATE YOUR MISSION WITH A MANTRA

Southwest Airlines is the most successful and most studied airline ever. One key factor was Herb Kelleher's relentless focus on the mantra "low-fare airline."

Herb once gave the media the following example: suppose that a new marketing employee suggested that people flying from Houston to Las Vegas might like a chicken salad entree, instead of getting just a bag of peanuts. What would you tell that employee?

Herb's answer was that you'd ask, "Will adding the entree help make us the low-fare airline?"

In *Made to Stick*, the Heath brothers suggest that this sort of mantra works because it creates a forced prioritization; it teaches people what to think and how to react.

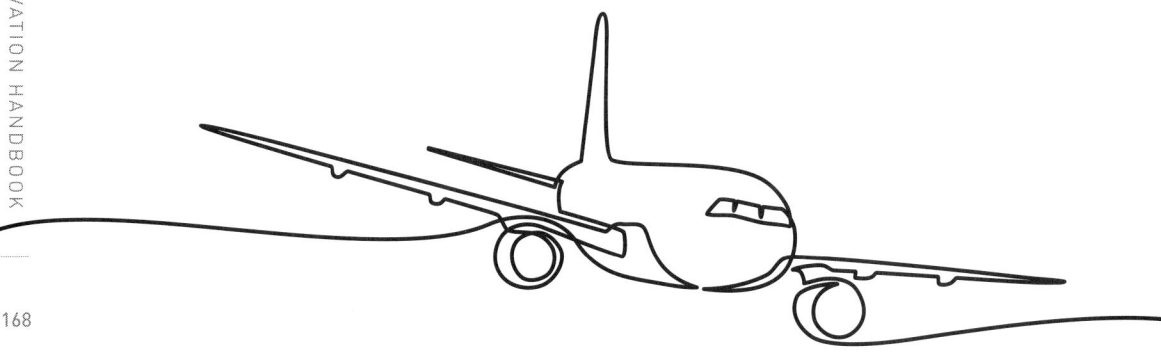

IN TIMES OF CHAOS AND DRAMATIC CHANGE, A POWERFUL MANTRA LEADS TO ALIGNMENT AND SUCCESS.

CONVEY YOUR PURPOSE
IN SEVEN WORDS OR LESS

In 1935 Henry Gustav Molaison was a happy nine-year-old boy, playfully riding his bicycle down a familiar street. Suddenly, he crashed, and his life began a course plagued by seizures.

In an attempt to help, neurosurgeons removed part of Henry's medial temporal lobes. The surgery left Henry with severe anterograde amnesia. He could remember everything prior to the surgery but could not encode new long-term memories.

Then, Henry's case became even more curious.

Although he couldn't remember anything from five minutes prior, the last 30 seconds were always crystal clear. He scored perfectly normal on all short-term tests and continued to enjoy playing bingo, solving crossword puzzles, watching television, and socializing with caregivers. Henry's case provided the first pieces of evidence that humans have a powerful short-term working memory.

Henry would go on to make great contributions to cognitive psychology and marketing, even influencing the length of your phone number.

The peculiarity is that the short-term memory appears to have a finite capacity. In 1956, cognitive psychologist George A. Miller suggested that this capacity was seven plus or minus two items.[68] Decades later it was determined to be roughly 2.5 seconds of information.[69] In English, that equates to seven plus or minus two words. In Chinese, it can accommodate 10 words.

Part of why Southwest's mantra works so well is that it is short and easy to remember.

PEOPLE ARE REMARKABLY BETTER AT REMEMBERING MESSAGES —— *WITH SEVEN WORDS OR LESS, SO KEEP YOUR MANTRA BRIEF!*

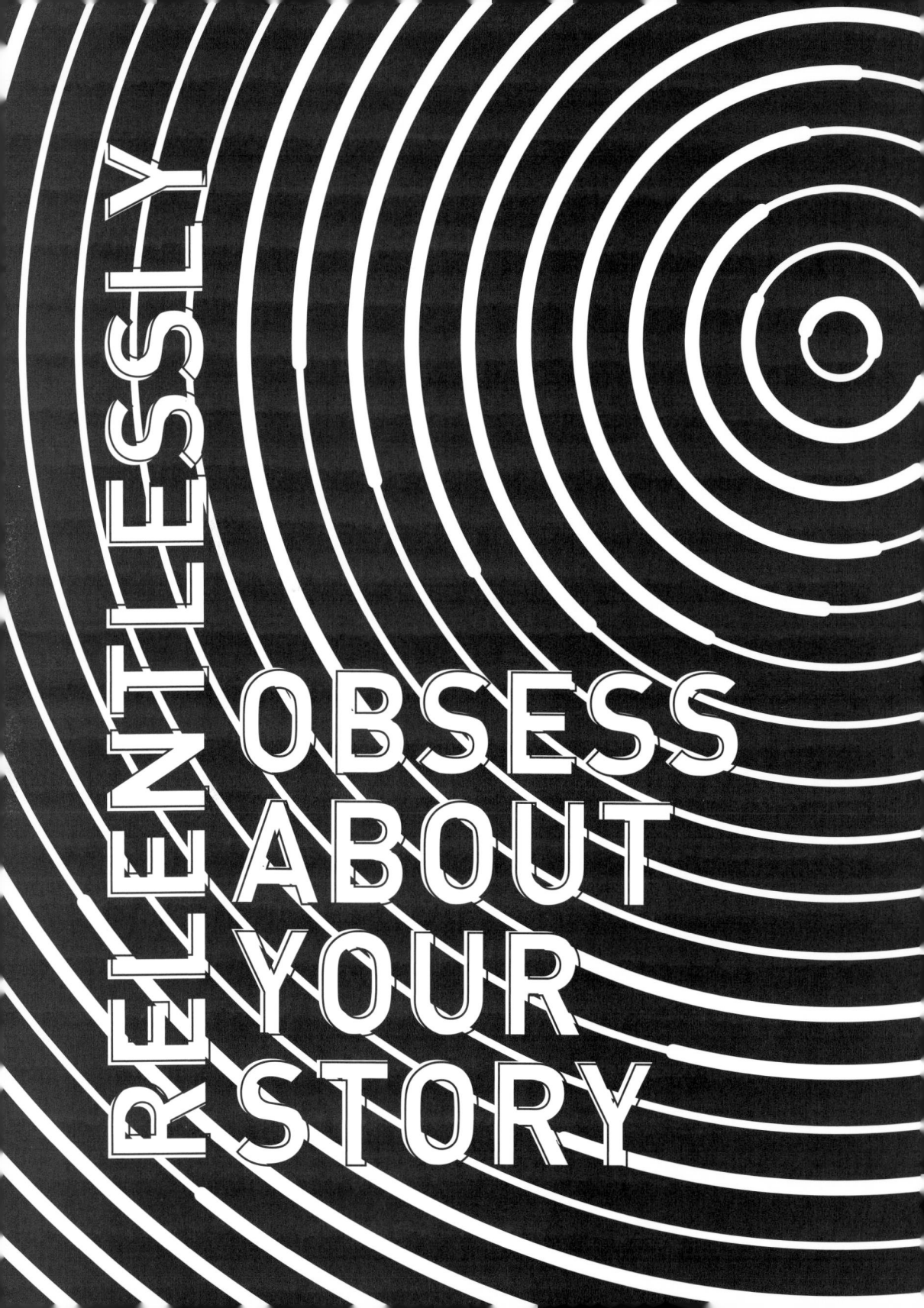

RELENTLESSLY OBSESS ABOUT YOUR STORY

THE TREND HUNTER TITLE FRAMEWORK

After attracting over 3 billion views, we have learned how to make messages that travel quickly. Our analysis led us to make sure every article we publish has a title that is: simple, direct, and supercharged.

Here's how our framework breaks down:

1. **SIMPLE (SUPERCHARGE WORD OF MOUTH):** As Jack Welch of GE put it, "Simple messages travel faster, simpler designs reach the market faster, and the elimination of clutter allows faster decision-making."[70] Similarly, author Seth Godin notes that simple messages "supercharge word of mouth."[71]

2. **DIRECT (ANSWER: WHY SHOULD I CHOOSE YOU?):** An outsider should understand your value proposition from your seven words. Your value proposition is your advantage. It's the unique attribute that explains why I should choose you.

3. **SUPERCHARGED (THE "I HAVE TO TELL SOMEONE TEST"):** Your seven words should pass the "I have to tell someone test." If they don't, why would someone else care? You can't expect your message to drive word-of-mouth exposure if you don't give people a supercharged story.

The Trend Hunter framework will lead you to a message that is much different than a traditional marketing approach.

EXAMPLE 1

The $5,000 Hamburger

Fleur De Lys is a unique restaurant at the Mandalay Bay in Las Vegas. On their menu they sell a very special hamburger, priced at $5,000, called "The FleurBurger 5000." Interesting name, right?

FleurBurger is a clever play on the name of the restaurant. It also conveys that the burger is classy. But it is not simple. It is not direct. It is not supercharged.

What if it was called "The World's Most Expensive Hamburger"? That message is simple and direct, but it's not totally supercharged. I don't have to tell someone about such a burger.

What if we called it a "$5,000 Hamburger"? That's what it is: literally a $5,000 hamburger. The $5,000 Hamburger is so expensive you even get a certificate to put up on your wall. What does it say? I have enough money that I can afford to eat a $5,000 hamburger.

FleurBurger is the wrong way to sell this burger. In comparison, the $5,000 Hamburger is simple, direct, and supercharged.

	The FleurBurger 5000	The World's Most Expensive Hamburger	The $5,000 Hamburger
Simple	✘	✓	✓
Direct	✘	✓	✓
Supercharged	✘	✘	✓✓✓

THE NEXT TIME SOMEBODY MENTIONS AN EXPENSIVE HAMBURGER, YOU'LL REMEMBER THE $5,000 HAMBURGER. THAT MESSAGE JUST STUCK.

EXAMPLE 2

The Heart Attack Grill

Sticking with the hamburger theme, I present you with this lovely beast. It's not the healthiest-looking burger, but being healthy is not its claim to fame.

You might expect a burger like this to come from the Fatburger restaurant chain. The Fatburger brand is simple and relatively supercharged.

But this burger comes to us from the "Heart Attack Grill®" in Phoenix, Arizona.

At the Heart Attack Grill, this burger is served to you by someone wearing a nurse's outfit. On the menu, it's called the Quadruple Bypass Burger®.

It comes served in a combo pack that includes three beers and three packs of cigarettes. If you finish the Quadruple Bypass Burger, the pretend nurse will roll you to your car in a wheelchair.

	Johnny's Hamburgers	Fatburger Cafe	The Heart Attack Grill
Simple	✘	✔	✔
Direct	✘	✔	✔
Supercharged	✘	✔	✔✔✔

MAKE STORY OBSESSION A LIFESTYLE.

EXAMPLE 3

Trend Hunter

These lessons of infectious messaging are not exactly easy. In my own case, I spent years trying to figure out the right seven words or less for my own company.

Originally, we plastered the slogan "#1 Trend Website" throughout our materials. It met the "Simple" criteria, and it was superlative. We were the biggest, so why not brag about it? The problem is that you don't *need* a trend website, so it didn't clearly relate to what we actually did. It was not "Direct."

Seven years into our journey, we adapted our slogan to be "Find Better Ideas Faster." I loved this slogan for several years. It wasn't as flashy as saying we were the "#1 Trend Website," but in other ways it spoke more. My team wants to help you find BETTER ideas, using crowdsourcing, AI, and big data. And we want you to find those ideas FASTER so that you don't spent years searching, like I did.

As we embark on our next level as a company, I realize that half of our work has come from discovering opportunity, but the other half has come from running key-notes and workshops to consult with CEOs and their teams about how to make change actually happen. Hence the other half of this book, "Create the Future," which has become our new slogan. In comparison, it is less direct but more supercharged.

	The World's Best Trend Website	Find Better Ideas Faster	Create the Future
Simple	✓	✓	✓
Direct	✗	✓	✗
Supercharged	✗	✓	✓✓✓

IN SEVEN WORDS OR LESS,
SPECIFICALLY WHY SHOULD I CHOOSE YOU?

CHAOS CREATES OPPORTUNITY

Raphael, Da Vinci, Michelangelo, Machiavelli, Copernicus, and Galileo. From the 14th century to the 17th century, humanity would be forever changed by the breakthroughs of the Renaissance. In philosophy, the humanist movement encouraged scholars to build upon knowledge rather than to break it down.

In art, traditional styles were eclipsed by the realism and perspective introduced by "the greats." Artists like Leonardo da Vinci blurred the lines between art, science, and invention. The Scientific Revolution began, marking the beginning of the modern age. In short, a new way of thinking emerged. Philosopher Jacob Burckhardt likened the Renaissance to a veil being lifted from the eyes of man.[72]

Shockingly, this remarkable period emerged from the 14th-century eruption of the Black Death, the deadliest pandemic in human history. Nearly half of the European population died, causing a state of chaos. But this chaos caused archaic social structures to collapse. It forced a period of remarkable adaptation.

In our lives, we are unlikely to experience an atmosphere of chaos that compares to the intensity of the Black Death. However, parallels of opportunity will be created as our history evolves. Chaos of any kind sends ripples through our culture, but it also gives birth to new opportunity. When outdated structures break down, the world becomes open to new ways of thinking. As we enter history's highest period of change and business disruption, it is clear that we have entered a new period of chaos.

You are closer to new opportunity than you have ever been. You have so much potential, well within your grasp. You have the potential to **CREATE THE FUTURE.**

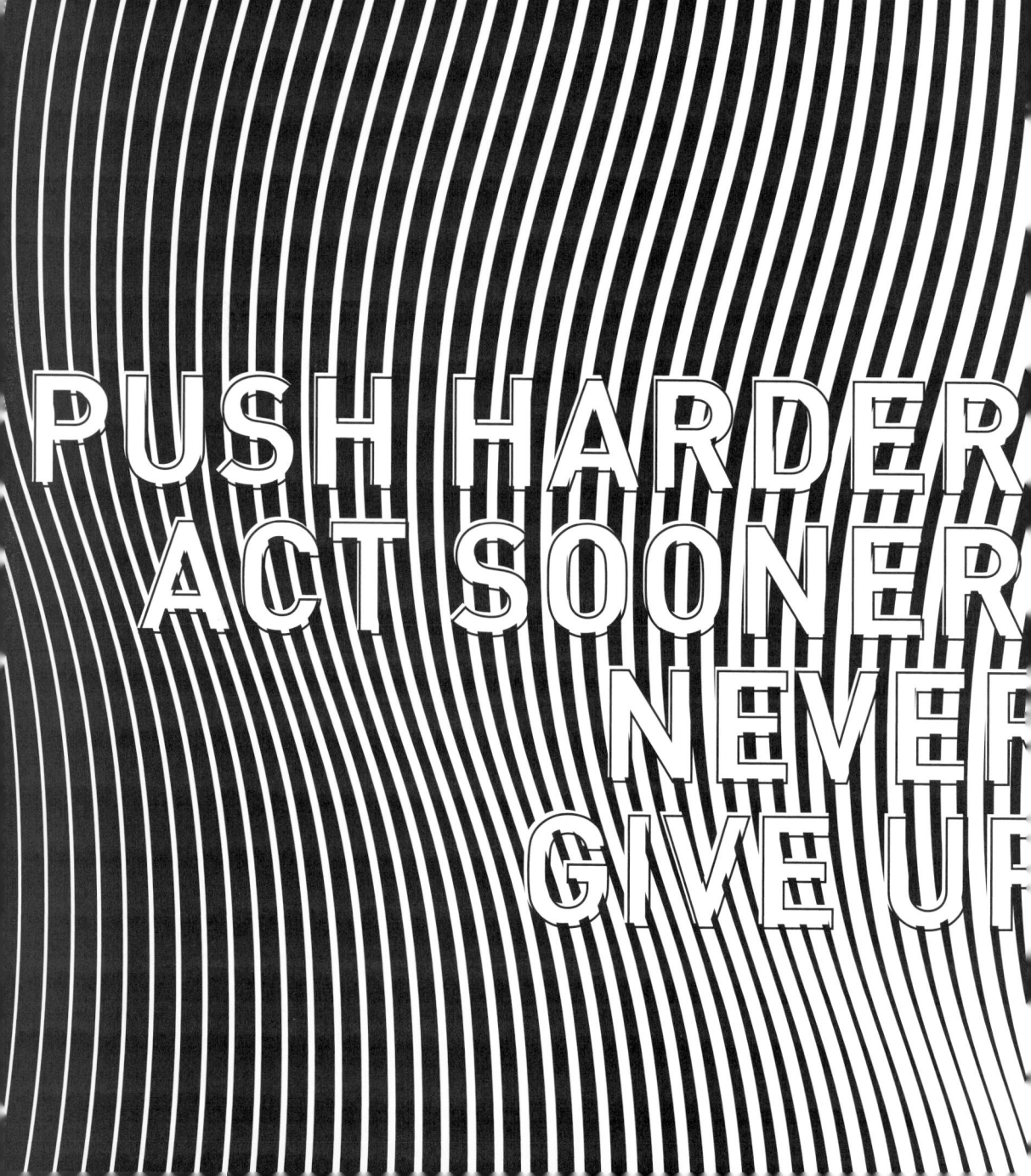

- Specifically what is it that you are trying to do?

- Why should I choose you, in seven words or less? (Make sure to be simple, direct, and supercharged.)

- How would you explain your business idea to a 12-year-old?

- Describe your idea in 20 words. Then ban those words and try again to describe it using completely new words.

TACTICS

1. Create a cultural purpose around your brand.

2. Deliberately try to be different.

3. Reconsider the importance of repetition and simplicity in your communications.

4. Recognize that simple word choice has an enormous impact on your destiny.

5. Take a course in public speaking, copywriting, marketing, or persuasive writing.

6. Hire or involve a copywriter in your key communications, internal or external.

7. Recognize that rule #1 is to relentlessly obsess about your story.

ACT NOW

AS A CREATIVE PERSON, you were no doubt thinking of many ideas as you read this book. What will you do with those ideas?

A young man once approached J. P. Morgan with a proposition: "Sir, I hold in my hand a guaranteed formula for success, which I will gladly sell to you for $25,000."[73]

Always curious, J. P. Morgan replied, "I do not know what is in the envelope, however, if you show me and I like it, I give you my word as a gentleman that I will pay you what you ask."

The man agreed, handing J. P. Morgan the envelope.

When J. P. examined the note, he reached for his checkbook and paid the man the agreed-upon sum of $25,000. In one of his presentations, Tom Peters revealed the advice that was on that piece of paper:

1. Every morning, write a list of the things that need to be done that day.

2. Do them.

IF YOU WANT TO CREATE THE FUTURE, THE TIME TO ACT IS ALWAYS NOW.

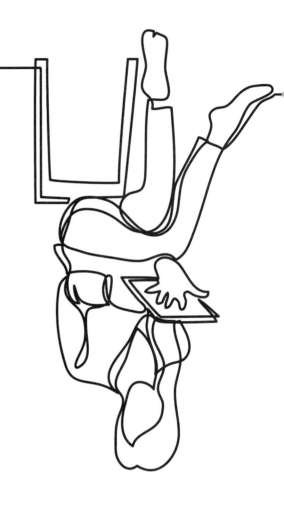

TAKE THE NEXT STEP

- FUTURE FESTIVAL—Join thousands of the world's top innovators—including adidas, Starbucks, Nestlé, Samsung, Disney, Universal, and NASA—at Future Festival, my team's exciting innovation conference. Now in more than a dozen cities! FutureFestival.com.

- INNOVATION ASSESSMENT—Figure out your innovation strengths and blind spots by benchmarking yourself to the world's top innovators. Plus, benchmark your team to get more personalized recommendations to make a culture of innovation. TrendHunter.com/Assessment/H2WTF.

- CUSTOM RESEARCH & ADVISORY—If you work at a large organization, join 750 of the world's top innovators who rely on Trend Hunter to help them predict and create the future. To date, we have conducted more than 10,000 custom trend reports and innovation workshops. TrendHunter.com/advisory.

- KEYNOTE VIDEOS & WORKSHOPS—Check out my YouTube channel if you want to see my other keynote video topics. Or better yet, I'd love to be part of your company's next big event. If my schedule won't allow for it, we have a team of futurists for keynotes and in-office workshops. JeremyGutsche.com.

- TRENDHUNTER.COM—Fuel your curiosity and spark new ideas by exposing yourself to thousands of micro-trends at TrendHunter.com, the world's largest site for trend spotting and innovation. You can also start a free portfolio to track your favorite topics. TrendHunter.com.

- FREE WEEKLY NEWSLETTER—Stay on the cutting edge by subscribing to the TrendHunter.com free Weekly Trend Report, which filters through all the noise to highlight the most interesting discoveries each week. TrendHunter.com/newsletter.

TREND HUNTER
FUTURE
FESTIVAL™

Get inspired and collide with the world's top innovators (and me!).

Now in a dozen cities: **FutureFestival.com**.

THANK YOU!

When I wrote my first book, it was much easier to think about all the people who made it happen. This time, it is more complex because my stories, tactics, and ideas have been shaped by my family, my team of 75 people, hundreds of clients, and all of those friends and mentors who have been part of Trend Hunter's epic 14-year journey. In addition, the first version of *Exploiting Chaos* had several pages of people thanked, and the original content continues to be inspired by each of those people.

For this version, in particular, I want to start by thanking my terrific mother, Shelagh Gutsche. As a family therapist and social worker, you taught me so much about understanding people, which is ultimately the foundation of any good business idea. You also tolerated (and encouraged?) a lifetime of my own "disruptive thinking," so it is fitting then that I have written a book about exactly that. I am also thankful for my inspiring sister, Kyla, and her talented kids, Alex and Alee, whose upbringing taught me about the raw creativity of children versus adults, a key inspiration for the section about myelin.

An enormous thank you goes to Taylor Klick for being my lovely inspiration and support network. In addition to the many ideas you've provided me, you also developed the art direction for the book and consulted on the design throughout, to make the book beautiful.

On the Trend Hunter team, I am grateful to Hannah White and Ellen Smith for editing the book and adding extra spicy headlines. I am thankful for Jaime Neely, our Chief Culture Officer, for development of our Innovation Assessment and for her Work Culture interlude in Part 2. Appreciation is also due to Armida Ascano and Rebecca Byers for their work developing our Megatrend Frameworks, which dramatically enhanced the section on trend spotting. Thanks to Jonathon Brown for the innovation tactics from your interviews and the launch strategies developed when we made *Better and Faster* a *New York Times* bestseller. Thank you to Samantha Read and

Sam Mollicone for finding all the line drawings and Trend Hunter designs that make the book pop. Lastly, thanks to our CMO, Rose Goring, for the launch strategies.

I am thankful to Tony W. Hunter, former CEO of the *Chicago Tribune*, for letting me be a part of your amazing journey, for your friendship, for your story in this book, and for all the support you have given to me and to Trend Hunter over the years.

Thanks to Malcolm Gladwell for your foreword and to Guy Kawasaki not just for your foreword, but for support of Trend Hunter since its inception. Thanks to Stephen King for your mentorship and thoughts on horses, space, and getting caught in a path.

On the Fast Company Press team, thanks to Lindsey Clark, the book's senior editor, Elizabeth Brown, the talented copyeditor, and to Tyler LeBleu for figuring out how to make an impossible timeline, possible. Thanks to Brian Phillips for the most beautiful book covers I could have ever imagined, and to both Brian and Cameron Stein for the interior layout and design. As well, thanks to Olivia McCoy for marketing strategy, Steve Elizalde for distribution strategy, Sam Alexander for brand strategy.

Thanks to Mark Fortier and Elena Christie from the Fortier PR team for the PR support and strategy related to the book launch.

Last, thanks to Jessica Sindler, the original editor of *Exploiting Chaos*, William Shinker, the original publisher, and Mark Melnick, the original designer. In addition, Judy Ng and Linda Ng who sourced the image rights for both editions of the book.

THANK YOU!

183

ENDNOTES

1. Haas Edersheim, Elizabeth and Peter Ferdinand Drucker. 2007. *The Definitive Drucker*. New York: McGraw-Hill.

2. Christensen, Clayton M. 1997. *The Innovator's Dilemma: When New Technologies Cause Great Firms to Fail*. Boston: Harvard Business School Press.

3. Charles O'Reilly. 2008. "Strategic Execution: The Ambidextrous Organization"(lecture). Stanford Graduate School of Business, Palo Alto. November 16, 2008.

4. Scott D. Anthony. 2008. "Disruption Is a Moving Target." February 26, 2008. *Harvard Business Review*. https://hbr.org/2008/02/disruption-is-a-moving-target.

5. Razeghi, Andrew J. 2008. "Innovating Through Recession." http://www.scribd.com/doc/7450921/Innovating-Through- Recession-Andrew-Razeghi-Kellogg-School-of-Management.

6. Caron, Sarah. "14 Big Businesses That Started in a Recession." InsideCRM.com. http://www.insidecrm.com/features/businesses-started-slump-111108.

7. Schwartz, Peter. 1996. *The Art of the Long View: Paths to Strategic Insight for Yourself and Your Company*. New York: Random House.

8. *New York Times*. 1990. "Venture Ties Acer and Smith Corona." September 27, 1990. http://www.nytimes.com/1990/09/27/ business/company-news-venture-ties-acer-and-smith-corona.html.

9. Frieswick, Kris. 2005. "The Turning Point." *CFO Magazine*. April 1, 2005. http://www.cfo.com/article.cfm/3786531.

10. Jupiter Media Metrix. 2001. "Global Napster Usage Plummets, but New File-Sharing Alternatives Gaining Ground" (press release). July 20, 2001. http://www.comscore.com/press/release.asp?id=249.

11. McBride, Sarah and Ethan Smith. 2008. "Music Industry to Abandon Mass Suits." *Wall Street Journal*. December 19, 2008.

12. Bangeman, Eric. 2005. "I Sue Dead People." *Ars Tecnica*. February 4, 2005.

13. Bylund, Anders. 2006. "RIAA Sues Computer-less Family." *Ars Tecnica*. April 24, 2006.

14. Borland, John. 2003. "RIAA Settles with 12-Year-Old Girl." Cnetnews.com. September 9, 2003.

15. Palenchar, Joseph. 2006. "XM Faces the Music in RIAA Copyright Suit." TWICE. May 22, 2006.

16. Out-Law.com. 2001. "RIAA Sues Internet Radio Stations." July 5, 2001. http://www.out-law.com/page-1778.

17. Allofmp3.com. 2007. Digital music press release. November 5, 2007.

18. IFPI. 2009. "IFPI Publishes Digital Music Report 2008." January 14, 2009. http://www.ifpi.org/content/section_resources/dmr2009.html.

19. *BusinessWeek*. 2006. "The Enemies of Innovation." April 24, 2006. http://www.businessweek.com/magazine/content/06_17/b3981401.htm.

20. Gerstner, Louis V., Jr. 2002. *Who Says Elephants Can't Dance?: Inside IBM's Historic Turnaround*. New York: HarperCollins.

21. Ayres, Chris, Alexi Mostrous, and Tim Teeman. 2009. "Oscars for Slumdog Millionaire—The Film That Nearly Went Straight to DVD." *The Times* (London). February 24, 2009. http://entertainment.timesonline.co.uk/tol/arts_and_entertain- ment/film/oscars/article5793160.ece.

22. Chouinard, Yvon and Tom Frost. 1974. "A Word." *Chouinard Equipment Catalogue*. October 1974. http://www.patagonia.com/web/us/patagonia.go?slc=en_US&sct=US&assetid=3316.

23. Arden, Paul. 2003. *It's Not How Good You Are, It's How Good You Want to Be*. London: Phaidon.

24. Sutton, Robert I. 2001. *Weird Ideas That Work: 11 ½ Practices for Promoting, Managing, and Sustaining Innovation*. New York: Free Press.

25. Heath, Dan and Chip Heath. 2007. *Made to Stick: Why Some Ideas Survive and Others Die*. New York: Random House.

26. GSD&M. 1987. Communication Arts.

27. McClure, Tim and Roy Spence. 2006. *Don't Mess with Texas: The Story Behind the Legend*. Austin: Idea City Press.

28. *BusinessWeek*. 2006. "The World's Most Innovative Companies." April 24, 2006. http://www.businessweek.com/maga- zine/content/06_17/b3981401.htm.

29. Sapolsky, Robert M. and Lisa J. Share. 2004. "A Pacific Culture among Wild Baboons: Its Emergence and Transmission." *PLoS Biology* 2(4). http://www.plosbiology.org/article/info:doi/10.1371/journal.pbio.0020124.

30. Alcoholics Anonymous. 2007. "Alcoholics Anonymous Fact File." http://www.aa.org.

31. Brafman, Ori and Rod A. Beckstrom. 2006. *The Starfish and the Spider: The Unstoppable Power of Leaderless Organizations*. New York: Portfolio Hardcover.

32. Yong, Ed. 2008. "The Spread of Disorder—Can Graffiti Promote Littering and Theft?" ScienceBlogs.com. November 20, 2008. http://scienceblogs.com/notrocketscience/2008/11/the_spread_of_disorder_can_graffiti_promote_lit- tering_and_th.php.

33. Lanier, Jaron. 2007. "Long Live Closed-Source Software!" *Discover*. December 2007. http://discovermagazine.com/2007/ dec/long-live-closed-source-software.

34. Peters, Tom. 2005. "Re-Imagine: Business Excellence in a Disruptive Age" (slides). February 2005.

35. Krames, Jeffrey A. 2004. *The Welch Way: 24 Lessons from the World's Greatest CEO*. New York: McGraw-Hill.

36. Dalio, Ray. "Bridgewater Philosophy." Bridgewater Company website. http://www.bwater.com/home/philosophy.aspx.

37. Powell, Colin. 1996. "18 Lessons in Leadership."

38. Trend Hunter Innovation Assessment.

39. Deloitte. 2012. "Core Beliefs and Culture; Chairman's Survey Findings." https://www2.deloitte.com/content/dam/Deloitte/global/Documents/About-Deloitte/gx-core-beliefs-and-culture.pdf.

40. Bennet, Mary. 2017. "A Breakdown of the Five Generations of Employees in the Workplace." Navex Global. https://www.navexglobal.com/blog/article/formal-introduction-five-generations-employees-your-workforce/.

41. SAS Institute Inc.

42. McKinsey Global Institute. 2017. "A Future That Works: Automation, Employment, and Productivity." https://www.mckinsey.com/~/media/mckinsey/featured%20insights/Digital%20Disruption/Harnessing%20automation%20for%20a%20future%20that%20works/MGI-A-future-that-works-Executive-summary.ashx.

43. Hire by Google. https://hire.google.com/.

44. Dell Technologies. 2017. "The Next Era of Human Machine Partnerships." https://www.delltechnologies.com/content/dam/delltechnologies/assets/perspectives/2030/pdf/SR1940_IFTForDellTechnologies_Human-Machine_070517_readerhigh-res.pdf.

45. C.S.T. Consultants Inc. "Inspired Minds Careers 2030." http://careers2030.cst.org/jobs/.

46. Rashid, Brian. 2016. "The Rise of the Freelance Economy." *Forbes*. https://www.forbes.com/sites/brianrashid/2016/01/26/the-rise-of-the-freelancer-economy/#7d5588603bdf.

47. Adkins, Amy. 2016. "Employee Engagement Stagnant in U.S. in 2015." Gallup. https://news.gallup.com/poll/188144/employee-engagement-stagnant-2015.aspx.

48. Hassell, David. 2015. "Infographic: How Important Is Communication to Your (Millennial) Employees?" 15Five. https://www.15five.com/blog/employee-communication-millennials/.

49. Landrum, Sarah. 2017. "How Millennials' Happiness Is Tied to Work Friendships." *Forbes*. https://www.forbes.com/sites/sarahlandrum/2017/01/09/how-millennials-happiness-is-tied-to-work-friendships/#1bab5c72133d.

50. World Health Organization. 1995. "Global Strategy on Occupational Health for All: The Way to Health at Work." https://www.who.int/occupational_health/publications/globstrategy/en/index2.html.

51. LinkedIn.

52. Guta, Michael. 2018. "The Stats on the Work-Life Balance of Your Employees (Infographic)." *Small Business Trends*. https://smallbiztrends.com/2018/02/work-life-balance-statistics.html.

53. Egan, Brendan. 2018. "Work-Life Balance Is Simple. To Succeed at Work, Get a Life." *Entrepreneur*. https://www.entrepreneur.com/article/311414.

54. Leibson, Hayley. 2018. "The Power of Purpose-Driven." *Forbes*. https://www.forbes.com/sites/hayleyleibson/2018/01/25/the-power-of-purpose-driven/#3714efb85dca.

55. McGregor, Jena. 2015. "There Are More Men on Corporate Boards named John, Robert, William, or James Than There Are Women on Boards Altogether." *The Washington Post*. https://www.washingtonpost.com/news/on-leadership/wp/2015/02/25/there-are-more-men-on-corporate-boards-named-john-robert-william-or-james-than-there-are-women-altogether/?noredirect=on&utm_term=.d48f58a3900b.

56. Adkins, Amy. 2016. "Millennials: The Job-Hopping Generation." *Gallup*. https://www.gallup.com/workplace/231587/millennials-job-hopping-generation.aspx.

57. Arruda, William. 2017. "The Surprising Things Millennials Want from Their Careers." *Forbes*. https://www.forbes.com/sites/williamarruda/2017/08/02/the-surprising-thing-millennials-want-from-their-career/#5d17f93824fc.

58. Deckers Outdoor Corporation. 2008. Annual Report.

59. Crocs Inc. 2008. Annual Report.

60. Kelley, Tom as told to Jancee Dunn. 2008. "Six Steps to Getting Unstuck," *O (The Oprah Magazine)*. September 2008.

61. Millward Brown. 2008. "Managing Your Brand in a Recession." www.millwardbrown.com/Sites/MillwardBrown/Media/Pdfs/en/KnowledgePoints/2828DF8B.pdf.

62. Schrage, Michael. 1999. *Serious Play: How the World's Best Companies Simulate to Innovate*. Boston, MA: Harvard Business School Press.

63. Kahney, Leander. 2008. *Inside Steve's Brain*. New York: Portfolio.

64. Cook, Brad. 2006. "Microsoft Confirms It Originated iPod Box Parody Video." iPodObserver.com. March 13, 2006. http://www.ipodobserver.com/ipo/article/Microsoft_Confirms_it_Originated_iPod_Box_Parody_Video/.

65. Ridley, Matt. 1993. *The Red Queen: Sex and the Evolution of Human Nature*. London: Penguin.

66. Ulrich, Dave, John H. Zenger, Jack Zenger, and W. Norman Smallwood. 1999. *Results-Based Leadership*. Boston: Harvard Business Press.

67. SK-II. "About SK-II." http://www.sk-ii.com/about.php.

68. Miller, G. A. 1956. "The Magical Number Seven, Plus or Minus Two: Some Limits on Our Capacity for Processing Information." *Psychological Review* 63: 81–97.

69. Baddeley, A. 1992. "Working Memory." *Science* 255:5044 (January 31, 1992): 556–559.

70. Slater, Robert. 1998. *Jack Welch and the GE Way: Management Insights and Leadership Secrets of the Legendary CEO*. New York: McGraw Hill.

71. Godin, Seth. 2001. *Unleashing the Ideavirus*. New York: Hyperion.

72. Burckhardt, Jacob. "The Civilization of the Renaissance in Italy." Boise State, Electronic Renaissance. http://www.boisestate.edu/courses/hy309/docs/burckhardt/2-1.html.

73. Peters, Tom. 2005. "Re-Imagine: Business Excellence in a Disruptive Age" (slides). February 2005.

READY TO THINK
DISRUPTIVELY?

FLIP THIS BOOK OVER FOR PART ONE:

CREATE THE FUTURE